THE INJURY INDUSTRY

The Injury Industry

and the Remedy
of No-Fault Insurance

by JEFFREY O'CONNELL

foreword by Daniel P. Moynihan

UNIVERSITY OF ILLINOIS PRESS
Urbana, Chicago, London

TO MIMI

In token repayment: True
repayment would take
much more than many
volumes from each of the
six of us.

Acknowledgments

I am grateful for their help in the preparation of this manuscript to my research assistants: Vincent Walkowiak of the University of Illinois College of Law, Class of 1971, and Theodore Bailey of the Class of 1972.

I also want to thank Mrs. Richard (Ursula) Tate, my secretary, for her expert secretarial help.

I hereby thank too Professor Alfred Conard, of the University of Michigan Law School, and his associate, Attorney Charles Voltz, who first used the phrase "The Injury Industry" in an August 1970 issue of *The Michigan State Bar Journal*. I also thank Professor Conard for reading the manuscript and offering several excellent suggestions for improvement.

I am grateful also to two individuals who, this time as so many times before, have read a manuscript by me and given me innumerable helpful comments: my brother, President Thomas E. O'Connell of Berkshire Community College, Pittsfield, Massachusetts, and my wife, Virginia (Kearns) O'Connell.

Finally, I cannot write on the subject of auto insurance without expressing my deep gratitude to my colleague, Professor Robert E. Keeton of the Harvard Law School. So many of my ideas in this area have been shaped by him. This is not to say, however, that he, or anyone, shares any responsibility for any shortcomings or errors in this manuscript. Several people have recently referred to Professor Keeton and myself as "the fathers of no-fault auto insurance." This ignores the many who labored in the vineyard before us. But, if it can be said that someone "fathered" the recent more intense upsurge of interest in no-fault insurance, it must be kept in mind that the nature of the procreative act renders it rather awkward for more than one man to be the father of any given offspring. Given that fact, it would seem more accurate, both factually and poetically, if you will, in light of his predominant role in initiating and executing our joint efforts, that Robert Keeton should be called "the father" of the recent interest in no-fault insurance and myself a very fond uncle.

July, 1971   Jeffrey O'Connell

Foreword

A recent publication of the European Cultural Foundation headed by Prince Bernhard of the Netherlands observed that industrial technology, which was the creation of European civilization, had become the foremost threat to its survival. It is useful—it is absolutely imperative—for Americans, preoccupied as they have been in recent years with problems associated with advancing technology, to realize that they are not alone. Other nations have problems of pollution and such like at least as bad as our own, and in many instances considerably worse. Similarly, there are situations in which other nations are doing considerably better. All in all, what we see is a typical pattern of industrialization, with a wide range of initiative and achievement, of the kind that characteristically leads to comparative advantages, and hence to trade. We do not yet think of social measures designed to control technology, or to ameliorate its effects, as being traded between or among nations, but that is in fact what is beginning to happen. It is a fact that gives special importance to Jeffrey O'Connell's work.

The response to the technological assault on our environment and sensibilities has been more or less bi-modal. There has been a large, or at least a very loud, element demanding in effect that we smash the machines: an approach to complexity that has ever appealed to simple minds. Another group, not as large, and certainly not as noisy, has taken the position that technology has profoundly affected the human condition, and very much for the better. So much so that we have become overenthusiastic about trying everything that comes along, too often to repent in leisure, and have been unwilling to change our institutional arrangements as rapidly as technology alters the outcomes produced by these arrangements.

The Bomb is, of course, the symbol of all this: the ultimate technological achievement that so many for so long now have assumed will lead to the ultimate conflict and an end to the whole Promethean madness. It may do so. And yet it is possible also that the existence of nuclear weapons will force peace on mankind, at least as between those nations possessing such weapons. The outcomes of technology are not as easily predicted as some would think; nor, as it has become fashionable to think, are they necessarily dehumanizing, alienating, desiccating.

It may seem odd to raise such matters in introducing a book which describes in devastating detail precisely the absurdities and even cruelties technology imposes on us in the form of automobile injuries and deaths and the subsequent allocation of costs. Yet it is appropriate to do so, for the essential thrust of Jeffrey O'Connell's work is the contention that technology does serve human needs, and will do so far better if only we will apply the same capacity for rational analysis to the second and third and fourth order effects of technological innovation as we do to developing the initial phenomenon.

The automobile was, of course, the great innovation. It has changed everything. No phenomenon save modern warfare itself has had anything like the consequences of this rather inelegant and relatively inefficient machine—an engineering success, as the saying goes, a scientific failure—developed in the late 19th century. Roughly speaking, Europeans invented it; and Americans learned to build it. Nothing has been quite the same since: or will ever be.

Right away there appeared an unprecedented form of morbidity and mortality. I mean right away. In 1896, when there were four motor vehicles in the United States, two were in St. Louis. They managed to collide with such impact as to injure both drivers, one seriously. For the longest while these events were described as "accidents," a pre-scientific term suggesting that rational preventive actions would not be of much use. But these crashes, and their effects, were not "accidents" at all. They were perfectly predictable outcomes of a particular transportation system utilizing a specific technology. (Recent research has demonstrated that insults to the body associated with such events as automobile crashes are in fact simply another form of disease, or rather partake of all those essential features which constitute disease.) In 1959, for example, Dr. William Haddon and I, in the crudest of calculations, estimated that one of every three automobiles manufactured in Detroit ends up with blood on it. The estimate may have been low. We argued that what might be rare for the driver was routine for the vehicle, with all the implications that follow. O'Connell now takes this line of reasoning further, pointing out statistically that nearly the entire universe of drivers is eventually involved in a collision.

The problem of "death on the highway" first attracted serious attention. By the late 1950's, it is fair to say that the problem had been solved, which is to say that it had been correctly defined, and that working solutions would follow fairly close upon applied efforts.

The late 1950's and early 1960's were heady days for those of us involved with the problem of traffic safety. It was then, as it remains and will continue to be for some time, a terrible problem, to which government directed great efforts, with almost no results (apart from highway design, which was greatly improved, following the good habits of professional engineers). One panacea followed another. One after another, they would fail. This merely strengthened the conviction of the "epidemiologists" that vehicle design was the heart of the matter; and that sooner or later the automobile manufacturers, possibly under legislative duress, as it were, would see this and act accordingly. I repeat that it was a heady time. As I have written elsewhere, it was rather as if in the late 1960's a group of twenty to thirty doctors, engineers, social scientists and lawyers had worked out a solution to the problem of crime in the streets which they were absolutely confident would work and, moreover, would eventually be put into effect. Only a matter of time. The problem had been solved. We knew it, and kept demonstrating it to one another in small conferences and in papers published in more or less obscure journals. Public interest was low, but morale was high. It was only a matter of time.

It came more quickly than we expected. During the Presidential campaign of 1960, I wrote a statement issued by John F. Kennedy calling for a scientific approach to traffic safety. I rather doubt that he ever even saw the document, but it constituted grounds for pressing ahead once he was elected. His successor, Lyndon B. Johnson, proposed the necessary legislation early in 1966; and it was enacted in a single session of the Congress. Once serious persons could be made to listen to the case for a rational approach to the problem, the battle was over: *so irrational and ineffectual was the approach then being pursued.*

One of the books that contributed to the passage of this epic legislation was Jeffrey O'Connell's *Safety Last,* which appeared in the winter of 1965-66, along with Ralph Nader's *Unsafe at Any Speed.* Earlier he had published a long and important law review article on the same subject.* As a professor of law he had instantly grasped the complex significance of the problem of traffic safety. The unavailing effort to limit the extent of death and injury was significant enough in itself, *but it was by no means the only or the most important consideration.* Basically, the thrust had been to use traditional techniques of law enforcement to bring about desired behavior. Unfortunately, no one could define the desired behavior: What does it mean to "drive safely"? What are the actual consequences in lower collision rates of observing arbitrary speed limits? What will be the effects on alcoholics of penalties for drunken driving? And, where one would be confident that the prescribed behavior would be maximal behavior, what impact does the pattern of arrest, trial and punishment have on the actual performance of one hundred million or so drivers? The answer had to be—it could be shown to be—very little impact. A waste. Just as importantly, a misuse of a precious and often fragile institution, that of law enforcement, through techniques and traditions that are fundamentally pre-technological. The essentially mundane purpose of running the highways, with objectives no different than those of the private concerns which ran the railroads, was beginning to overwhelm and to distort the fundamental processes of law enforcement. Americans, for example, were becoming accustomed to regarding arrest by an

---

*O'Connell, "Taming the Automobile," 58 Northwestern University Law Review pp. 299-399 (1963).

armed officer of the law as a routine event. Something was wrong here, and O'Connell quickly saw the implications of it all.

To move from the problem of traffic safety—what might be termed a second order effect of the technological innovation of the automobile—to that of "accident" litigation—a third order effect—was altogether logical, just as it is altogether clear that the nation will eventually be very much in the debt of Professor O'Connell and his colleague Professor Robert Keeton for the conceptual breakthroughs that have pointed the way to "solving" this dilemma. (Nothing is more self evident and obvious than a hard problem that has been solved.)

At this time the judicial process is being used to allocate the costs of motor vehicle crashes. (Indeed, from the point of view of an economist, that is all that is involved. There are certain costs: who bears them?) The judicial system cannot do this efficiently or even, it would appear, fairly. The rules of evidence and the legal fictions about the nature of the events under scrutiny are such that it just doesn't come out right. Who can reconstruct a complex accident? "Tell the jury which way the bullet was travelling when it entered the victim's heart." "At what approximate speed would you say the bullet was moving at the time of entry?" O'Connell points out that "about 45 per cent of those seriously injured in traffic accidents [get] . . . absolutely nothing from automobile liability insurance." It would appear that this half of the victim population is disproportionately made up of persons who can least afford such losses.

But this is only a part of the problem. Just as in the case of traffic safety, the most serious consequence of our present system of allocating collision costs is that it has brought on a near breakdown in the judicial system itself. The courts are overwhelmed, swamped, inundated, choked. In a futile quest to carry out a mundane mission—deciding who hit whom on the highway when every day there will be thousands and thousands of such events routinely arising from a particular transportation system—we are sacrificing the most precious of our institutions: the independent judiciary, which dispenses justice and maintains the presumption and perception of a just social order that is fundamental to a democratic political system.

This is what is at issue. *This* is what concerns O'Connell. This is what has led him to the single-minded pursuit of no-fault insurance over the past six years. If I am not mistaken, it is what will lead, ultimately, to the success of his efforts. He is confident of this: very much as were the traffic safety reformers of a decade or so ago. The clarity, openness and urgency of his arguments are the marks of a man with an idea whose time is coming.

There are problems; he knows and describes them. The interests of the legal profession—the trial bar—are very much involved here. These are legitimate interests and should be looked to in any general shift to "lawyerless" insurance. There are men and women whose careers will change if we change our system of allocating the cost of automobile collisions. But their careers need not be diminished. On the contrary, it is precisely because they are so much needed in the central pursuits of the legal profession that they ought not to be "wasted" in the conduct of litigation which is fundamentally futile from a social perspective, and all too frequently unjust from the point of view of the individual victim of a motor vehicle collision. For this reason one may hope that lawyers in particular will read this eminently readable, thoroughly lawyerlike book.

Daniel P. Moynihan

July, 1971

Contents

Chapter   Page

I   The Maw of the Law................................   1

II   'Who Dunnit?'   9

III   Injuring the Injured.............................   15

IV   Paying for Pain..................................   28

V   A Pound of Flesh (All About Lawyers' Contingent
        Fees)   37

VI   . . . To the Hounds (All About Ambulance Chas-
        ing)   54

VII   Let the Buyer (not only) Beware (but be gone)..   69

VIII   The Untouchables (All About Assigned Risks)...   81

IX   No-Fault Insurance —What and Why...........   94

X   Lower Price—Higher Value.................... 106

XI   Defending the Indefensible.................... 122

XII   Where from Here?............................. 139

        Epilogue 155

        Appendix I—Provisions for Property Damage.... 157

        Appendix II—An Optional No-Fault System..... 161

        Appendix III—Complete or Partial Abolition of
        Fault Claims? 169

        Appendix IV—Excerpts from the Summary Report
        of the U. S. Department of Transportation Auto
        Insurance Study 176

        Notes 224

        Index 249

Chapter I

The Maw of the Law

As a surgeon I am weary of the urgent night calls [from traffic accidents], the usual milling cluster of police and scared relatives, the trail of blood down the corridor to the battered girl with a smashed face and a fractured pelvis, vomiting blood over an avulsed eye. [Other doctors] . . . are sick of it too. I believe that God himself is nauseated.[1]

1

Start from the premise that each of us is going to be involved in a traffic accident: More than half of us (56 per cent) who drive motor vehicles will have an accident in the next three years; 75 per cent of us will have an accident in the next five years; 94 per cent of us will have an accident in the next ten years; 99 per cent of us will have an accident in the next 20 years.[2] In other words every one of us, as a practical matter, is inevitably going to have an accident sooner or later; most of us sooner.

And all this is likely to cost us very dearly—both as individuals and as a society.

According to the recent Department of Transportation study, auto accidents in 1968 involving serious injury resulted in 5.1 billion dollars of "compensable economic loss," *e. g.,* medical expense, wage loss and car damage.[3]

With that kind of predictable and staggering loss, obviously it is incumbent on a sensitive and sophisticated society—and especially a society in which insurance plays a very large role— to devise an insurance mechanism which will spread that loss not only efficiently and effectively but with at least a measure of courtesy and compassion.

Have we devised such a system?

On the contrary.

We have devised just about the worst system imaginable: A system that not only fails to spread most of that loss but is cruel, corrupt, self righteous, dilatory, expensive and wasteful while it grimly goes about the business of failing.

If all that sounds extreme, consider the massively documented shortcomings of the present auto insurance system:

—Auto insurance premiums are too high.

—Payments to traffic victims are long delayed.

—Auto accident cases clog the courts.

—Many traffic victims—especially among the seriously injured—are not paid at all, or paid only a fraction of their loss.

—Many other traffic victims—especially among the trivially injured—are often overgenerously paid.

—Temptations to suppress or fabricate evidence are constantly present because in order to be paid a traffic victim must arrange his version of the accident so that it appears to be solely the fault of the other party.

—Much too much of the auto insurance premium is chewed up in insurance overhead and legal fees compared to what is received by traffic victims themselves.

—Auto insurance is difficult to purchase and/or continue in effect, especially among those in inner cities and among the young, the old and those in the military.

—Many insurance companies—especially among those insuring so-called "bad risks"—have gone into insolvency leaving policyholders and victims without protection.

The basic difficulty with the present automobile insurance system is that the insured event is too complicated, turning as it does on *legal* liability. You can be paid for a traffic accident only by traversing very tricky terrain. First, you must claim against the other driver's insurance company, which obviously owes no loyalty to you. Second, you must claim that the other driver was at fault in causing the accident and you were free from fault, when it is oftentimes extremely difficult to know just what happened in the split second of an agony of collision. Third, you must claim for a totally uncertain amount which includes not only your out-of-pocket loss for medical expenses and missed wages, but payment for so-called pain and suffering, which is obviously almost impossible to translate into dollars and cents. These needlessly complex legalisms, in the words of *Consumer Reports,* the magazine of Consumers Union,

> are particularly conspicuous when contrasted with other kinds of insurance written by the same companies or their affiliates. When you die, your life insurance company does not refuse to pay your widow on the ground that you contributed to the unfortunate result by smoking too many cigarettes or eating too much. When your

house burns down, your insurance company does not refuse to pay on the ground that you should have had your roof reshingled with fire-resistant materials. When you are hospitalized for a broken leg, your health insurance company will not refuse payment on the ground that if you had replaced that burned-out bulb over your staircase, you wouldn't have fallen down the stairs. Yet, defenses parallel to these are the common grist of automobile liability cases.[4]

The result is not a system for paying people automobile accident insurance after automobile accidents, but a system for *fighting* people about paying them automobile accident insurance after automobile accidents. The result is a system where the traffic victim—already battered enough from the accident itself —cannot know after the accident *when* he will be paid, *what* he will be paid or *if* he will be paid. A 1.6 million dollar study of the present automobile insurance system was recently completed by the U. S. Department of Transportation (DOT) after two years of effort. It reveals, in the words of Richard J. Barber, formerly Deputy Assistant Secretary of Transportation for Policy, "a system that is working very poorly and very inadequately. It is indeed startling and indeed terribly disturbing from both an economic and a human standpoint."[5]*

The biggest problem presented by the present fault automobile insurance system is the extent to which many traffic victims—especially among the seriously injured—are not paid at all from automobile insurance, or are paid only a fraction of their losses. The Department of Transportation study found— as a study by the University of Michigan had found ten years previously—that about 45 per cent of those seriously injured in traffic accidents got absolutely nothing from automobile liability insurance.[6]

The DOT study found also that, with compensable losses totalling $5.1 billion in serious injury and death cases, auto

---

* For the essence of the Summary Report of the DOT study, including its findings and recommendations, see Appendix IV *infra*.

liability insurance paid out only $800 million, or 15 per cent of compensable losses.[7]

Not only is auto liability insurance failing to pay most of the loss but it is cruelly misallocating what relatively little it does pay. In the words of Professor Alfred Conard of the University of Michigan, who conducted the monumental University of Michigan study of auto accident payment, "If there is one thing which [all] the surveys have shown conclusively, it is that the [fault] . . . system overpays the small claimants who need it least and underpays the large claimants who need it most."[8]

The DOT study documented how little those who suffer the most in measurable economic loss ($10,000 or more) received from fault claims. Approximately 60 per cent got nothing from fault claims. Among those with $10,000 or more in economic loss who did get something from a fault claim, 95.6 per cent got less than their economic loss; 85 per cent got less than half their economic loss, and only 0.6 per cent received more than two times their loss. At the other end of the scale, among those with economic loss less than $1000 who received fault payments, none got less than half their losses, 87 per cent got more than their loss, 41 per cent got more than twice their loss, and 14 per cent got four times their loss or more.[9]

The following chart reveals this pattern of payment:[10]

Portion of Loss Paid	$1 to $999 loss	$1,000 to $2,499 loss	$2,500 to $9,999 loss	over $10,000 loss
Less than ½ of loss....	0	11.0%	36.3%	85.5%
Equal to or more than loss	87.4%	55.9%	32.5%	4.2%
Two times loss or more..	41.5%	18.4%	6.1%	.57%
Four times loss or more..	14.0%	1.3%	1.4%	0

According to another study by insurance companies themselves, those with under $100 of economic loss who retained a lawyer received on the average over *seven* times their loss.[11] Even with payments from other than fault claims added, such as Blue Cross

or sick leave, the pattern remains of great overpayment of
small claims and great underpayment of large claims.[12]

Not only is payment under the fault system often nonexistent
or a fraction of true loss, but it is long delayed. According to
one of the DOT studies, on the average, 16 months elapses
between the accident and the time of final payment. In addition, the larger the loss, the longer the delay. For losses over
$2500, the average delay rose to 19 months.[13] According to
another comprehensive study of auto insurance by the Insurance
Department of the State in New York, traffic victims face average
delays in payment from fault liability insurance that are *ten*
times as long as the delays in collecting under such no-fault
coverages as homeowners or burglary insurance, and *forty* times
as long as delays under accident and health coverages! The
Insurance Department reviewed a sample of 7000 insurance
company files of insurance claims paid throughout the state
during September, 1969, of which 1000 were fault liability claims
for bodily injury to persons. The findings were as follows:[14]

Interval Between Claim and Payment	Auto Bodily Injury Liability	Auto Physical Damage [No-fault coverage on one's own car]	Home-owners	Burglary	Individual Accident and Health
2 months or less	23%	79%	92%	64%	98%
6 months or less	49	98	99	97	99
1 year or less	71	99	99	99	100
2 years or less	83	100	100	99	—
3 years or less	88	—	—	100	—
Average period (months)	15.8	1.5	1.6	1.9	0.4

Note that these figures demonstrate that the delays are long
for traffic claims both in and out of court and in and out of metropolitan areas. Of course, as has long been known, auto claims
that go to big city courts "encounter truly incredible delays—
between four and five years in the largest counties in [New York]
. . . State," according to the New York Insurance Department
study.[15] Indeed, court delays of auto cases in metropolitan areas

throughout the country have become virtually legendary. The officials of the Institute of Judicial Administration speak of the continuingly "dismal picture of untoward civil delay in personal injury cases in . . . metropolitan areas." [16] The *average* trial delay in counties over 750,000 in population is about 30 months, or two and one-half years. In Philadelphia County, Pennsylvania, it is 47.7 months; in Bronx County, New York, 58.1 months; in Cook County (Chicago), Illinois, 60.7 months. [17] (If you are involved in a traffic accident in a metropolitan area in the United States, you'd better hire yourself a young lawyer.)

The other principal characteristic of the present auto insurance system beside delay is its profligate waste. Over half of the auto insurance dollar—56 cents—is chewed up in insurance overhead and legal fees, with only 44 cents left for actually paying traffic victims. [18] Waste and delay are the inevitable consequences of the insurance business turning over the definition of the insured event to the lawyers: *any* business that allows itself to be turned over to lawyers gets itself in very bad trouble—especially with delay and waste. Lawyers have traditionally been notorious for being dilatory and extravagant operators.

This is illustrated not only in auto accidents but in other areas where society has been foolish enough to give lawyers free reign to indulge their penchant for ignoring time and cost. Probate, real estate transfers and bankruptcy, for example, are similar areas where lawyers run wild with costs and procedures totally disproportionate to any real need. All this is just another illustration of the wisdom of Winston Churchill's injunction that experts should be "on tap" not "on top." In auto insurance, lawyers are "on top" with predictably disastrous consequences.

It was this sort of situation, perhaps, that led Dick the Butcher in Shakespeare's *King Henry VI* to shout, "The first thing we do, let's kill all the lawyers." An understandable urge —at least from a nonlawyer. But as a lawyer let me suggest a somewhat milder course. "Let's put the lawyers back where they belong." Let's structure things so that we don't need them as a normal necessity, but only as a last resort: as with accident and health insurance—and almost every form of insurance. How often does anyone have to hire a lawyer to get a health insurance claim paid? Or a fire insurance claim? Or a life insurance claim? Rarely indeed. The courts, after all, are not clogged with any but *auto* insurance claims.

And so we should transform auto insurance to make it like most other forms of insurance—payable automatically by your own insurance company, as long as you didn't *intentionally* try to injure yourself. In other words, we should switch from "fault" insurance to "no-fault" insurance. By doing so, insurance payments to traffic victims would be much prompter, much surer, much more efficient and infinitely less abrasive than under the fault criterion. And at the same time, *mirabile dictu,* auto insurance would cost much less money and be available to many more people.

This "miracle" can be worked because the lawyers, and the ever-present threat of lawyers, with their incredible cumbersomeness, will have been barred from the everyday.

There are very few major problems facing this country susceptible of simple solutions. The problems of national defense, of the environment, of civil rights, of the poor, of disenchanted youth assuredly are not. Nor are other smaller—if major—problems facing the consumer in particular. Not auto safety, for example, nor the delivery of health care, nor shoddy goods. But the major problem of auto insurance *can* be solved with relative ease. And given deep disenchantment—conceded on all sides—with government and elected officials, surely a primary need is for government and elected officials to move on any major problem that can be readily solved. John Kennedy's old friend, journalist Charles Bartlett, put it best, "The great counterrevolutionary task is to deal as quickly as possible with all the aggravations that can be remedied. Auto insurance deserves urgent ranking on this list." [19]

Chapter II

'Who Dunnit?'

In 1936, a senior law student at Duke named Richard M. Nixon succinctly summarized the law applicable to auto accidents —and the difficulties plaguing it:

> Despite the insistent contention of counsel in the early cases that the [no-fault] . . . liability of the keeper of vicious dogs or evilly-disposed mules should

be imposed upon the drivers of "devil wagons" [so the automobile was once labelled], the courts from the beginning held that the automobile driver should be subject to liability only if his conduct were at fault and then only to plaintiffs whose conduct was free from fault. "Fault" was defined in terms of a departure from the common law standard of ordinary care. The courts thereby took upon themselves the problem of determining in each case whether the parties had exercised the required degree of care. In the days of poor roads and low speeds, the fact of an accident could be reconstructed in the courtroom with some degree of accuracy, and the problem of determining fault did not present unusual difficulties. But with high-powered cars and concrete highways, the probability that an accident—often the consequence of a fractional mistake in management—can and will be described accurately in court has become increasingly remote, especially where court congestion has delayed the time of trial.[1]

The difficulties of determining who was at fault in the typical traffic accident have been graphically illustrated by a recent film produced by the American Trial Lawyers Association (ATL), the organization of plaintiffs' personal injury lawyers, in cooperation with the University of Michigan Law School. The film, based on an actual case, shows the complete proceedings of a "representative civil case"—an auto accident case—from the time of accident through the entire trial.

In her first interview at her lawyer's office, the plaintiff in the film—a middle-aged lady—says, in describing the accident, "Since I was going to turn left I had my signal on. Out of the corner of my eye, I suddenly saw the other car. Then there was a terrible shock. I just can't explain it. It was an awful feeling."[2] Later in taking the plaintiff to the scene of the accident to reconstruct it, her lawyer says to her, "Like every accident, it probably happened pretty fast. I know your recollection is pretty confused, and that's only natural. It probably happened with startling suddenness and, in addition, a great deal of time has elapsed since it happened." The plaintiff readily agrees to each of these assertions.

At the scene of the accident, the following exchange takes place:

Says the woman, "I came to a full stop. I remember there were two—no—three cars to my left and I waited for each of them to clear the intersection and then I pulled out slowly. Then this other car plowed right through the stop sign and hit me."

"You didn't see the truck go through the stop sign, did you?"

"No, but it must have been the way it hit me."

"Did you see the truck when it hit you?"

"No, not exactly. I sort of saw it out of the corner of my eye, the way you see things that way."

"How far away was the truck when you first saw it?"

"Well, how can I tell, I can't say."

"How fast was it going?"

"Well, it was traveling fast, I'll tell you that. It's been such a long time. I wasn't paying that much attention. In addition, I'm just no good at distances and speed."

At that point, plaintiff's lawyer tells her bluntly that she will *have* to remember. Then as the scene fades out, the narrator comments that the lawyer explains the rules of negligence to his client, making clear that, if she is to be paid, she must establish negligence on the part of the other driver. The lawyer is then shown saying to the client, "You are going to have to try to remember. Whether you like it or not, you are going to have to recall distances and speed."

Of course, this exchange is not surprising to any lawyer who has ever tried an automobile accident case. This prodding of witnesses and clients to remember the unrememberable—and making very clear the unfortunate consequences to a client of *not* remembering—is standard procedure in automobile accident cases. What emerges, of course, is not so much "the truth, the whole truth and nothing but the truth" but rather "half truth, quarter truth or no truth at all." Auto accidents are unique— except for divorce cases, a horrendous can of worms in their own right—for the amount of misrepresentation and perjury they generate. (It is perhaps no coincidence that the solution to the mess created by divorce law is increasingly seen as no-fault divorce law, variations of which have been passed in California and New York.)

Thereafter, throughout the preparation for trial in the film, it is made abundantly clear that no one can remember very precisely what happened. Certainly the defendant's memory is diametrically opposed to the plaintiff's. According to him, he stopped but she turned suddenly without using her turn signal. In addition, wholly differing views on whether the defendant or plaintiff drove properly are advanced from varying witnesses. (One witness, who purports to be positive on this point, is proven to have been situated where he couldn't possibly have seen what he says he remembers.) Indeed, after all the prodding of plaintiff by one of her lawyers, another of her lawyers, in speaking of her recollection to a witness, says, "Keep in mind that my client may be mistaken. She has told us certain things which I am sure she means in good faith, but she may be telling us things she really doesn't know or that are wrong. Everyone at an accident sees things differently and remembers things differently."

In addition to the problems of just remembering what happened in the fleeting, panic-filled moment of collision, there is also the pride that most people take in their own driving, and their reluctance to admit that they were at fault—especially after an accident. And even if they (1) do remember, and (2) are willing to "tell it like it is," the years of delay between accident and trial will mean, as law student Richard Nixon suggested, that memories will blur and other witnesses disappear.

The thorny difficulties of determining who was at fault in the typical accident are so great that, when claimants' and insurance lawyers were asked to name the principal issues they fight about in trying to negotiate settlements of auto accident cases, they agreed—with remarkable statistical accord—that the issue of trying to determine who was at fault led all others.[3]

Keep in mind, too, that even if the plaintiff in the film had been able, from the welter of confusion surrounding her accident, to prove that the other driver had been at fault, her task would still only be partially done. She would still have to prove that she herself had not in any way been at fault. This is because, as fledgling lawyer Richard Nixon also indicated, in order for an injured party to be paid, not only must he be the victim of a wrongdoer, but he must himself be free of wrongdoing. This rule of so-called "contributory negligence" was formulated in 1808 by a singularly obtuse English judge, Lord Ellenborough ("whose forte was never common sense," according to one prominent American legal authority).[4] Like so many other bad English legal rules, it was immediately seized upon and adopted in the United States. The result was a rule that held that no matter how slight the plaintiff's fault in comparison to the defendant's much greater wrongdoing (lacking some wanton behavior on the defendant's part), the plaintiff is *completely* barred from any payment. Writes William Prosser, a noted American authority in the law of torts, "[n]o one has ever succeeded in justifying that as a policy, and no one ever will." [5] And yet, according to Prosser, the rule has been like a "chronic invalid who will not die." [6] It remains the law in the overwhelming number of American jurisdictions today, despite the fact that England and most other countries have long since seen its folly and abandoned it. In point of fact, until very recently only six American jurisdictions—Arkansas, Georgia, Mississippi, Nebraska, South Dakota and Wisconsin—had seen fit to abolish the rule of contributory negligence in place of the rule commonly prevailing elsewhere in the world—the rule of so-called comparative negligence. Under this rule, the negligence of the parties is compared and damages allocated accordingly. Thus, for example, if the defendant's fault were determined to be twice as great as that of the plaintiff, the plaintiff would be paid two-thirds of his losses and bear the remainder himself. Recently five more states— Hawaii, Maine, Massachusetts, Minnesota and New Hampshire— have switched to comparative negligence.

But the rule of comparative negligence is scarcely a panacea. Although it probably means more people being paid at least something, it complicates the already overly complicated process of ascribing fault. Now not only the *fact* but the precise *amount* of fault must be determined, calibrated to precise percentages: Surely an illusory process at best.

Note too that the rules of both contributory and comparative negligence add the puzzle of establishing just how the plaintiff reacted in the instant of an accident to the problems of precisely dissecting the defendant's conduct.

What a field day for lawyers!

Chapter III

Injuring the Injured

Once the lawyers and the insurance adjustors have finished their wrangling and haggling over (1) whether the defendant was at fault, (2) whether the victim was at fault, and (3) often over the *degree* that each was at fault, the hapless victim is scarcely home safe even if it is determined that he is one of the privileged group entitled to be paid.

Next comes the wrangling and haggling over the *amount* to be paid.

15

The fault system's way of measuring the injured person's damages seems really designed to do it badly. A truly accurate measurement, after all, has to be *ex post facto*—after the event so that the loss can be identified and precisely determined. This doesn't mean that you would necessarily have to wait months or years for all the effects of a serious accident to be manifested before any payment could be made. One could make periodic payments for losses as they accrue—that is, as wages are lost or medical bills are incurred. Given the inordinate delays in final settlement of auto accident claims (see Chapter I), such a procedure would seem not only desirable but essential. Part of the reason this is not done under the fault system lies in the fact that very often the delay ensues because the parties are arguing about whether any payment at all is due, in light of a dispute over who was at fault. The insurance company can hardly be expected to make periodic partial payments on a claim the entire validity of which it disputes.

But suppose there isn't really any dispute that at least a certain amount is due. Is there any way the claimant can get something on account? Or suppose it's agreed that the insurance company is going to have to pay, but the claimant is going to continue to have to undergo medical treatment for an indeterminate period and amount. Can the claimant have his medical bills paid as they accrue (subject to being reasonable)? Unfortunately, the fault system does not provide for any such sensible procedures. Rather it prescribes only one lump-sum payment, including not only all those damages that have already accrued, but also a *final* estimate of all the damages that will ever occur in the future—because, once the damages are assessed by a settlement or verdict, ordinarily the amount cannot be redetermined even if it is found to be woefully inadequate or grossly excessive.[1]

This process often leads, incidentally, to the unedifying spectacle of a plaintiff's doctor grossly exaggerating the aftereffects of an injury, while the insurance doctor equally grossly disparages them—with a hapless jury in between left to decide.

The "whore"—a term for the doctor whose slanted expert opinion is consistently available for purchase by either claimants or insurers—is too familiar a figure. Indeed, too often the plaintiff's lawyer will urge the plaintiff to be treated by a doctor not because of the doctor's medical expertise, but because of his compliance about testifying in accordance with the lawyer's wishes.

The fact of a lump-sum payment can have other disastrous effects on medical treatment. Because any victim will rightly fear getting less if he appears before a jury fully healed or rehabilitated (with, for instance, an artificial leg that he can expertly use), sometimes he will forego treatment or rehabilitation during the long delay between accident and trial in order to appear before a sympathetic jury as pathetically handicapped as possible.[2] This scandalous situation has led Professor Alfred Conard at the University of Michigan Law School to speak of "the schizophrenic choice between 'recovery' in the medical sense and 'recovery' in the legal sense."[3]

This was beautifully illustrated—with uncomfortably little exaggeration—in the shooting script from the movie *The Fortune Cookie*. Jack Lemmon portrays Harry, a slightly injured accident victim, and Walter Mathau plays his brother-in-law and lawyer, Willie Gingrich. (Willie has "a brain full of razor blades. He would have run afoul of the law a long time ago if he didn't have a slick lawyer—himself.")

> WILLIE (In hospital room). And what are you doing walking around?
>
> HARRY. I'm trying to get some circulation in my legs. Do you mind?
>
> WILLIE. Circulation? That's the last thing we want. Now . . . just get back in bed.[4]

Actually, little has been written on why the law has felt it must straightjacket itself and allow only one lump-sum award, imposing, as that rule does in the words of Yale law professor Fleming James, "the difficult and uncertain task of prophecy."[5]

Juries are understandably often puzzled about why future losses cannot be left for subsequent determination—in a manner analogous to alimony cases, for example.

The reasons for the law's rigidity in insisting on lump-sum payments were originally based on historical and legal technicalities. But, as a practical matter, the attraction to lawyers of receiving their fees in lump-sum—and their concomitant distaste for piecemeal payment—has had something to do with the retention of the rule. Certainly, under Workmen's Compensation, which calls for periodic payments, lawyers are notorious for pressing their clients to choose optional lump-sum payments in order that they (the lawyers) can get their fees in convenient form, regardless of the well being or needs of their clients.[6] At any rate, unquestionably, in the words of Professor James, ". . . the single recovery rule is often both capricious and inflexible in its operation so that damages in accident cases, even where they are awarded and actually paid, often fail to do the job they should if accident law is to perform its function of administering accident losses efficiently in the public interest."[7]

One of the cruelest problems stemming from the rule of lump-sum payments is that most victims are simply unaccustomed to the management of relatively large sums of money, and thus amounts paid are often dissipated in frivolous luxuries, such as color TV sets, as opposed to being spent constructively in mitigating the losses they are designed to "repair."[8]

Discussion of rehabilitation points up again the deep-seated inconsistency between legal and medical treatment of the injured. The National Council on Rehabilitation defines rehabilitation as ". . . the process of restoration of the [injured] . . . to the fullest physical, mental, social, vocational and economic usefulness of which they are capable."[9] According to a member of the Committee on Trauma of the American College of Surgeons:

> Rehabilitation should commence on the day of injury and be continued until the limit of improvement is

reached. Many a temporary partial disability has become a permanent partial [disability] or even permanent
total [disability] because emphasis was placed entirely
on the legal rather than on the medical facet of the
problem.[10]

Rehabilitation should obviously be a prime aim of every
insurance scheme, not just to relieve the victim's own misery,
but to reduce the total loss to both him and society. But not
only does the fault system not promote rehabilitation—it hinders
it: Rehabilitation must begin promptly, whereas the fault system delays payment; and rehabilitation is most often needed by
the seriously injured, whereas the fault system pays him pro-
portionately the least.[11]

The recent DOT studies confirm the tragic failure of the
fault system to foster rehabilitation. Says John Henle, formerly
Director of Rehabilitation for Nationwide Mutual Insurance
Company, in the DOT report devoted exclusively to "Rehabilitation of Auto Accident Victims," the "traditional settlement environment for . . . auto bodily injury claims [under the fault
system] offers nothing to encourage and much to preclude the
early introduction of rehabilitation." [12] "It cannot be stressed too
often that the settlement environment of [the fault liability
system, whereby claims are made against the other driver's
insurance company] . . . is the antithesis of the [proper] rehabilitative environment. . . ." [13] Thus, despite attempts by some
insurers to inaugurate programs for rehabilitation of traffic victims under fault claims, according to the DOT study, "of the
11.3 per cent of seriously injured victims to whom rehabilitation
has been suggested, only 2.1 per cent were referred by an insurance company." [14] As a result, the report concludes, "the difficulties encountered in employing rehabilitation techniques under
the present [fault] . . . liability system suggests strongly the
need for the development of . . . 'without fault' system [whereby
the victim deals with his own insurer]." [15]

If the benefits of a prompt start at rehabilitation are axio-
matic, conversely the devastating effects of allowing an injury

to "harden" are equally so. And yet one often hears lawyers protesting that a case cannot be disposed of until the injuries *do* "harden," i. e., become fully developed so that one will know how much finally to bargain for. Concomitantly, the delay in payment (and therefore often in treatment) is a bargaining counter the insurance company does not want to give up lightly. The insurance adjustor can—and does—suggest with great effect that the victim should take a lesser sum now rather than be forced to wait—as the insurer can force him to do—the months or, more likely, years before final payment will be due.

The basic problem here lies, as the DOT study suggests, in the adversary nature of the typical personal injury claim. You are claiming, as stated earlier, not against your own insurance company, which has a built-in loyalty to you as its customer, but typically against the insurance company of the person who injured you—a company which has no loyalty to you, a company to whom you are a total stranger. Thus the ideal solution for the insurer becomes not satisfaction to you, but "claim denied" or, at a maximum, the smallest payment possible, perhaps after the longest delay possible, through shrewd and flinty bargaining. As long ago as 1936, a young social scientist, Emma Corstvet, described the vulnerable bargaining position of the seriously injured traffic victim—a situation often as true today as it was then. The traffic victim with permanent disability, for instance, often a family bread winner with a relatively low income, without resources and with mounting expenses, finds himself in a pathetically inadequate bargaining position against the insurance company whose position, because of the very nature of bargaining, concomitantly grows stronger with delay:

> [T]he great disadvantage to the injured is that while the buyer of a waiver of future claims [the insurance company] is not anxious to buy at all unless the horizon is really threatening, the seller [the injured] must sell to this buyer or none at all. His costs have been forced from him, he must recoup what he can. And, if the outlay has been serious, the injured often needs money and

at once. [The victim's income and obligations ordinarily leave] . . . little leeway for unforeseen emergencies. The family doctor may wait, the landlord be generous, the grocer, up to his limited means, give credit. But a nurse is not a capitalist and needs her wage at once, a specialist is not the family doctor, the need for coal and light, medicine, special sick foods and some unavoidable necessities of family living goes on. The result is that the families most in need of compensation can often least afford to hold out for an adequate price, *i. e.,* a price commensurate with expenditure and as great as those who can afford to wait might obtain.[16]

This baleful eyeing of each other by adversaries after an auto accident so thoroughly permeates the fault insurance system that in order for the system to function "properly," the hostility must begin from the first moment after the accident. Listen to the cautionary advice given by the California Bar Association for "proper" behavior after a traffic accident:

(1) If anybody falsely accuses you of wrongdoing, deny it promptly and shortly. If the accusation is true merely state "That's your view." Silence in the face of an accusation may provide damaging evidence against you.

(2) Don't say "I have insurance. They will take care of everything" to the other driver. A civil suit may be filed if there is car damage or personal injuries.

(3) Don't make payments of any kind to the other party until you get some legal advice. It may weaken your position.

(4) Don't make any settlement without legal advice.[17]

Perhaps, under the system now in effect, the state bar is rendering drivers a genuine public service by such advice, but surely it is urging conduct that society from a humanitarian point of view ought to find shameful.

In 1963, insurance executive Arne Foungner pointed out that the present system, poisoned by the atmosphere of mutual hostility and suspicion, had developed to the point that—far from encouraging prompt and effective medical care for traffic victims—

> no single liability carrier in this country has yet adopted a system under which money is advanced to legitimate victims as a standard procedure to defray normal and necessary medical expenses, even in the face of clear liability and adequate coverage. I doubt if there is a handful of top [insurance] executives who would admit, publicly at least, that such a procedure would be both desirable and feasible. At the mere suggestion that it should be our way of life, a vast majority would join "Mr. Casualty Insurance" in [exclaiming] . . . : "Are you crazy, man, suggesting that we start financing our enemies?" [18]

To a limited extent, this has changed. Insurance companies are beginning to recognize—albeit not uniformly and often begrudgingly—that a new approach to accidents is necessary. It is obvious from what has been said that the framework of negligence law and negligence liability insurance has traditionally not placed primary emphasis on the victim and his care and rehabilitation. Rather the purpose of liability insurance has been to protect the assets of the negligent wrongdoer from being used to pay for any liability for his wrongdoing. In the words of Paul Wise, President of the American Mutual Insurance Alliance, a trade organization of mutual casualty insurance companies:

> As originally conceived more than half a century ago, an automobile liability policy was designed to protect the driver of the car against law suits, not to compensate the accident victim. Legally this is still the case. But public expectations have shifted more and more toward protecting the person who is injured. [19]

Reflecting this trend, insurance companies began a few years ago what they call an "advance payment" technique. Under this new method, where a company's insured is clearly liable, the insurance company offers to advance the victim money for his medical expenses and wage losses as they accrue, without requiring any release and with only the promise that the sums advanced be deducted from any ultimate negligence settlement or verdict. This is a reflection not so much of a humanitarian instinct as a recognition of the advantage to all concerned—even monetarily to the insurance company—from such an approach. According to Dr. Harriet E. Gillette, Secretary of the American Academy of Physical Medicine and Rehabilitation, "insurance companies are finally realizing that the physiatrist (doctor of physical medicine) is right when he says a paraplegic can be rehabilitated for $10,000 but it might cost $80,000 to maintain him in custodial care for life." [20] The change in insurance companies' approach and attitude is illustrated by the remarks of Dr. William J. Erdman, II, Director of the Department of Physical Medicine at both the University of Pennsylvania and Philadelphia General Hospital and a consultant to the advance payment-rehabilitation program of the Insurance Company of North America, one of the nation's largest casualty insurance companies. "In injury cases, we have often had trouble getting an insurance carrier to admit financial responsibility for a patient, and a hospital can't afford to carry them merely hoping for a settlement later on," says Dr. Erdman, who "couldn't believe" the switch when INA announced its new program.[21]

Not only is more effective and rapid—and less expensive—treatment fostered by the new technique, but some insurers are convinced that advance payments actually help to "control the claim" and keep it from being inflated in other ways. Insurers explain that if a victim becomes convinced that an insurance company is generally interested in his welfare, he will be less likely to go to a lawyer and perhaps push for a maximum settlement. But seeing an attorney doesn't stop the advance payments. According to Merle McCartney, Director of Claims Policies for Nationwide Mutual Insurance Companies, Columbus, Ohio, "[our] continuing to show an interest in the plaintiff's economic welfare will certainly contribute to favorable negotiations and

reasonable disposition of the claim at a later date." [22] The Wall
Street Journal has recounted

the case of Mrs. Marion Barbero of Wayne, New Jersey,
who was left with severe facial scars after an accident
in which the car in which she was riding was struck by
another whose driver was insured by Hartford Accident
& Indemnity Co. She had 35 stitches taken in her
face and emergency treatment, and Edward VanValen,
claims manager [for the Hartford Company] in the
Passaic, New Jersey, office, could see that the company
was exposed to a potentially large claim.

The Barberos agreed, at Mr. VanValen's suggestion,
to see a plastic surgeon he recommended (they were
driven there in a limousine arranged for by Hartford),
and got a quotation on the cost of surgery. Mr. Van-
Valen then told them the company would pay for everything without their signing a release, and that if they
weren't satisfied they could still get a lawyer and sue for
damages. He asked only that they agree that any money
spent by the company be credited against final settlement.

Mrs. Barbero had the plastic surgery which she says
has turned out "perfectly." Hartford was able to settle the
claim, which also covered minor injuries to her husband,
for a total of $4,140.00; it estimates that it saved several
thousand dollars on the case. "Without advance payments a settlement would have taken a couple of years
in this case," explains Mr. VanValen. "The Barberos
could not have afforded on their own the treatment that
Mrs. Barbero got, and by the time they received a settlement the scars would have adhered too well for such
successful plastic surgery. The case probably would
have been worth $7500 to $10,000 then."

As for Mrs. Barbero, she is grateful to Hartford for
its help. "We just felt that if they were going to be so

generous and take care of everything, we weren't interested in getting a lawyer," she says.[23]

The same Wall Street Journal article also reported on a similar case whereby Nationwide Mutual Insurance Company

worked closely with the Pennsylvania Bureau of Vocational Rehabilitation to restore mobility to a 49-year-old man who suffered severe fractures of both legs in an auto accident involving a [Nationwide] policyholder. Nationwide Mutual consulted with the state agency on his case, sent him to a private rehabilitation center where hip surgery was suggested, found an orthopedic surgeon, and arranged for the operation plus home nursing care afterward.

The man has regained 95% of his former mobility and Nationwide Mutual settled the claim for $6,000. Without fast action, says a company official, corrective surgery would have been more difficult and the case would have gone to its $10,000 policy limit.

"We saved a modest amount here," says John Henle, the company's manager of rehabilitation, "But if a company insists on coming out ahead on each case, it is going about rehabilitation all wrong. We expect to save money overall, but a good program must be based on all the potential values to the company, not just dollar savings." [24]

But the advance payment technique—while a welcome change from the uniformly hostile adversary process—has built-in limitations which prevent it from being a panacea for the many ills plaguing the fault system. In the first place, not all companies, by any means, are employing it. And even those who are using it do so only in those cases where liability is "clear"—although a few companies are experimenting with it on cases of "probable" liability as well. But this raises a further difficulty: These definitions are highly elastic and thus the whole program can turn on the whims and whirls in attitude of a given company or even its claim department. The basic problem is that the rights of the victim cannot be made to turn on the continuing largesse of a profit oriented organization, such as an insurance company, waiving its legal rights as to whether and when it may pay. Nor have they been waiving those rights very often in practice.

According to a DOT study, advance payments—despite all the fanfare about them from the insurance industry—have been made for only 8 per cent of seriously injured traffic victims, leaving all the rest out in the cold.[25] The continuing hardships stemming from the lack of payment, the underpayment, and the delay in payment for a typical traffic victim under the fault system were graphically documented in recent DOT studies. Many accident victims, in the words of DOT Deputy Assistant Secretary Barber are affected both "seriously and grievously, both economically in very plain personal terms." [26] For instance, for 22 percent of the most seriously injured victims, another member of the family was forced to seek employment; 14 per cent were forced to move to cheaper housing; 30 per cent had to draw on savings; 28 per cent had to borrow money to meet expenses; 29 per cent missed credit payments, and 45 per cent were forced to change their standard of living.[27] All this confirms the findings of the Michigan study that where the fault-insurance settlement produced a major part of the payment, there was too often "great financial stringency while the settlement was awaited. The survey showed many injury victims suffered deprivations pending settlement." [28]

According to the Michigan study:

> The length of time from injury to settlement is very important to injury victims. During that time there is likely to be hesitation to obtain the fullest desirable medical treatment, for fear of the burden of paying for it. If the victim is a wage earner, the family may well go on reduced rations, and even become a "relief case" while awaiting the settlement.[29]

"Advance payments," then, are only a flickering indication of what a genuinely compassionate and sensible insurance arrangement could be like. In the meantime for the overwhelming number of traffic victims, the old adversary game based on fault —with all its harshness, delays, unfairness and waste—goes on.

In sum, the fault-adversary system consistently commits that most unpardonable sin: adding insult to injury.

Chapter IV

Paying for Pain

Martin Mayer, in his best-seller of a few years ago, *The Lawyers*, was generally quite complimentary to law and lawyers: But not about auto accident law. "From any angle of approach," he wrote, "the realities of the legal consequences of [auto] accidents are an unconscionable mess."[1]

The most disheartening feature of that mess is that we spend so extravagantly to achieve it. The 56 cents of every auto insurance premium dollar spent in administrative and legal costs are in disturbing contrast, as Colston Warne, President of Consumers Union, has pointed out, to "an administrative cost of 3 cents in Social Security, 7 cents for Blue Cross, [and] 17 cents for health and accident plans . . . ."[2]

Actually, the waste of the fault insurance system as applied to auto accidents is even worse than Warne's comparison would indicate. Very little of that paltry 44 cents that filters through the lawyers and insurance men to the occasional traffic victim actually pays for what insurance is really supposed to pay for— namely, genuine out-of-pocket loss. The overwhelming percentage pays either to duplicate payments already made from health insurance or sick leave, or to buy off small "nuisance" claims.

Why should insurance money be paid for losses already being paid by other coverages? Under the legal rules of the fault system, surprising as it may seem, a settlement or verdict, supposedly to reimburse a victim for his losses, is not in any way diminished by the fact that a victim has not, in fact, suffered a loss in that he has already been paid from some other source, such as Blue Cross or sick leave.[3] This rule grew out of the understandable premise that the wrongdoer ought not to benefit —in having what he owes diminished—by the fact that the victim was prudent enough to have other sources of compensation, which he was probably paying for. At a time when other sources of compensation were meager, the effect of this rule may have been marginal. But one of the most significant occurrences in the field of injuries in the last thirty years has been the phenomenal growth in health and other forms of no-fault insurance. This growth has been so great that about two-thirds of what is paid to traffic victims now comes from the victims' own no-fault sources such as life insurance, health and accident insurance, Social Security, etc.[4] This means, of course, that fault insurance payments are often going to duplicate payments already made, rather than to cover genuine out-of-pocket losses. And, given the ever-increasing amounts of both government and nongovernment no-fault benefits (think for example of the impact of Medicare and Medicaid, not to speak of the growing availability of group health and accident insurance through employment), the waste is ever becoming that much worse.

Actually, the picture is even blacker than this black view. The waste stemming from the rule that ignores payment from other sources feeds on itself to produce even more waste when combined with the rule that allows a fault claimant to be paid not only for his out-of-pocket loss, such as wage loss and medical expenses, but for the monetary value of his pain and suffering as well. How do you measure pain and suffering? How do you translate physical discomfiture or agony into an insurance claim made up of dollars and cents? Value is defined in the law as: What a buyer, willing but not obliged to buy, would pay to a seller, willing but not obliged to sell.[5] Not a bad definition, when you think about it. At least it works when one is talking about a piece of real estate, or a used car, or even a plumber's services. But it fails almost completely when one is talking about pain and suffering because the unalterable fact is that there is no market for pain and suffering. It is not for sale. How can you decide, then, what my aching arm is worth? Actually the jury is forbidden the one yardstick that perhaps most naturally suggests itself: "What would I charge to suffer this pain myself?"[6] But, any way the question of how to value pain and suffering is formulated reveals how unanswerable it is. And yet this measuring the unmeasurable is what must be done in every personal injury case.

And because it must be done—and must be done constantly —a fairly expeditious, but potentially disastrous, way has been found: Quite simply, this involves paying a multiple of the out-of-pocket loss (called by the lawyers and insurance adjusters "the special damages" or often "the specials"). This entails multiplying by three, or perhaps four, or perhaps five or even ten, the amount of the medical bills or wage loss to arrive at the monetary value of pain and suffering (called by lawyers and insurance adjusters "the general damages").[7] But note the *tremendous* waste encouraged by having pain and suffering measured as a multiple, say, of medical expenses. For every dollar of medical expenses a victim can pad on—often needlessly and often paid for by some other insurance company, such as his health and accident insurance company—he will get back in the eventual settlement or verdict from his fault claim, not only one extra dollar but an additional three dollars or more, supposedly for his "pain and suffering." This is really a new way of coining money! The claimant already has, most likely, some accident and health insurance. He hires a lawyer at no risk to himself on a contingent fee (which means that the lawyer gets paid only if the claimant wins, whereupon the lawyer gets a percentage—usually one-third —of the payment) ; the lawyer knows—and the client learns soon enough—that all the client need do is utilize his accident and health insurance, once again at no risk to himself, to enable him to reap a prodigious profit (300 percent or more!). Could anything encourage more shameful and even fraudulent misuse of precious medical and insurance resources—both already sky-rocketing in cost because of *legitimate* demands on them?

The claims supervisor for one insurance company describes the process:

> To build up their case [attorneys] will tell their client to . . . "stay home for a few weeks especially since [he] . . . get[s] paid salary anyway," to lend credence to the claim that he was so badly hurt that he couldn't go to work. Or else they will send him down the street to the general practitioner for two or three visits to check on his neck—they'll do that and then they'll send him to an orthopedist for an examination which will cost us $50 and then, for those headaches the fellow has been having, they'll send him to a neurologist and then that will be another $50; and then to a radiologist. . . . Here we are talking about a case that, if the attorney wasn't there, might have accumulated $50 in medical bills and gone back to work. [Instead] with the advice of the attorney, he would have stayed away from work and gathered up about $300 to $400 of medical bills and a couple of hundred dollars worth of lost pay. So if an attorney is on the case, you set your sights . . . higher when it comes to [preparing to pay]. . . .[8]

The beauty of this kind of "build up" is that it is so hard to detect. It is very hard for an adjuster to argue that a certain amount of medical treatment is unnecessary, especially in a small case where there is a variety of petty complaints. As Professor H. Laurence Ross, a sociologist who has extensively studied the settlement of auto cases, has stated, "Most claims will support a modest amount of 'building,' and attorneys may take advantage of the opportunity."[9] Unfortunately, finding doctors who are willing to aid in such a medical build up is all too easy for lawyers, so that inflating minor personal injury claims into major ones has become big business. This practice—along with exaggerating the medical prognosis referred to earlier (see Chapter III *supra*)—has caused Martin Mayer to assert that the "money in personal injury law suits has corrupted two professions."[10]

Not long ago, a west coast professor was visiting a large eastern city between semesters. Driving his brother-in-law's car on a Saturday afternoon, he was in an accident when another driver banged into his rear, causing some damage to the car but, as far as he could tell, no injury to himself. On the advice of his brother-in-law, he went to see a lawyer who, in turn, referred him to a doctor. The professor expected an X-ray or two to be taken to be sure there was in fact no injury. But he was startled when the doctor, after taking the X-rays and finding nothing, stated, "Well, we'll put you in the hospital for several days anyway."

"The hospital!", exclaimed the professor. "I don't need to go into any hospital. Besides I've got to be back on the west coast by Monday to begin teaching."

"Professor," said the doctor, "it's going to cost you about $2,000 to teach your classes on Monday. Is teaching those classes worth that kind of money to you?"

In other words, the build up was on, and getting off would mean sacrificing a hefty windfall indeed. The professor—tempted as he was—decided he wanted no part of it. But how many of us would have similarly resisted? Especially since it was all so plausible and even "respectable"?

It would be a mistake to imagine, however, that any formula for measuring pain and suffering simplifies the settlement negotiations to the point that payment becomes expeditious. Claims are not paid on a formula basis except in completely routine cases—and most cases are not routine. When plaintiffs and defense lawyers were asked to name the principal source of controversy between them in negotiating over claims, they agreed that evaluating pain and suffering was second as a point of contention only to evaluating who was at fault.[11] The unpredictability of the negotiating process can perhaps best be appreciated by listening to a claims adjuster discuss the extent to which he uses, as a basis of settlement, the formula of medical expenses (or specials) multiplied by a given number:

> Assuming you're dealing with reasonable specials, assuming that you're dealing with all other factors being equal (and there's so few cases that fit this), I believe you can use that method, but there has to be so many other factors that are the same. I believe that it's fallible to use it as a god . . . . You cannot use it as a god because it's so—there's so many things wrong with it. For instance, I use it with attorneys where it works to my favor, where you get real small specials, then I'll talk this three times the specials. If he has built-up specials then I tend to play it down. I don't mention it or I don't bring it up because it's grossly wrong. It's useless to use it on some cases . . . . I use it and I don't use it, but I would say that for the average, run-of-the-mill case is to have it in the back of your mind and not being tied to it. It can be helpful, especially for a new adjuster who doesn't know where to start. He has no idea where to go. We occasionally mention this to him, but we say, "Don't think this is an authorization or that you can always use this 'cause it will throw you way off in many cases."[12]

In other words, the setting of a formula is only a rough approximation of a point to begin bargaining. Other factors, such as the conduct of the defendant, the age, sex, and appeal of the parties, can be highly influential, though often logically unrelated to the amount of the damages. The degree of fault—including outrageous behavior of the insured—forms one such instance. An adjuster may evaluate a case as worth more—though the claimant's damages remain unchanged—where the insured defendant was guilty of drunk driving in the accident, or engaged in a game of "chicken." In addition, it has been informally suggested that the value of a disability increases by 10 per cent for every 10 years over age 40 and that disability to a woman is worth 20 to 25 per cent more than the same disability to a man. Similarly valuable beyond any objective measurement are injuries to a young child.

Note that adjusters emphasize how much more the smaller claim is subject to the "build up." This is a function of the "nuisance value" of smaller claims. It costs insurance companies so much to negotiate and defend any fault claim—no matter how small, since each has its own nettlesome issue of appraising who was at fault and the value of pain and suffering—that an insurance company is sorely tempted to pay an inflated value, knowing how much more, comparatively speaking, a full scale defense of the claim will cost.[13]

Given, say, a cost of about $800 to defend the average claim, a claimant's lawyer says to the insurance company, "My client has $40 in out-of-pocket losses. I demand $400 in settlement."

"Why in the world should we pay you $400?" asks the company.

"Because you and I know it will cost you $800 to beat me. I'm actually saving you $400 by agreeing to settle for that amount." And he's right. So the claimant gets paid ten—or maybe only five—times his out-of-pocket loss.

A company is especially tempted to pay early what might seem even an inflated claim, as long as the dollar figure is relatively low, knowing how easy it will be for the claimant to keep building up his claim by the methods just outlined. Thus the intractable issues of evaluating who was at fault and the amount of pain and suffering work to the advantage of the claimant in small cases: His potential for "bothering" the insurance company with the expense of having to find out who was at fault and perhaps having to pay a comparatively large amount for pain and suffering gives him a disproportionate bargaining power. *The result is that in small cases the company often caves in by paying far more than the claim would seem to be worth.* This is reflected in the fact, as we have seen, that the claimant with only $100 or less of economic loss gets, on the average, over seven times his economic loss.[14]

Conversely, however, the intractable issues of evaluating who was at fault and the amount of pain and suffering work to the advantage of the insurance company in large cases. There the injured party's needs are likely to be so great (with his sick leave and accident and health insurance, if he has them, having run out) that he cannot afford the risk of losing, or even a long delay in negotiating. *The result is that in large cases the claimant often caves in by accepting far less than his claim would seem to be worth.* This is reflected in the fact, as we have seen, that the claimant with large out-of-pocket losses so often receives less than half his losses.[15]

This, then, is the overall situation: most of the money paid to traffic victims is supposedly paid for pain and suffering. (In the aggregate, the amount paid for noneconomic loss under the fault system averages about 1.5 times the amount paid for economic loss.)[16] But, in fact, those suffering pain the most are paid for it the least, and those suffering pain the least are paid for it the most. Indeed insurance companies, in paying above economic loss, most often are paying not for claimants' pain and suffering —though those are the terms used—but for relief of their own vexation. That vexation is caused by the nuisance value inevitably imparted to smaller claims where the criterion for payment is cumbersome and uncontrollable. What is really involved in all this business about paying for pain and suffering, then, is not the *claimant's* pain but the *company's*. In other words, it is not so much that the claimant has a real pain in the neck as that his untrammeled ability to profit by claiming a possibly false one gives the company a real one.

The result of all this is that the 44 cents (out of the original one dollar of insurance premium) that reaches the traffic victim breaks down as follows:

8 cents for economic loss already reimbursed from other sources.

21.5 cents for other than economic loss (largely for the nuisance value of smaller claims).

14.5 cents for genuine out-of-pocket loss not reimbursed from other sources.[17]

Genuine out-of-pocket loss is what most people believe they are insuring against. If told that only 14.5 cents out of the premium dollar they pay reimburses the essential insured loss, they would feel badly used indeed. And rightly so.

Chapter V

A Pound of Flesh
(All About Lawyers'
Contingent Fees)

A very large portion of the money being diverted from the pockets of traffic victims is going to their lawyers.

The traffic victim's lawyer is paid on what is called a contingent fee—that is, a fee contingent on his winning the case. Nationally, this fee averages about 33 per cent of whatever is paid the victim[1]—with nothing paid to the attorney if nothing is paid to the victim. The percentage is sometimes lower (e.g., 25%) if the suit is settled prior to trial and often higher (e.g., 40% or more) if the case is appealed.[2] This method of payment is in contrast to the way the attorneys are paid when they defend insurance companies. Then, they are usually paid, win or lose, on an hourly basis, plus extra fees for days in court.

The lawyer's contingent fee contract with an accident victim often gives the lawyer the right to take his percentage of the winnings before deducting the various costs and expenses (such as court filing costs, witness fees, etc.), thus placing all these costs on the claimant.[3] Oftentimes, however, these items are in fact deducted before the split is made, thus causing them to be shared in the proportion which sets the fee.[4]

Lawyers have often seen to it that their interest in contingent fees is protected by law. In several states—by law—lawyers must be paid before hospitals.[5] In addition, a claimant may find it very expensive to change attorneys in midstream. Conceivably, he could end up having to pay two full fees: one to the discharged lawyer and one to the successor lawyer. If each attorney had a contingent fee contract calling for the customary one-third to one-half of the recovery, the claiment's net recovery could approach zero.[6]

The contingent fee has long been the subject of intense controversy. Insurance people view it as the source of many, if not most, of the evils in the present personal injury system. In their view, it encourages attorneys—by making them, in effect, co-owners of the claims—to seek out claimants greedily and then to cause clients to pad their claims. "The contingent . . . fee is a cancer," says one insurance executive.[7] Many lawyers not engaged in personal injury practice tend to agree, asserting that the greedy overreaching, so characteristic, in their view, of personal injury claims, is due to the incentive to lawyers through the contingent fee to increase their take by increasing the size of the claim.

The late Reginald Heber Smith, a distinguished member of the Boston Bar and a lawyer who was particularly concerned with legal services for the poor, wrote 50 years ago:

> The contingent fee . . . attracted undesirable persons to become members of the profession. Because the stakes were high and the players essentially gamblers, it induced the unholy triumverate of lawyer-runner-doctor conspiring together to win fraudulent cases. It has degraded expert testimony and served as a cloak for robbery through extortionate fees. Unquestionably, it has done more than anything else to bring the bar into deserved disrepute.[8]

The contingent fee is unethical almost everywhere in the world but the United States.[9] It would be considered most unseemly for lawyers elsewhere to "own" a portion of a claim. Indeed, in the early development of Greek and Roman law, an advocate arguing someone else's cause was said to be carrying out a duty based on friendship and family. Since his was a "noble" act, and since being paid might lead to abuses, under early Greek, Roman, French and English law the advocate performed his services without any right to compensation. As a remnant of this, today, in England, the English barrister still is barred from suing a client for a fee. Rather, in that delightful world of make-believe in which the English choose to live so much of the time, the *formal* rule is that the barrister may accept an honorarium as a gesture of the client's gratitude but for which there is no obligation.[10] This is a charade, of course; the barrister expects and receives payment as routinely as his American counterpart.

The spur of the contingent fee—with the opportunity for lawyers to share in the return of a law suit—has led to the exploitation of the whole concept of pain and suffering as a major portion of personal injury damages in the United States. In some measure (except for corruption, which, God knows, exists—see Chapter IV *supra*), most items of damage are *relatively* unelastic. Medical expenses and wage loss, within limits, are based on objective facts. But "pain and suffering" is truly a protean concept—almost unlimited in the manner in which it can be expanded. Couple this with the fact that personal injury cases in the United States are tried before relatively sentimental and susceptible jurors, whereas elsewhere in the world judges sitting alone hear such cases, and with the fact that personal injury lawyers get a piece of the verdict. The result has been a development of this pain and suffering concept as an element of damages on a scale unimagined elsewhere in the world. Writing in 1964, a German legal scholar pointed out that the "highest amount adjudicated [for pain and suffering] since the end of World War II is 50,000 marks [$12,500]. In this case the plaintiff had suffered incredibly grievous injuries."[11] In the United States, such a case could have brought many hundreds of thousands—or perhaps even millions—of dollars to the claimant and his lawyer.

Of course generous payment for pain and suffering—especially in cases of grievous injury—has a *great* deal to recommend it, given the frightful misery that an injury can inflict. The trouble has been, as we have seen, that on the whole the potential for greatly expanded verdicts for pain and suffering, except for an occasional sensational verdict, has most often meant more nuisance value for smaller claims than actual compensation for pain in larger ones. (See Chapter IV *supra*.)

A significant factor in the growth of verdicts and settlements for pain and suffering in the United States has been the rise and growth of the American Trial Lawyers Association (ATL)—the organization of attorneys who represent the injured in personal injury suits.

The American Trial Lawyers Association was founded in 1946 by 11 lawyers specializing in representing injured employees in Workmen's Compensation cases. Originally, the organization was known as the National Association of Claimants Compensation Attorneys—often shortened to "NACCA." The newer and more euphemistic title was adopted in 1964. Since then, the organization has had such a phenomenal growth that it now numbers over 25,000 members. "In the process," according to *The New York Times*, "its members have wrought a revolution in civil litigation."[12]

A key part of the revolution has been a striking increase in the value of pain and suffering, as plaintiffs' lawyers have become ever more skilled in wringing ever larger amounts from juries. The principal weapon in this part of the revolution has been the use of so-called demonstrative evidence—evidence other than oral testimony that brings home, usually to the jurors' visual senses, the point counsel is trying to make. Says *The New York Times*, "By developing graphic techniques for demonstrating to juries the monetary value of disability, disfigurement, mental anguish, pain and suffering, [plaintiffs' lawyers] . . . made it possible for the most lowly victims to salve their hurts with handsome jury verdicts."[13]

What are these graphic techniques? Pictures or movies, for example, showing the tortuous exercises the plaintiff with a bad back must undergo on a typical day as the result of his injury. According to one lawyer, use is made of

> color pictures of the patient at various stages of his ordeal . . . . There is nothing like a bloody shot of a client shortly after his injury, or a martyr-picture of him in the hospital, up to his eyes in bandages and with his leg in a cast pulled up at an awkward angle with ropes and pulleys. You can feel the excruciating agony of the fellow trapped in this rack of torture, especially at the height of [his lawyer's] . . . final argument, when he screams with anguish, "This poor, helpless fellow has waited much too long for his money!"[14]

(Conversely, the defendant will sometimes show surreptitiously taken movies of the supposedly crippled plaintiff painting his house or playing golf.) Demonstrative evidence also includes large x-rays, diagrams, drawings, charts, "models, experiments, . . . skeletons and other medical exhibits, . . . surgical instruments, splints, crutches"[15]—in short, anything that will convey facts vividly to the jury. In one case, counsel had a mother remove a girl's glass eye right in front of the jury in a suit for injury to the eye. In another case, counsel had the plaintiff demonstrate the numbness of her leg by sticking pins in it.

One especially controversial technique of trial lawyers is the so-called "blackboard technique" whereby counsel uses in argument to the jury a mathematical formula stating that specific sums per day, hour, minute, or even per second should be allowed as damages for pain and suffering. In one case, for example, plaintiff's counsel put on the blackboard the time of the operation (1 hour and 6 minutes), the time of the general anesthesia (2 hours) and the number of hours in the hospital (53 hours). Counsel also then broke down the plaintiff's life expectancy into 233,600 hours and placed this on the blackboard for consideration by the jury. His aim was to suggest to the jury a specific value for each segment of pain, subdivided into periods of time. Some idea of the astronomical values that such techniques can impart to personal injury cases can be seen from the remarks of the appellate court in this case, "If one cent were used for each second of pain, this would amount to . . . [$36] per hour, to . . . [$864] per 24-hour day, and to . . . [$315,360] per year. . . . [Y]et a penny a second for pain and suffering might not sound unreasonable."[16]

Because of such astronomical figures, some courts—including the court in the case just referred to—outlaw such a blackboard argument; but others permit it on the ground that it is as valid as any other way of arguing about the "value" of pain and suffering.

Not only have the members of the American Trial Lawyers developed such techniques, they have aggressively encouraged their use by lawyers everywhere. ATL has for years conducted seminars throughout the country—and at law schools—disseminating information on techniques for high verdicts. These seminars are taught by their top members and are widely attended. According to *The New York Times*:

> In fact, the [recent] rise in verdicts coincided with the growth of the organization, and was due in large part to its vigorous training efforts. Where 20 years ago a claimant could not find a lawyer in many communities who could compete with the skillful insurance advocates who represented most defendants, now the A.T.L.A. holds clinics in about 100 cities each year.
>
> . . . "You don't hear all about that insurance-company baiting anymore," said A.T.L.A. lawyer J. B. Cobb

of Memphis [at a recent A.T.L. meeting], gazing . . .
down the row of skeletons and other training devices.

"Now we beat them with brains and training."[17]

In the wake of these efforts, personal injury cases in the
United States, in the words of an earlier work by Professor
Robert Keeton and myself, have been turned into

theatrical extravaganzas, rather than rational, dispas-
sionate hearings. Elaborate techniques are carefully
wrought to appeal to the jurors' weaknesses—their
"sympathy, bias, credulity, gullibility, susceptibility to
impression to a good speech, a good display and a good
show." Expensive, multivolumed tomes are published
to instruct [plaintiff's] counsel in great detail how to
play upon the jury's weakness—"how to invest his
working capital in a production designed to take the
fullest advantage of it, and how to cash in."[18]

As Dean Prosser has said, "European lawyers view the
whole thing with utter amazement."[19]

Unquestionably, the lawyer's contingent fee can take a savage cut out of the victim's payment—keeping in mind that *all* of
the payment is designed, in theory at least, to reimburse the
victim for his loss, with no extra amount being tacked on for
attorney's fees. Thus, the contingent fee almost literally comes
out of the plaintiff's hide. A study in Michigan showed that
whereas the mean collection expenses—consisting mostly of attorneys' fees—were around 33%, they ranged in some cases up
to more than 60% of the settlement.[20] Thirteen per cent of traffic victims in Michigan incurred collection expenses of between
40 to 59%.[21] A study of retainer statements filed in New York
City revealed that, prior to the institution of rules restricting
the amount of contingent fees, about 60% of the 188,000 retainers
filed were for a 50% fee, though the eventual fee may have been
less in many cases.[22]

In the words of former Judge David Peck, when the contingent fee approaches the 50% level, "it ceases to be a measure
of due compensation for professional services and makes a

lawyer a partner or proprietor in the lawsuit."[23] In point of fact,
when the lawyer is getting the standard contingent fee of one-
third, he is also, to a significant extent, a partner in the litigation
—owning, when you stop and think about it, fully half as much
as the victim himself.

It is this proprietary interest in the claim, it is argued, that
causes lawyers to indulge in ambulance chasing; to cause groundless and even fraudulent suits to be brought; to employ professionally partisan witnesses, especially medical witnesses who are
ready to slant their testimony; to pad claims; to suppress less
favorable facts and to exaggerate more favorable ones; to use
improper coaching of witnesses; to use overly sensational demonstrative evidence designed to play on the sympathy and emotions
of the jury; and to indulge in sharp and even unethical trial
tactics.

One report of a disbarment proceeding illustrates the more
corrupt aspects of the contingent fee. An Illinois lawyer, William W. McCallum, employed numerous "runners" in several
midwestern states to "chase ambulances" and to solicit cases for
him. Although he told the clients that his fee would be 33%,
he actually had them sign a contract agreeing to a 50% fee
by telling them they were signing an accident report for the
Interstate Commerce Commission. He would then put the client
up in a Chicago hotel, pay his hotel bill, his medical bills, court
costs and even advance him money, taking a note in return.
When payment on the claim was received, all these costs and
the 50% fee were deducted, often leaving very little for the
client, which even then might not be paid without a fight.[24]

But the evils of overcharging under the contingent fee lie
not so much in spectacular instances of chicanery. Rather, it is
argued, contingent fees in the *normal* cases are exorbitant for the
services performed. In the words of F. B. McKinnon, who conducted for the American Bar Association the most thorough
study ever done on the contingent fee:

> As the fee is payable without regard to time spent
> on the case, it may be to the lawyer's advantage to set-
> tle it quickly, spending as little time as possible on the

small claim where the increment in value through rigorous bargaining or trial, while significant to the client, is not significant or perhaps even compensatory to the lawyer. For example, the addition of $100 to the recovery of a claim for which an offer of $300 has been made will add $25 to $50 to the lawyer's fee, but may require more than that amount of his time. However, the additional $50 or $75 may be very important to the client. It is financially more profitable to handle a mass of small claims with a minimum expenditure and time on each than it is to treat each as a unique case and fight for each dollar of the maximum possible recovery for the client.[25]

To encourage the lawyer to devote more time to a case, sometimes the contingent fee contract is graduated so as to afford additional compensation according to the stage of litigation at which payment is obtained. Here, too, though, "the increase in the rate of fee may lead the lawyer to bring suit or start trial . . . solely to increase his rate from 25% to 33⅓%, without actually doing that much additional work, and without the likelihood of a comparable increment to the client. (Studies show that bringing a case to trial does not, in itself, increase the value of the claim.)"[26] Insurance company lawyers are often guilty of the same conduct. Defense attorneys are paid for their time, and more for days in court. According to a Pennsylvania survey, "There is evidence that a significantly large number of cases in Allegheny County are settled only after a jury is sworn in order to allow the [defense] attorney to collect his fee for a 'day' in court." In the words of *The New York Times*, "Lawyers are touchy about this [lack of work in personal injury contingent fee cases], but in a profession where a man's earning capacity is too often tied to his available working hours, these windfall cases can make the difference between a good and a bad earning year."[27]

Although the contingent fee means that the lawyer typically owns half as much or more of the claim as the claimant, oftentimes the problem is not that the interest of the lawyer and client are identical (though, as we have seen, this can be a problem in destroying the lawyer's professional objectivity about the case), but that their interests conflict. For example:

¶ For the lawyer who has a great backlog of personal injury cases, delay is not an acute problem. On the contrary, he is busy with many claims and regards an individual case, according to McKinnon, as "one of a series . . . ripening on the vine."[28] On the other hand, the Michigan survey showed that delay in settlement of claims is very disturbing for many claimants.[29]

¶ A lawyer will not uncommonly delay receipt of a large settlement in order to put it over to the next year when he expects the effect on his income tax will be better for him. Conversely, a lawyer may capitulate and accept a quick but unwise settlement because he—not the client—needs the cash.

¶ Although, as we have seen, the lawyer may be tempted to settle a case quickly rather than spend more energy on it with little return to him as opposed to his client, occasionally the converse is true. A lawyer may be tempted to fight a case through a court verdict, win or lose, just to "keep the insurance company honest." In other words, a lawyer's bargaining position with an insurance company through the years is determined, among other things, by how willing he is to fight. If the company has offered, say, $6,000 on a case where the lawyer has demanded $7,000, it might clearly be in the interest of the client to take the $6,000 in view of the chances of losing and getting nothing. But the lawyer in the interest of building up his reputation as a fighter for use in future claims may turn down the settlement. Perhaps this tactic benefits his clients as a group as well as himself, but the interests of the individual client clearly may be sacrificed. Conversely, a lawyer may be dissuaded from pushing hard on a given claim by an insurance company representative who insists that he will "make it up to him later in other cases." Here again, perhaps the lawyer's clients as a group may benefit; but the individual client clearly has been prejudiced.

¶ One other tactic which is to the advantage of the lawyer but detrimental to at least some of his clients is the "group settlement" whereby a lawyer will "wholesale" a large group of claims he has against a single insurance company in a "package deal." This arrangement may be to the advantage of both the lawyer and the insurance company because it disposes of a whole group of claims in one fell swoop, saving time and labor for both sides. The lawyer, too, gets a nice slice of the big package. But obviously individual claimants may have their interests sacrificed; many claims may be diminished to make up for the weaknesses of several in the pile. The lawyer, too, then assumes arbitrary power in doling out the proceeds of the group settlement to the individual claimants on a basis which may be very different from their individual due.[30]

Of course, attorneys taking advantage of clients is not unknown in other areas of the law. But the extent to which the lawyer is tempted to serve his own interests rather than his client's is probably unique in auto accident cases. In the words of Professor H. Laurence Ross:

> The attorney's relationship with his personal injury client has struck some observers as being of a different order from the relationship usually envisaged between client and attorney. [Researchers Roger] Hunting and [Gloria] Neuwirth, for instance, suggest that there might be a degree of exploitation here that is not found elsewhere in legal work:

> ". . . [W]e find that the traditional attorney-client relationship of trust and reliance, the intimate counselor and adviser usually thought of when 'attorney and client' is mentioned, is far from the relationship that often exists when the client is the victim of an automobile accident. There, instead, we find two strangers who deal with each other only in passing. The client may be, in the eyes of the lawyer, only the source of a piece of lucrative 'raw material' to be processed to a settlement while the lawyer is, in the eyes of the client, only a necessary professional aid in extracting from the insurance company enough money to compensate him for expenses and suffering."[31]

All this chicanery by lawyers can lead to strong public reaction. Judge John Van Voorhis of the New York Court of Appeals, in upholding judicial regulation of contingent fees (which was challenged by a group of New York trial lawyers), warned of the "growing public resentment" of excessive contingent fees and upheld the Court's power to regulate "lawyers who are trying to sail too close to the wind."[32] Similarly Bernard Botein, a very respected jurist who has recently left the bench to return to the practice of law, warns that present excesses with reference to contingent fees "may be inviting a public revulsion that could shake our courthouses to their foundations."[33]

But the contingent fee has its passionate defenders—especially among personal injury lawyers. Indeed, public criticism of the contingent fee causes them to leap up and sputter about its virtue with an indignation that it should be challenged. (In point of fact, whenever people are as supersensitive to criticism as personal injury lawyers are about contingent fees, isn't there probably something to be sensitive about?) In the first place, personal injury lawyers argue that the contingent fee enables the impecunious, who could never otherwise afford expert counsel, to hire a lawyer able to compete with the highly skilled adjusters and lawyers employed by insurance companies. They argue that given the inherently disproportionate bargaining power between the confused, isolated, injured individual and the experienced, massively financed, impersonal insurance company, the necessity for being able to readily obtain counsel is acute for the injured victim.

This justification of the contingent fee is surely somewhat undercut, however, by the fact that lawyers will not normally take a personal injury case on *other* than a contingency fee no matter how wealthy the client. In other words, while the contingent fee may have developed as a means of allowing the person of limited or average means to seek redress in the courts, the fact that, as a practical matter, lawyers insist on its use whatever the financial condition of the claimant suggests that in substantial measure its use is widespread today because it is so profitable for lawyers.[34] (It is true that recently—but only recently—the Canons of the American Trial Lawyers Association have called upon ATL members to make available to clients the choice of a non-contingent fee[35]—for example, an hourly fee based on time spent—but, given the uniform preference and practice of its members in using only a contingent fee in personal injury cases, one can only be very skeptical at how much difference this formality has made or will make.)

Lawyers often justify the contingent fee by the risk that they run in taking these cases. Says one prosperous lawyer, "Look at the risk I take. If I lose the case, I get nothing for the time and effort I've invested." While there are risks to personal injury suits, to justify the contingent fee on the grounds of the risk the plaintiffs' lawyers run may be difficult indeed. In point of fact the risk to the lawyer of getting nothing is very small. A study in New York City showed that, when lawyers are retained, payments are made about 90 per cent of the time.[36] Said former New York Judge Botein, "There is very little that is contingent about the contingent fee. . . . [T]he dread contingency of no recovery and therefore no fee is pretty remote."[37]

The real justification for the contingent fee, if there is one, is that lawyers can be said to earn it. Thus studies tend to show that hiring a lawyer not only increases the chance and amount of payment but leaves more net payment for the claimant even after deducting his lawyer's fee. According to one statistical study conducted at the Columbia Law School, "the claimant who retains an attorney improves his chances of recovery"; and, in addition, "the increment to the victim who retains an attorney is large enough so that, even after the attorney's fee is deducted, he will 'net' more than if he had handled the case himself."[38]

Insurance companies seem willing to pay claimants, when they retain lawyers, a sufficient increment to more than cover the lawyer's cost. In other words, in the tough test of the market place, the contingent fee seems to prove its worth. What this seems to mean is that, given the tremendous variables that go into a claim for personal injury, the contingent fee, in the words of Professor Alfred Ehrenzineig, is a necessary corrective of all the "risk[s] involved in the gamble of a negligence suit."[39]

When no one can be sure of what—if anything—is due, an expert seems necessary to guide the inexperienced up the tortuous path to payment. The value (and perhaps danger) of the lawyer's services is illustrated by the story of the client who complained bitterly that the lawyer was taking 50 per cent of *"my* recovery in *my* case." "It isn't *your* recovery in *your* case," snapped the lawyer. "The case *you* came in here with wasn't worth anything. It was *my* case that won the recovery."

One thing seems clear: Contingent fees in personal injury cases mean big money for the American lawyer. According to a study in Illinois, more money is spent on legal expenses arising after accidents than for medical treatment.[40] One expert has informally estimated that personal injury litigation provides for one-third of all lawyers most of their income individually and represents a full one-half of the bar's collective income. Similarly, J. Harry La Brum, a prominent Philadelphia insurance lawyer, estimates that "more than 50 per cent of all private law practice, in terms of dollars, flows from automobile accident cases . . . ."[41] Others find this too high, and, in point of fact, no firm figures are available. Two studies—one in New York City and the other in Ohio—both arrive at the conclusion that approximately 15 per cent of the bar's gross income comes from contingent fees in personal injury cases.[42] A recent study of the Department of Transportation indicates that lawyers earn about one billion dollars annually from traffic accident claims, with plaintiffs' lawyers earning $794 million, insurance company lawyers $180 million, and each side spending about $55 million in other litigation expenses.[43] Given about 200,000 lawyers in private practice in the United States, one billion dollars works out to about $5,000 per lawyer.[44] In point of fact, the money is not, of course, distributed evenly; rather some lawyers earn many hundreds of thousands of dollars and others little or nothing from auto accident cases. Some idea of the wealth that contingent fees can mean for some lawyers is indicated by a report on a New Jersey lawyer:

> He has been in practice for 18 years, [and] . . . isn't at all well known outside Essex County, New Jersey. He

isn't an officer of the trade association of personal injury lawyers, the American Trial Lawyers Association; he doesn't get interviewed the way Melvin Belli does; he doesn't have the fame among other lawyers that Jacob Fuchsberg and Harry Gair of New York do in this field. In fact, . . . the vast majority of the lawyers in the New York metropolitan area have never heard of this forty-two-year-old attorney. Yet year in and year out he is good for a *net* of nearly $350,000 a year from contingent fees. And even more—if he had not paid out some $280,000 to other lawyers for referring cases to him.[45]

Whatever the precise figures and spread, the dependence of *many* lawyers on auto cases (which probably constitute about 85 per cent of all personal injury cases) is widespread. Says attorney Alfred W. Gans, formerly the editor of the *American Law Reports,* "The basic bread-and-butter of almost all individual lawyers today [i.e., lawyers practicing alone] is the occasional negligence case."[46] Maurice Rosenberg, one of the country's leading experts on procedure and litigation, has stated that, if personal injury cases were removed from the courts, "about two-thirds of the bar in New York State . . . would feel the pinch badly."[47]

Keep in mind that for every three or four dollars paid to plaintiffs' lawyers to get or increase payment in auto cases, approximately one dollar is paid to defense lawyers to deny or reduce payment.[48] Thus, despite the bitter and often personal antagonism between plaintiffs' and insurance lawyers, they rally together in an unholy alliance to preserve the fault insurance system that serves them both so well.

Plaintiffs and defense lawyers try to play on their role as strange bedfellows by stating that the agreement of such long-standing foes on any issue must prove how right they are. But Representative Anthony Scariano of the Illinois House of Representatives, long a colorful battler for the underdog and an early sponsor of no-fault auto insurance (despite the fact that he is a lawyer), has viewed it somewhat differently:

The best indication that the [no-fault] . . . plan is a good plan is that you find both those who represent the defense and those who represent plaintiffs against it. Just as whenever labor appears with management on the same side against any bill in the legislature I know it is a good bill, whenever the representatives of the defense and the plaintiffs get together against a bill, I know it must be a good bill.[49]

Even the contingent fee—so deeply resented by the insurance industry—may not be so deeply resented by the industry's lawyers. John D. Phelan, President of the American States Insurance Company of Indianapolis, pointed out in a speech to insurance counsel the indirect fondness of defense lawyers for their opponents' lavish fees.

Let's recognize that the defense attorney presently may feel he has a great economic stake in the continuance of the contingent fee. . . . Unlimited contingent fees have seemed good to the business side of the practice of defense law. The economic theory is simple. Unlimited contingent fees generate suits in quantity. Suits in quantity require defense [lawyers] . . . in quantity.[50]

Indeed even non-personal injury lawyers—those specializing in real estate, say, or probate—can be viewed as having a stake in the preservation of the fault insurance system and its concomitant contingent fee. For years lawyers not engaged in personal injury practice have recognized what a disaster the fault system has been for the insuring public, for the court system and for traffic victims. Almost all of them will readily admit that in private. But with discouragingly few exceptions, these other lawyers have refused to speak about the problem in public, not to mention actually supporting reform. Part of this is the *noblesse oblige* among professional brethren, each specialty of the law being left to pursue its own interests in its own bailiwick, without any outside professional interference. But, partly, it may be the fear—probably irrational (see Chapter XI *infra*)—that removing the necessity for lawyers in auto cases by no-fault insurance would, in the words of Lewis C. Ryan, a past president of the

American College of Trial Lawyers, not only ruin the "50 per
cent of the legal profession" dependent on such cases, but also
"adversely affect the other half because the industrious, imaginative and skillful trial lawyers who specialize in tort litigation
would quickly invade and master the other fields of practice in
which the other groups excel."[51]

Chapter VI

. . . To the Hounds (All About Ambulance Chasing)

There is more than enough money involved in auto accident cases to make "chasing" those cases well worth it—although doing so is strictly illegal and subjects a lawyer to disbarment.

Ambulance chasing is big business. Just how big was suggested by a recent newspaper investigation by the *Chicago's*

American (now *Chicago Today*): "Ambulance chasing is one of the safest and most lucrative rackets in America . . . ." But, unlike "dope, gambling and prostitution . . . it is all but unpunishable . . . ."[1]

In Philadelphia alone, a report of the Philadelphia Bar Association's Committee on Censors recently revealed that about 75 lawyers were earning about 10 million dollars a year from the "unethical solicitation of personal injury cases."[2]

It is just as well that newspapers are willing to talk about ambulance chasing. Lawyers often are not. The Philadelphia Bar Committee's report was published only because it was leaked to *The Philadelphia Bulletin*. Indeed the report itself was an interim report, "drafted in an effort to head off attempts by some members of the Bar to kill off a final report . . . . The Board of Governors [of the Bar Association] had earlier refused to grant the committee another year to investigate the evidence it was uncovering . . . . The . . . committee . . . decided not to make public the interim report. Despite this, however, *The Bulletin* obtained a copy."[3]

At about the same time as the Philadelphia revelation, in Illinois *The Chicago Tribune* reported an accusation by the Law Practice Study Committee of the Illinois House of Representatives that, in the words of the Committee chairman, "the Chicago Bar Association has taken absolutely no action" to disbar or suspend some 50 lawyers in the city suspected of using ambulance chasers. The Committee chairman was referring to lists of lawyers' names submitted to the Legislative Committee by Chief Judge John S. Boyle of the Cook County Circuit Court, which lists had been turned over to the Chicago Bar Association for scrutiny some nine months earlier. James Velde, the Bar Association president, responded that the Bar "lacks sufficient funds and personnel to initiate investigations of these 50 suspect lawyers."[4]

The apparent reluctance of the Philadelphia and Chicago Bars to act against widespread and notorious ambulance chasing is all the more damaging when it is realized that in Illinois, as in Pennsylvania and some other states, while the most readily

applicable law forbids "any person not an attorney at law to
solicit . . . any claim for personal injuries . . . ,"[5] attorneys are
not covered by the law. Thus, if the Bar won't act against attorneys, the chances of anyone else doing so are greatly reduced.

Ambulance chasing began—and has grown up—with the
automobile accident.[6]

Just how does ambulance chasing work?

Keep in mind that being in a traffic accident, in addition to
causing one a lot of misery, can be worth a lot of money.
(Chapter IV *supra*.) But this "asset" of being an accident victim
is worthless to the average untutored victim who does not know
anything about such arcane matters as tort law, with its rules
of negligence and contributory negligence, the collateral source
rule (whereby one is entitled to get one's medical bills and wage
loss paid for again and again) or the right to recover payment
for one's pain and suffering. Not only is the typical traffic victim
ignorant of such matters; he is often from a lower socio-economic
level, knowing not only no law but no lawyers as well. On the
contrary, law and lawyers genuinely frighten him. So there he
is with his inchoate "juicy asset" and no knowledge of its existence, or at any rate no knowledge of how to exploit it. Couple
this with two other interrelated phenomena: First, lawyers are
strictly forbidden, under their Canons of Ethics, from advertising
or soliciting business. Second, insurance companies know that
most people don't know anything about the law of automobile
accidents, and that lawyers are not allowed to seek them out to
tell them about it. So if insurance adjusters can get to victims
promptly, they can settle the case for a fraction of what it will
cost if it chances to drift into the hands of a lawyer. Enter
therefore the person who not only *does* know what a bonanza an
auto accident can be, but whose job (unlike the lawyer's) legiti-
mately enables him to learn when an accident has occurred
almost as soon as it happens. These people include policemen, tow-
truck drivers, ambulance personnel, hospital orderlies, nurses,
interns, doctors and garage mechanics, as well as others who,
in the words of one lawyer, are "in a position to get cases—if
people are in an accident, they find out."[7]

In Chicago, chasers get a minimum of a $100 "a head" for sending an accident victim to a given lawyer but the fee could go to $1500 for a case with serious injuries. "For a badly injured person," according to the *Chicago's American* investigation, "a chaser can command a percentage of the lawyer's fee—usually one-third. In a prime case he might ask for bids."[8] In Philadelphia, according to the Bar Committee report, chasers "are paid $150 when the injured person is 'signed up' as a draw against 10 per cent of the attorney's fee."[9] Chasers run the gamut from "amateurs," such as individual former clients occasionally in a position to refer a case, to highly professional corps of operators. Says one lawyer who receives over one-half his personal injury cases on recommendation from prior clients and others:

> If a colored guy sends me a case, a 200 dollar case, I give him 10 dollars. If you don't, he won't remember you the next time. . . .
>
> . . . I don't have any professional chasers, I'm too frightened to use them. Mine come from referrals. With certain ones I don't give a gratuity. . . . My brother has an associate doctor, and they get nothing except free legal advice. And I don't give friends money. For 20 per cent I have to give gratuities. With colored you have to give them something, and they're very appreciative—and they're good for getting business. Fifteen per cent of my clients are colored. They're warm, good-hearted people, and if they trust the lawyer they trust him down the line.[10]

At the other end of the spectrum is a law office with "100 to 150 cases in the works, promising fees running to seven . . . figures. At one time, an even two dozen full- or part-time chasers drummed up business for the lawyer under the guidance of a dispatcher or master of hounds, who was paid $10,000 a year just to route them around."[11]

Legal sociologist Jerome Carlin has described a large scale chasing operation. He mentions:

. . . a few very successful personal injury lawyers who rely almost exclusively on highly organized methods of solicitation, cooperating with chasers and others who have made it their business to locate the potentially most rewarding cases. These people, armed with retainer contracts in blank, have developed quite elaborate and seemingly efficient procedures that enable them to be first in time to reach potentially lucrative clients. They have contacts with police, particularly in accident squads, and contacts in hospitals with interns, doctors, nurses and ambulance drivers. It is well known, for example, that certain hospitals are "controlled" by certain chasers. As one lawyer put it:

> _____ [a well-known personal injury lawyer]
> makes a million a year from _____ Hospital.
> If I went in there, the police would escort me
> out. An outsider can't get in — I'd be picked
> up for unethical practice.

The best-organized chasers have automobiles patrolling hospitals with two-way radios and can be informed almost instantly of . . . an accident case. A chaser, often working with one of the doctors or interns, will be at the patient's bedside with a contract ready to "sign him up" as soon as the patient has recovered sufficiently to write his name. The lawyer quoted above reported just such an incident:

> At 2:15 a court reporter came over, and
> we went out to a client's home to take a state-
> ment. He was badly hurt and had been taken
> to a hospital; and, when he regained con-
> sciousness, the doctor assigned to him — gee,
> I hope this will be confidential — introduced
> a young man to him saying, "He'll be your
> lawyer, sign here." In addition, they took
> his savings account book. I've got a sworn
> statement from the court reporter. The

> patient wanted to hire me. He had been referred to me by his employer.[12]

So great is the competition in urban areas between chasers and insurance adjusters, and among chasers themselves, that the *Northwestern University Law Review,* speaking of Chicago, describes it as "an exciting version of cops and robbers which might be called 'ambulance chasers and insurance adjusters.' "[13] Each strives to get to the injured first, the adjusters to get a settlement and the chasers to sign up the victim for their lawyers. One writer has written of the "frantic haste" of a chaser's work, which is "lively, competitive, full of stratagems and spoils," with instances of "chasers who climb hospital fire escapes to get to a victim's side."[14] Says one lawyer, "There isn't a lawyer in Chicago who doesn't do it—some kind of [payment] . . . to people who bring in business."[15] According to a claims supervisor of one insurance company:

> A large percentage of the legal representation of personal injury clients in Chicago is got by unethical means. The national average is 25 per cent representation by counsel; in Chicago 75 per cent are represented by counsel. If the police are called to the scene of an accident, there is no foreseeable chance but that an active and vigorous solicitation will follow. Corrupt politicians are on the payroll of chasers . . . .[16]

That chasing entails a violation of professional ethics—and, in most states, laws—means that rank corruption is pervasive. For example, the Philadelphia Bar report indicated that, of the "27 professional runners" it uncovered, "virtually all of [them] . . . have criminal records."[17] The chill cast on the whole business is described by one personal injury lawyer:

> That type of business [using chasers]—first, something about it is abhorrent. These chasers put you under pressure—they run the lawyer, the lawyer doesn't run them. You become dependent on them, and if you depend on them it could hurt you if they turn from you. They'll keep you busy if you do a volume of business.

And their demands are exorbitant. Some want 40 per cent, some 50 per cent—the good chaser wants more than a third.[18]

The injection of corruption can indeed reach ugly proportions. Both the Philadelphia and Chicago investigations indicated that the corruption of ambulance chasing encompasses *extensive* padding of chased claims by doctor-chasers and others. Nor is the chicanery limited to padding claims. Recently, an indictment was returned by a federal grand jury in Chicago against ten persons, including seven lawyers, charging the ten with engaging "in a fifteen million dollar ambulance chasing racket . . . by submitting phony and inflated personal injury and auto repair claims arising out of minor fender-bender accidents," including "false medical claims."[19] Nor is the corruption limited to faking medical claims outright; it even extends to staging "fictitious" accidents.

Consumer reporter Sylvia Porter has described such a racket:

Typically, an unscrupulous lawyer hires two or three people in two different cars to stage an auto accident in which a fender or two are damaged fairly badly —enough to make physical injury appear a possibility. Then, with the cooperation of an unethical doctor, the lawyer files a fat claim against the insurance company of the "hitter" on behalf of the individual who allegedly suffered a whip-lash injury.

The hitter, of course, is well protected by a liability insurance policy, although his car may have been rented. The "injured" individual plays his part—by being admitted to a hospital, feigning injury, etc.[20]

There is so much money to be made of auto accident cases that tiers of "chasing" are created—with each tier taking a fat cut from the pie. First, the chaser refers his case to what sociologist Carlin calls a lower-level personal injury lawyer, in return, oftentimes, for a percentage of the lawyer's fee: If the case is a significant one, the lower-level lawyer then refers it to an upper-level personal injury lawyer, in return for a percentage of the second lawyer's fee. This latter practice is called "broker-ing." It too is a naked violation of the legal Canons of Ethics. Canon 34 of the American Bar Association's Code of Ethics flatly forbids any division of fees between lawyers where there is no actual division of labor or services in the case. And yet, in the overwhelming number of instances where cases are for-warded, the forwarding lawyer simply obtains the case (by fair means or foul) and sends it along to a lawyer capable of actually trying it, if need be. Certainly, the typical attorney who is for-warding many cases couldn't even begin to conduct an actual trial. Hence the name "broker." He does not in fact function as a lawyer. He has an illicit system set up to get cases; he negotiates the easier and smaller ones and forwards the bigger and more complicated ones to a "real" lawyer, if you will. Soci-ologist Carlin has described such a "law" practice:

> The personal injury practice of half the specialists in this area—the lower-level practitioners—is restricted to building up a file and to efforts at negotiation with claims adjusters. The paperwork is routine and rela-tively uncomplicated. Contact with the courts is gen-erally limited to filing complaints or motions and an occasional appearance; only one such lawyer mentioned that he ever tried a case. The bigger cases are referred out to other lawyers if they cannot be readily settled.[21]

According to Carlin, the lower-level personal injury practi-tioner "reads nothing in the way of legal material and engages in no research. His paperwork is reduced to a rather simple routine."[22] Says one of the breed, "I'm ashamed to tell you [I don't even spend] . . . an hour a week [reading legal material]. You can say I get by on cursory knowledge of the law. . . . [As to preparing legal documents], I use a form, filling in the date, and so on, so it doesn't take too much time. If it's in the Circuit or Superior Court it's just a simple two-page document. . . . If you don't go to court, almost any lawyer can handle a personal injury case . . . . It's not complicated."[23]

Referring cases and sharing fees, despite no work done, is not confined to hacks specializing in brokering personal injury cases. A New Jersey upper-level personal injury specialist comments as follows:

> A man is hurt in an accident. He goes to his family lawyer or more likely just the lawyer who handled his home closing or a relative's divorce. Most people don't *have* lawyers. They *go* to someone. The case sounds pretty good and the lawyer, who wouldn't know a sacroiliac from a sacred fount—and *knows* he doesn't know—calls me because he has done business with me before. And that's *all* he does. *I* want it that way. I got my methods and forms; I don't want him sticking his two cents in and lousing me up. Oh, maybe if it's one of those rare cases that actually goes to trial he comes around one day and sits at counsel table. It looks good, you know. He knows I am on the up-and-up. He is going to get his check for a third of my fee the day after the insurance company check is in my office.[24]

Typically, then, such a forwarding lawyer would receive "a third of [the] . . . fee, which would be, in a typical 6,000 dollar award, about 650 dollars for making a phone call and listening to the client for maybe a half hour."[25]

So common is this improper practice of fee-splitting that, according to one prominent Washington attorney, "The practice of dividing fees with another lawyer, who has done no more than refer a client, is so widespread among certain segments of the bar that the phrase 'the usual forwarding fee' is commonly employed . . . ."[26]

Thus, the typical upper-level lawyer in many urban areas, who can and does try cases, is heavily dependent on referrals from other lawyers. It is not uncommon for well over half their business to be obtained in this manner. The referring lawyers are willingly paid a third to a half of the final fee.[27] So the "broker" pays a good cut to the chaser, and the "lawyer" pays a good cut to the "broker," with no real complaint, since there is more than enough to go around. Of course, all this is coming out of money supposedly being paid to compensate the victim for his loss and suffering; and it's also obviously coming out of the pocket of the consumer paying the premium on his insurance policy.

Another form of corruption permeating much of the present auto compensation system is the support given by lawyers to traffic victims for their medical fees and lost wages, etc., pending the settlement or verdict. The necessity for such payment is a natural outgrowth of the fault system's rule calling for only one lump-sum payment at the end of all the negotiating, which rule militates against any periodic payments. (See Chapter III *supra.*) Thus, without such outside support from their lawyers, many victims simply could not hold out and would be forced to capitulate and accept far less than they might be entitled to. The trouble is that advancing such living expenses to a client is, according to a American Bar Association study, considered "professionally improper, if not illegal, by most courts."[28] Like the rules against the contingent fee elsewhere in the world, this rule stems from the abhorrence in English law, as crimes of champerty and maintenance, of any conduct whereby a person acquires an interest in another's law suit or supports him in his prosecution of it.[29] Despite its illegality, advancing not only the costs of litigation but living expenses is widespread in order to keep a client in line and in order to compete for the client in the first place.[30] According to one personal injury lawyer, this requires "large working capital."[31] A report on one personal injury lawyer indicates that normally he might have $100,000 outstanding on such "loans" to clients[32] ("loans" automatically forgiven, of course, in the remote possibility that no settlement or judgment is forthcoming).

Where are the Bar Associations in the face of all this flaunting of their Canons of Ethics? Right there—doing nothing, as the experience in Philadelphia and Chicago suggests. The enforcement of the Canons of Ethics by Bar Associations for any transgressions is minimal at best. But in the area of automobile accidents—where violations have long been most notorious—enforcement has long been a joke. Oh, occasionally a gesture is made, but one almost wonders why the Bar bothers, judging by the timing and size of the gesture. Former New York Justice Bernard Botein has pinpointed the cynicism and futility of the enforcement:

> The fastest way for a young, unscrupulous lawyer to clean up is to follow the ten-year rule. For some reason that perhaps the experts on cycles ought to look into, most large metropolitan areas seem to have ambulance-chasing investigations about every ten years. Suddenly there is a great hue and cry and investigation, and the papers are filled with details of lawyers and their chasers and accident faking and the padding of medical and hospital bills. A few lawyers are disbarred, several doctors get their wrists slapped, the bar issues an earnest statement, and a month later—things are back to normal. Now all a lawyer would have to do to benefit from this cycle is to come to a city that just had an ambulance-chasing investigation and proceed to rip and tear for ten years and then leave in time. Then [go to] the next city that's just had an inquiry, and so on.[33]

Why should this laxity persist?

Partly, of course, it is the simple reluctance of most professions to chastise those in the brotherhood. In addition, however, there is probably a tacit recognition that ambulance chasing serves a social purpose if kept within bounds (though there's the rub—keeping it within bounds). Recall, if you will, the ignorance of the typical traffic victim concerning his rights. A recent survey at the University of Illinois found that, among a representative sample of Illinois traffic victims who received payment under the fault criterion, at the time of the accident over 70 per cent didn't know about their possible right to potential payment for their pain and suffering.[34] Insurance adjusters learn to play on such ignorance. A prime aim of adjusters, as pointed out earlier, is to keep the claimant from getting to an attorney where he will learn about his rights. According to a recent study, generally quite favorable to insurance company claims practices, "A great deal of the adjuster's work is directed to maintaining the claimant's unrepresented status, closing the claim without the intercession of an attorney. This is called keeping the claim under control."[35] And "control" is a good word for it, because with an unrepresented claimant, given the ignorance of the typical claimant, all the expertise is in the hands of the adjuster. Thus, adjusters will commonly try in routine cases to get away with paying only the claimant's out-of-pocket loss, paying nothing for pain and suffering and nothing for loss already paid by other insurance, although in fact, as we know, the claimant is entitled by law to both of the latter.[36] And all this does not take into account the heart-rending cases most lawyers can report on where adjusters have taken savage advantage of a badly injured—but ignorant and desperate— victim by getting him to sign a release for a comparative pittance.

In light of these factors, many chasers and personal injury lawyers look upon themselves "as the protectors of unsophisticated accident victims from heartless claims adjusters." In the more sedate words of a study sponsored by the American Bar Association,

> Not all lawyers view solicitation [of cases] as an evil. While not condoning the excesses of "ambulance chasing" in its many forms, some lawyers argue that they are rendering a valuable service to the public in taking the initiative in bringing the opportunity for legal counsel to the attention of potential claimants. They say this is particularly useful in the face of aggressive tactics of insurers in seeking releases. They argue that the image of a lawyer waiting in his office for clients is inconsistent with the patterns of modern life in urban centers.[37]

This last point raises a fundamental issue: The conflict between "proper" business getting and the reality of an urban practice. This conflict was pointed up long ago by law professor Karl Llewellyn when he stated that "the Canons of Ethics on business-getting are still built in terms of a town of twenty-thousand (or, much more dubiously, even fifty thousand)—a town where reputation speaks itself from mouth to mouth. . . . Turn these same Canons loose on a great city, and the results

are devastating in proportion to its size."[38] As Professor Carlin
has pointed out, the model for the present Canons of Ethics of
the American Bar Association was a code of ethics adopted in
1887 by the Alabama Bar Association which was, in turn, largely
based on an essay by a judge with the reassuringly 19th century
sounding name of Sharswood, published in 1854. In Carlin's
words, "the image of the profession that is unmistakably conveyed by the Canons is of the small-town bar, consisting of
lawyers who are highly visible not only to one another but to
their prospective clientele, and who are capable, therefore, of
attracting clients by establishing a reputation in the community
as competent practitioners. These conditions, of course, do not
exist today in the large metropolitan centers."[39]

The Canons are particularly out of touch in relation to
traffic claims. For much legal business of a commercial or relatively affluent nature, such as lucrative wills or real estate
transfers, a lawyer can indirectly advertise by a membership in
a country club, by community service or by using the old school
tie. Such indirection is appropriate and effective because the
affluent already have a general idea of when they need lawyers,
and relatively little reluctance to employ them. Many lawyers
will tell you that joining a country club—tax deductible because
of this—will pay for itself many times over in clients gained.
In other words, lawyers know where the money is and—indirectly, it is true—arrange to get in its way. But how do you
"indirectly" get in the way of traffic victims—especially since
most of them are working class people who don't frequent places
that lawyers do, and don't know when they need a lawyer or
how to get one, and indeed distrust the whole process of law
and lawyers?

Think of how unique the traffic accident is in this regard:
Millions of people are continually acquiring a *very* valuable asset
—their traffic claims. But the asset, as we have seen, is a
peculiarly frustrating one. Without an expert—a person schooled
in the jungle of personal injury law—the asset is not only often
relatively worthless, but even unrecognized by its unknowing
owner. Couple this with the fact that it is a wasting asset that

is going to arbitrarily disappear in several years due to the statute of limitations. ("Due to the *what*?") And from the moment the asset is created, a skilled opponent (an insurance adjuster) is trying to take advantage of the owner's ignorance by "buying" his asset at a fraction of its value. Where else in our society does the gamut of mankind—including the ignorant and unsophisticated—constantly come into such inchoate, fleeting, mysterious but very valuable assets?[40] And if they do, where else are those relatively few individuals in a position to help market the asset forbidden from contacting the owner, while at the same time the only people in a position to buy the asset (insurance companies) are trying to buy it at a huge discount before the owner learns about its value? Given this situation, the Canons are bound to crumble. Bridges will *inevitably* be built between the ignorant and frightened owners of the asset and the experts who alone can help them get value for it. And as long as this explosive situation exists, the countless and interminable suggestions and campaigns for "cracking down" on ambulance chasing and for regulating contingent fees are going to be about as effective as enforcing Prohibition. Human nature being what it is, you *cannot* prevent, by ethical exhortation or otherwise, the few people qualified to turn very valuable assets into economic reality from having access to the otherwise helpless owners of those assets. Especially is this so when the supposedly unethical or illegal activity can be justified in the minds of its perpetrators by the necessity of helping the ignorant injured from being taking advantage of.

What is the answer? By now it should be a familiar refrain: Remove from the insurance system the needless difficulty and variability about being paid. Pay only for out-of-pocket loss and pay it automatically on the occurrence of an accident. When the traffic victim's rights are clear—when the criterion for payment is simple, both as to when and what he is to be paid, and when the chances for quick and unconscionably high profits are removed—the need for chasers and lawyers will largely disappear.[41] After all, whoever heard of ambulance chasers running after life insurance claims, or fire insurance claims, or accident and health insurance claims? The answer to the corruption of ambulance chasing and unconscionable contingent fees is no-fault insurance, just as that is the answer to so many other ills plaguing automobile insurance.

Chapter VII

Let the Buyer (not only)
Beware (but be gone)

The prodigal waste of the auto insurance system creates especially acute problems for both individuals and society in that auto insurance is (1) so expensive, (2) so inflationary and (3) so necessary.

Automobile insurance costs have long been one of the fastest rising items in the nation's economy. A report in 1966 stated that the meteoric rise in medical care costs in the preceding ten years had been exceeded only by the rise in the cost of "automobile insurance, domestic help and local transit fares"[1]—the latter two items, along with medical care, being legendary for their inflation in recent years. In 1970, the Cleveland Trust Company published a list of the 15 items in the consumer price index that have risen the fastest. The list included a "weight" factor to take account of the importance of the item in the consumer price index since, in the words of *The New York Times,* "obviously, big items like food and housing have more weight than seldom used ones such as . . . an item like cracker meal." On the Cleveland Trust list, auto insurance ranked fourth behind meat, home repairs and mortgage interest rates, but ahead of doctor's fees, local transportation, property taxes and hospital services. "Armed with this table," said *The New York Times,* "the consumer can take some specific actions to avoid goods or services where the price rise has been most significant."[2] But alone on the list is an item *required,* in effect, by the government to be purchased and therefore truly unavoidable by almost all—namely auto insurance. Auto insurance is not, then—like steak—a dispensable luxury, or even—like medical care—an item one can often to some extent cut down on, but a compulsory item.

In the words of the recent report of the New York State Insurance Department, "[A]utomobile insurance is expensive. The average premiums for the liability insurance whose purchase is required by law is now $125 a year. For some one-car families, the necessary insurance can cost as much as $429 a year."[3] And note that such insurance covers only minimum compulsory coverage—$10,000 to cover the insured's liability to any one person injured in an accident, $20,000 to cover all liability to any number of insureds in the accident, and $5,000 to cover property damage negligently inflicted by the insured. But, given the nature of present day automobiles—machines that can accelerate from zero to 60 miles per hour in nine seconds and which can reach speeds of 100 miles per hour and above—and given the corollary amount of injuries and damage that even a minor accident can cause, coverage of $10,000 is very minimum coverage indeed. According to the New York State Insurance Department report, "Expensive as it is, the compulsory amount of automobile liability insurance. is not enough either to assure victims of full compensation or to protect the vehicle owner against personal liability in case of serious loss. . . ."[4] Truly adequate limits could cost an owner of a car with a good driving record as much as $1500 a year in New York City.

And costs continue to rise. The cost of automobile insurance has just about doubled in the last twenty years; and, according to the New York report, "the prospects are for it to continue to go up."[5]* From 1950 to 1970, the typical average premium rate in New York State for compulsory automobile liability insurance has been:

Year	Amount	Per cent Increase from 1950
1950	$ 69.63	—
1955	86.98	24.9
1960	108.67	56.1
1965	112.87	62.1
1970	135.60	94.7[6]

Perhaps, then, it should not be surprising that the number one complaint concerning automobile insurance is its high cost. According to a recent survey done by the Survey Research Laboratory at the University of Illinois, when people were asked to list their complaints about automobile insurance, 41 per cent listed the high cost of auto insurance as their prime cause of dislike, with the second highest category (that insurance is often cancelled or made unavailable) reaching 10 per cent.[7] Some comments from the respondents to the Illinois poll are illustrative of public discontent:

> "The premiums are too high. It is ridiculous what one has to pay for present-day [automobile] insurance."

---

* Confirming this prediction is this item from the front page of *The New York Times*, February 5, 1971: "Automobile insurance rates will go up sharply throughout New York State by the end of this month or early in March." For a pro and con discussion of a possible contrary indication for the immediate future, see Wall Street Journal, May 28, 1971, p. 1, col. 6; June 11, 1971, p. 6, col. 6; July 6, 1971, p. 7, col. 1.

"[I]t keeps going up in price whether you have an accident or not."

"You have to pay more for the insurance than the car is worth."[8]

Insurance men and lawyers often decry complaints about the high cost of auto insurance on the grounds that any rise in automobile insurance prices is explained by the fact that such costs only reflect the fast rising items which automobile insurance pays for—medical costs, lost wages, automobile repair costs, etc. They point out, for example, that during the same 20-year period that automobile liability insurance rates rose by 94.7 per cent, the U. S. Consumer Price Index for medical care rose by 114.4 per cent, and for automobile repairs by 83.1 per cent, while earnings for production workers and manufacturing establishments in New York State rose by 118.4 per cent.[9] But the fact that automobile insurance is tied to some of the fastest rising items in the economy is all the more reason (1) to be concerned about its waste and (2) to search to find ways to cut its costs. This is still more essential when it is recalled that since automobile insurance is in effect required of every motorist in every state, rises in its cost adversely affect so many. And, finally, it is even more essential given the fact that more and more Americans are being forced by our patterns of living to buy two or more cars, thereby greatly increasing the effect on them of inflation in auto insurance.

A further irony in all this is that despite soaring rates, auto insurance companies insist that they are losing huge sums. These plaints have often in the past taken on a somewhat disingenuous air when one realized that the companies were speaking only of their *underwriting* losses. They refused to take account—and, if they could help it, refused to let others, such as insurance commissioners, take account—of the millions they earn as investment income on the vast sums they hold as a result of carrying on automobile insurance. According to *Consumer Reports,* "[T]he insurance companies cry that they have lost billions of dollars over the years in their automobile liability underwriting—that is, they have paid out, in expenses and claims, more than they have taken in. They tend not to emphasize that the red ink is dyed black again by investment income."[10]

But even including investment income in the rate making process—as some insurance commissioners, including New York's, have done—does not dramatically alter the overall auto insurance picture nor remove the undeniable price squeeze that auto insurers find themselves in. This was probably especially true recently, with reduction in portfolio values stemming from declines in the stock market.

Faced, then, with rising costs, insurers have naturally enough sought to get approval of rate increases from state insurance commissioners. But, because auto insurance costs so much and delivers so little, insurance commissioners, who are, after all, political appointees, have felt reluctant to allow price rises in a product so plagued with causes for dissatisfaction. Granting price rises—or at least price rises on the order requested by insurance companies—has been political dynamite. In the words of Professor Robert E. Keeton of the Harvard Law School, automobile insurance "is a basically unsatisfactory product. It is unattractive to consumers. . . . In turn, public dissatisfaction makes it difficult for insurance companies to obtain regulatory approval for premium rates that are adequate. . . ."[11]

Faced with such a response, according to the recent New York State Insurance Department report,

> [A]utomobile insurers thrash around for ways to control their costs, to bring order to a seemingly irrational and unpredictable business environment. It is no wonder that when financial institutions the size of casualty insurance companies begin to thrash around, they can do real damage to their surroundings.[12]

How do insurance companies thrash around? By refusing or shedding as insureds anyone they think will be a bad risk. In this respect, insurance companies have accelerated a trend which has long since rocked the automobile insurance industry. A little history at this point will help to fill out the picture.

Prior to World War II, nearly all drivers who sought insurance could readily purchase it. Most insurance was sold through old-line, sometimes rather sleepy, stock or mutual companies operating through independent insurance agents. These agents received a substantial commission (usually 20 per cent of the premium—generous recompense since the agents were selling a product, in effect, required to be purchased). Agents could place the business with any one of several companies they dealt with. There was little rate differentiation since insurance companies—considered by court decision and then by Congressional enactment exempt from the antitrust laws—all charged the same so-called "bureau" rates. (Bureau rates are set by a rating bureau which is, in turn, set up and supported by an aggregate of insurance companies.) According to a recent DOT study, "Competition in the automobile insurance industry had been limited prior to World War II. Most insurers participated in cooperative ratemaking arrangements; price competition was limited; and profits were favorable."[13]

The period following World War II, however, saw a mushrooming growth both in the number of automobiles and in the number and cost of accidents. According to a DOT study,

> In the intervening years [since World War II] the economic, social, and legal environment for the automobile insurance industry . . . changed radically. Automobile ownership is now widespread. Currently, 80 per cent of all households own one or more automobiles, with over one-quarter owning two or more. This represents a substantial increase over earlier years. In 1950 only 59 per cent of all households owned one or more cars and only 7 per cent owned two or more. . . .

> Concurrent with the growth in automobile ownership has been an enormous increase in the expenditures on automobile insurance. Premiums paid increased tenfold between 1938 and 1958 and doubled again through 1968. Current expenditures exceed $11 billion.[14]

As insurance costs increased after World War II, an increasing number of insurance companies broke out of the old non-competitive mold and began to compete on the basis of lower prices. This was accomplished in two ways: First, a growing number of companies began to bypass the high expense of sales commission by selling directly to the consumer. So-called "direct writers"—the leading ones being State Farm and Allstate—captured more and more business from the so-called agency companies by using exclusive agents or salaried employees, as opposed to expensive independent agents working on commission. Other companies made marketing inroads by using mail order sales. As a result of such tactics, State Farm and Allstate, which in 1949 collected 5.1 percent of automobile insurance earned premiums, have raised that share to 20 per cent at the present time. Direct writers now write over 40 per cent of premiums written for automobile liability coverages.[15]

If the new price-cutting marketing techniques had been limited to cutting down on expensive middle men, few—except the middle men—would have had cause for complaint. Unfortunately, the second price cutting technique pioneered by direct writers—and later copied by their increasingly desperate agency competitors—has spawned disastrous results for the public and, indeed, for the insurance industry itself.

Complementing their efforts to cut marketing costs, direct writers sought to reduce claims costs by writing insurance for only selected risks, i.e. insureds least likely to cause accidents. Thus the process of "creaming" the market began. It quickly spread to the old line agency companies who instructed their agents to restrict the type of business they wrote. But this selective process was often extremely crude in the way it operated, ruthlessly casting aside many perfectly adequate risks whose only offense was being young or old or black or divorced or living in the wrong neighborhood. According to the New York Insurance Department report,

> Insurance companies are large organizations, in which such mass operations as individual underwriting decisions [i.e. selecting those to be insured] have to be delegated to a large number of employees and agents. For that reason, insurance companies try to standardize

the underwriting process and make it routine. They are forever casting about for simple, objective, readily identifiable, present characteristics of an insured that the subordinate underwriter or agent can conveniently use to distinguish a "good" from a "bad" future risk.[16]

The result, in turn, was an often irrational and even outrageous denial of an essential commodity to millions of Americans. Reporter James Ridgeway has described how insurance companies,

> are locked in ruinous competition to insure preferred risk drivers—people between 30 and 50 who don't drive their cars around much and haven't had any accidents. . . . Those not included in the prime risk category are paying more for insurance and in some cases find it hard to get policies from reputable companies. The squeeze is especially severe on people between 16 and 25 or over 65, or anyone owning a car living in a metropolitan center. Some companies will simply not write any business in poor Negro neighborhoods.[17]

As former Pennsylvania Insurance Commissioner David Maxwell said recently, "Buying a car only takes money, but getting auto insurance is more like joining a country club"[18]— with the addition that in the case of auto insurance there are laws which, in effect, require you to find a club to join.

In the words of *The New York Times,* "Horror stories are widespread about how insurance companies treat their customers."[19]

¶ An Auburn, Washington, youth, age 19, with a perfect driving record had his coverage cancelled when he enlisted in the Air Force. He had the choice of giving up driving or taking a policy with a high-risk company, at twice the premium.[20]

¶ A Sibley, Iowa, farm couple in their 70s had their insurance company refuse to renew their policy. The husband had had one claim last year, the couple's first in 35 years of coverage with the company.[21]

¶ After a businessman had applied to an agent for auto insurance, the typical industry process followed whereby an investigator visited the businessman's home to speak with him. In writing up his report, the investigator mentioned that he had noticed several paintings of nudes on the wall. The businessman was turned down for the insurance as a moral hazard![22]

¶ A man in Virginia was refused insurance after a neighbor had told an investigator that the applicant drank too much, a story that later turned out to be false.[23]

Karl Herrmann, the insurance commissioner of the State of Washington, testified as follows before a U. S. Senate Committee investigating auto insurance when he was chairman of the Joint Interim Committee on Insurance of the Washington State Legislature:

Our committee is continually amazed at some of the deceptive techniques employed by a number of insurance companies to avoid fair treatment of the policyholder. One such case involves one of the biggest insurers of autos doing business in our state.

Our files have the complete record and photostat copy of the correspondence that took place in this particular case.

A graduate student in economics at the University of Washington, in Seattle, had his auto insurance suddenly cancelled. The letter, which lacked specific reasons for the cancellation, was signed by a Mr. "T. Case." The student tried to reach Mr. Case repeatedly by telephone, but could never locate the signer of the letter. He was always told by the insurance company's telephone operators that "Mr. Case is out to lunch," or "He's in conference" or "He's sick today."

One day the student was discussing his problem with an official of the university. A secretary whose husband worked as an adjuster for the company involved overheard the conversation and explained why it was that "Mr. Case" was always out. "That stands for 'Tough Case,'" she said. "There is no such person. It's the way the company has of avoiding further discussion with cancelled policyholders." Signing phony names on letters to customers is not the solution to the public's growing demand for better treatment at the hands of the auto insurance industry.[24]

Nor are these isolated instances—shocking as they are. On the contrary, they are part of a planned, pervasive design by the insurance industry as a whole to restrict ruthlessly those who can obtain insurance.

Thus, Charles W. Gambrell, South Carolina's insurance commissioner, stated that in South Carolina there is a requirement that insurance companies disclose the "guides" that insurance agents follow in writing insurance policies. According to Gambrell, 83 per cent of the insurers writing 65 per cent of the insurance in this state will not write new business for aged drivers (between the ages of 62 and 70). Similarly, 16 per cent of the companies will not write divorced people. Gambrell hypothesizes that the categories of poor risks listed in the guides as "suspects" are applicable throughout much of the country and, in fact, are just a veiled way of discriminating against Negroes.[25]

The following is from the transcript of testimony before a Senate Committee by Orman L. Vertrees, a reporter on the *Seattle Post-Intelligencer:*

MR. VERTREES. . . .

. . . [A series of articles on automobile insurance] triggered a staggering response from our readers. In a matter of just a few weeks, we received in excess of 500 letters and telephone calls on insurance matters, most involving complaints from the insurance consumer. . . .

An analysis of insurance complaints received by the *Post-Intelligencer* showed that automobile coverage was by far the most critical area. There were numerous instances of cancellation or failure to renew policies without any explanation from the company to agent or policyholder. There was evidence of mass cancellations. Seattle's central area, populated largely by minority groups, found its rates higher and coverage harder to obtain. Those in certain occupations, such as longshoremen, bartenders, servicemen, waitresses, entertainers, and of all people, aircraft workers—the Boeing Company employs thousands in the Seattle area, its headquarters—were frowned upon by some auto insurers. . . .

A little over a year ago, a Seattle insurance broker sent me a copy of a pamphlet, then in its 15th printing, entitled "Automobile Underwriting Pointers." The manual had been circulated by Safeco [Insurance Group] to several thousand of its agents. . . .

The manual warned agents to look with disfavor upon the "lower laboring classes, aircraft employees, longshoring classes, etc.," where auto insurance was concerned. It said that if someone liked to be called by a nickname, such as "Shorty" or "Scotty," he might not be conservative enough in outlook to qualify for auto insurance. It also warned that how a child's hair was cut should have a bearing on whether or not the family auto was to be insured.

THE CHAIRMAN [Senator Warren G. Magnuson of Washington]. You know, back home I am known as "Maggie." I suppose that could have some bearing on my auto insurance.

. . . . .

MR. VERTREES. You might have trouble, Senator.[26]

Another factor exacerbating the restrictiveness of the auto insurance market is caused by insurance companies' worry about the kind of witness its insured will make in court. This is especially pertinent under auto insurance, given the much greater likelihood, relatively speaking, of litigation under this coverage. T. Lawrence Jones, President of the American Insurance Association, has admitted that examining each applicant for an insurance policy as a potential defendant in court ". . . unfortunately leads to the reluctance of some [insurance companies] . . . to make auto insurance available to young people, minority groups and people with occupations that are judged to be in less favorable light."[27] This, coupled with the fact that insurance people tend to be prototypically middle class, conservatively oriented people, means that any deviance from the norm can be viewed with alarm.

A pervasive factor in restrictive auto insurance underwriting is race (or perhaps one should say racism). For example, Retail Credit Company, an Atlanta, Georgia based organization, in 1966 made 20,000,000 inspection reports on people who applied for insurance to determine whether the applicant should be given coverage. Retail Credit's Handy Guide lists the points that should be covered in the inspection report. Under a section headed "West Indian Island Races including Puerto Ricans," it asks:

Is applicant pure Caucasian or a mixture? Describe the individual if a mixture of races to show whether predominantly Caucasian or Negro. It is not practicable to attempt to estimate percentages.

And the guide has the following questions about applicants for insurance who are Mexican-Americans:

Is he a permanent resident or the floater type?

Does he occupy a hovel type of residence or a good substantial home?

Does applicant associate with Mexicans or with Anglo-Saxons?[28]

References to race pervade the guide. On a church applying for fire insurance, for example, the inspector must note "whether Baptist, Episcopalian or Methodist, etc., and whether the congregation is composed of Negro or white people, or general racial makeup of congregation." On apartment houses, information, according to the report, should include "racial descent" of tenants.[29]

Upon being asked about the guide, W. Lee Burge, President of Retail Credit, replied that the company was revising "all the sections dealing with race in an effort to delete those references."[30]

It is questionable, though, how much good that will do. According to an insurance commissioner of a midwestern state, one insurance company routinely assigns Negro applicants a code number beginning with the number seven, and he has discovered that a suspiciously large proportion of these "sevens" are turned down. "You can't prove discrimination," he says, "because the word 'Negro' is never used on the application form."[31]

Chapter VIII

The Untouchables (All About Assigned Risks)

For a long time, insurance companies piously denied there was any real problem of access to insurance, grinding out public relations releases indicating that the problem was being "grossly exaggerated . . . by politically ambitious legislators and state officials."[1]

A shell game of sorts was played, with insurance companies citing the supposedly infinitesimally small number of policies they ever cancelled, deliberately suppressing their technique of not cancelling but simply waiting a few months and refusing to renew a given policy. When that dodge was discovered, an insurer might proudly and loudly announce a non-cancellable policy, good for several years. Unmentioned and overlooked in the publicity generated by this technique was the fact that rates could, and often would, sharply rise after an accident. Unmentioned too was the fact that insurers, in supposedly guaranteeing maintained coverage, could simply tighten their criterion for originally insuring applicants. In that case, if the back door was shut, so was the front, so that any way you looked at it, the motorist would still be left out in the cold.

Typical of the meaningless hoopla generated by insurers trying to convince the public (and public officials) that there was little or no problem of access to insurance was the press conference called late in 1967 by the National Association of Independent Insurers, an association of some 350 auto insurance companies writing more than half the private auto insurance in force in the United States. The member companies of the association, according to the association's president, Vestal Lemmon, wanted to "try to do something positive and affirmative to offset these criticisms" of the way insurance was made available to the public. The result was the publication at the news conference of a new code of "guiding principles" for members to follow in dealing with policyholders and applicants, designed, in the words of one news dispatch emanating from the news conference, "to discourage such practices as arbitrary cancellation of policies and discrimination on grounds of race, occupation or advanced age. [The code] . . . calls for 'individual consideration' of each application of insurance." The association took pains to distribute, along with its own release, a prepared statement by Senator Warren Magnuson (D. Wash.), one of the auto industry's severest Senatorial critics. Said Magnuson, "In vowing to eliminate discrimination based upon race or age, occupation or other arbitrary classifications, independent insurers are moving to meet a major source of discontent."

But when Lemmon was pressed under questioning at the news conference, he admitted that the code involved "very little change as a matter of fact" in the organization's policy on the matters covered. Not only was the code meaningless in terms of effecting any change but it was toothless as well. Lemmon admitted there were no procedures for enforcement of the code, and if any members of the association were "unhappy with the principles, they would probably get out" of the association.

In effect, the association said, "We are not doing anything wrong and we promise to stop; but then again, our promises don't mean much."

Lemmon did acknowledge "isolated instances of unfair practices" by some member insurance companies. "If companies are guilty," he said, "we want to correct it. [But s]urveys we have made indicate they are not."[2]

Of course, a lot can turn on what you define as "isolated instances." Many insurance executives have attempted to dismiss as negligible rejections, cancellations, and failures to renew policies in that these acts affect only, say, three per cent of the market.[3] But three per cent of what? Three per cent of a market of 100,000,000 drivers is 3,000,000 people. Scarcely negligible by any standard. But is it really three per cent? A recent study of the Department of Transportation has given the lie to repeated insurance industry deprecation of the dimensions of the problem. According to the comprehensive DOT study, auto insurers have cancelled or refused to renew 14 per cent of all policyholders at some time in their lives. Fifty-five per cent of policyholders have heard of others whose policies were cancelled and not renewed.[4] "Thus does anxiety in the motoring public spread like ripples around those directly involved," stated *Consumer Reports*.[5]

Nor is this by any means always a question of insurers skillfully separating good from bad risks. Says a DOT report on insurance accessibility, "While a few drivers with very bad accident records have always had difficulty in obtaining insurance, an increasing number of drivers, even those with good records, have been rejected by standard insurance companies in recent years."[6]

When standard insurance companies reject an applicant, he is forced to seek coverage under so-called assigned risk plans or in so-called substandard companies. Neither alternative is a very happy one; and yet, according to the DOT study, "currently 8 per cent or more of all drivers are unable to obtain insurance through standard channels. In some states the substandard market ranges as high as 20 per cent."[7]

Under assigned risk plans, which are set up in every state to handle the so-called "high risk" or "hard to place" market, motorists rejected by standard companies in the voluntary market are assigned to insurance companies for coverage on a rotating basis, dependent on the amount of insurance written in the state by the various companies. But although, in the words of the DOT study, "assigned risk plans [were] originally conceived as the solution to assure insurance availability," they have scarcely lived up to that promise.[8]

In the first place, they serve no more than half the substandard auto insurance market, with the remainder scrambling elsewhere for coverage, keeping in mind that the scramblers already have been excluded from the standard voluntary market.

Even when a person is accepted as an assigned risk, his troubles are scarcely over. Most often his rates will be higher, perhaps by as much as 150 per cent or more. According to the DOT study,

> The hard-to-place driver faces extreme price variability when obtaining insurance coverage. In some cases prices attain levels which seriously tax the driver's ability to pay. For example, a youthful operator in West Virginia might pay as much as $1,077 for basic liability coverage as an assigned risk.[9]

The assigned risk also usually will be provided only with the inadequate minimum liability coverage, being denied really adequate liability limits as well as supplementary coverage such as collision insurance (covering damage to his own car) and medical payments insurance (covering his own medical bills and those of his family). Nor can one overlook the general unpleasantness of being classified as an assigned risk—a cast-off—forced upon an insurance company rather than being a normal sought-after customer. In the words of *The New York Times,* the assigned risk "stigma is so overpowering that most people in the plan are ashamed to admit it."[10] The insurance industry, with its ever-present instinct for windowdressing as opposed to real solutions, "has succeeded—with the consent of state regulatory agencies in at least 30 states—in changing its official name from the emotional-sounding 'assigned-risk plan' to the more neutral sounding 'automobile-insurance plan.' "[11]

But, if this were not bad enough, many persons in the substandard liability market, as indicated above, do not even get assigned risk coverage. Actually, more than half of the total substandard market is served outside the assigned risk plan, many of them "voluntarily" choosing to forego the assigned risk plan.[12] They do this not only because of the inadequacies of assigned risk coverage, but also because insurance agents oftentimes don't tell their customers about the availability of an assigned risk plan, since agents get higher sales commissions selling for a company selling in the substandard market. Those in the substandard market seeking voluntary coverage enter a jungle of so-called "high risk" insurers, whose coverage "provides no escape" from the high prices of the assigned risk plan.[13] Perhaps even more significantly, the price variations fluctuate even more wildly than under the assigned risk plan. For example, in West Virginia, a young driver with three traffic violations and one accident could pay as little as $395 or as much as $1,119, depending upon which high risk insurer covered him.[14] Although more than minimum coverage is often available through "high risk" companies, the price for such broader coverage can be very high indeed—often double the premium for basic rates.[15] In addition, in the words of the Department of Transportation study:

While voluntary high-risk specialists offer broader ranges of coverage than do assigned risk plans, too often their insurance is of inferior quality. Most insurance insolvencies in recent years have been substandard insurers. This has resulted in losses to policyholders and has left some innocent accident victims uncompensated. In addition, there is evidence that claims service provided by high-risk specialists is frequently inferior to that of standard companies.[16]

Generally speaking, insurance insolvencies have risen sharply in recent years. Between 1960 and 1965, at least 58 automobile insurance companies, with an overall premium volume of $179 million, went into receivership, leaving at least 1.2 million policyholders to face the resultant hardship. While it is true that premiums of insolvent insurers represented only .43 per cent of countrywide auto insurance premiums during the period 1960-65, insolvencies have created a much more serious problem for high risk insureds. According to an investigation into automobile insurance failures conducted by the Senate Subcommittee on Antitrust and Monopoly, 73 out of 350 companies engaged in high risk automobile insurance failed between 1960 and 1966. The high risk automobile insurance segment of the industry had a failure rate of 4.2 per cent per year—a rate six times as high as the failure rate for automobile insurance business in general. According to the subcommittee, high risk automobile insurance accounted for 106 out of 108 failures among insurance companies writing automobile insurance during the period 1958-68.[17]

In addition to the greater risk of insolvency, as the Department of Transportation study indicated, high risk insurance often constitutes an inferior product. A special study of complaints about insurance made to state regulatory bodies showed a disproportionate number of complaints about high risk insurance companies. Although their market share ranges from 5 to 11 per cent, the share of complaints concerning high risk companies ranged from 14 to 48 per cent. In Illinois, high risk companies accounted for almost half of all the complaints.[18] As to the merits of the complaints, for high risk insurers in Illinois the per cent of valid complaints (37 per cent) exceeded the percentage which were groundless (20 per cent), with the opposite being true of standard insurers. In point of fact, 63 per cent of all the valid complaints concerned high risk insurers, although their market share amounted to only 11 per cent.[19]

As a result of the marketing squeeze presented by automobile insurance, not surprisingly many motorists are just simply unable to buy insurance—especially younger drivers, who are generally our most dangerous drivers. The latest data indicates that about 20 per cent of the private passenger cars in the United States are uninsured for liability coverage. In 14 states, less than 75 per cent of vehicles are insured. This would mean that more than one in four cars coming at you in those states are uninsured! In Alabama, Arkansas, Georgia and Nevada, the situation is even worse with one in three cars uninsured. And, as suggested, the uninsured drivers are the worst drivers. Nationally, approximately 25 per cent of the drivers under age 25 are uninsured. According to the DOT study, "this suggests that the uninsured population is composed in large part of young drivers who could not obtain or could not afford coverage."[20]

Keep in mind the far-flung social effects of an inadequate auto insurance market. In addition to the obvious hardship on victims of uninsured or underinsured motorists, consider the effects on the premium-paying public—especially those in minority groups. Bayard Rustin, the prominent black civil rights leader, has criticized the so-called Kerner Report of the National Advisory Commission on Civil Disorders "for not dealing in any adequate way with transportation," and has pointed out the problems faced by the "poor people in the city ghettoes [who are without means of getting] to where the job market is opening up in the suburbs."[21] Similarly, Professor Alfred Conard, whose book *Automobile Accident Costs and Payments* is a leading source on many aspects of automobile insurance, stated before a Congressional committee:

> [T]he soaring costs of liability insurance are making automobile ownership impossible for many poor Americans. If they cannot own automobiles, they can-

not emerge from the congested cities where public transportation is available and cannot hold jobs at outlying factories. The present system of reparation produces two kinds of victims—those who are inadequately compensated for their injuries, and those who are charged the high premiums required by a wasteful system.[22]

Andrew Biemiller, the director of legislation of the AFL-CIO has made the same point with reference to many laboring people.

> Working people are among those hardest hit by soaring car insurance costs and arbitrary cancellations. With factories now so widely dispersed and beyond the reach of obsolete public transit systems, their car is for many workers the life line to their jobs. But insurance companies can, and all too often do, threaten that life line through their ability to withhold insurance, or at least to extract crushing fees for it.[23]

And this tightening market for auto insurance is apparently getting rapidly worse. Recently Liberty Mutual Insurance Company, one of the country's largest auto insurance writers, fired 25 per cent of its salesmen who sell private passenger auto insurance and instituted other curbs. According to M. B. Bradshaw, Liberty Mutual's administrative vice president, "all liability insurers" face the same deteriorating picture for auto insurance, in that "deterioration in these lines has come with a suddenness and degree of severity never seen . . . before."[24] State Farm Mutual, the nation's largest auto insurer, is also attempting to slow down new business.[25] (State Farm is not completely candid about the availability of its insurance. Although Consumers Union in its comprehensive report on the performance of various auto insurance companies—which was very favorable to State Farm—reported that State Farm sold in every state except Rhode Island,[26] it subsequently reported that State Farm had "misinformed us about the availability of its car insurance. We have since learned that State Farm has only one or two agents in Connecticut and Massachusetts and that it will not sell new policies to residents of those states.")[27] Similarly, the Insurance Company of North America, another major auto insurer, recently indicated its abandonment of more and more of the auto market. John T. Gurash, chairman of INA, announced that the company "is cutting off property and liability insurance coverage in areas where it isn't any longer profitable." So eager have auto insurers become to abandon large chunks of the auto market that they are apparently, at long last, willing to concede the racial biases of their restrictive underwriting. Gurash admitted that INA's cutback in auto insurance in unprofitable areas subjected the company to criticism for cutting off coverage in ghetto areas, but said the moves were nonetheless necessary. "Let's face it, a Watts or a Detroit were never contemplated in insurance rate structures."[28] Nothing indicates so clearly the critical nature of the auto insurance market as the announcement in September, 1970, by Nationwide Mutual Group, the nation's fifth largest auto insurance company, that it was instructing its agents to stop *all* new sales of auto insurance.[29]*

So critical is the marketing situation at the present time that in New York, according to *The New York Times*, "The offices of State Attorney General Louis J. Lefkowitz and the State Insurance Department are being inundated by a wave of consumer complaints about insurance companies' unwillingness to renew automobile policies."[30]

Of course, it is true that other lines of casualty insurance besides auto insurance, including particularly theft and fire coverages, also face restrictive markets. But the auto insurance situation is much more widespread, not by any means confined to urban or ghetto areas. The "real culprit" behind the uniquely bad auto insurance market, according to the New York State Insurance Department," is the concept of [an adversary proceeding]. . . . and the need to fix the blame for an accident before an insurance company begins to pay off."[31]

---

* By February 1971, Nationwide was willing to begin selling to new customers "on a limited basis" and "with caution," *The National Underwriter* (Prop. & Cas. Ed.), February 12, 1971, p. 39, col. 3.

The auto insurance market is also all the more scandalous in that, at least with other forms of insurance, when you succeed in getting coverage, you have something worthwhile. With auto insurance not only is it hard to get or harder to pay for, but it is hardest of all to get any real value from it once you've got it.

The real solution here is not legislation requiring insurance companies to insure more and more people at a loss. Rather, the solution is to recognize that the deteriorating market for auto insurance is most of all a symptom of the disastrous fault system. The most effective solution here, as elsewhere for other ills of auto insurance, is to change to no-fault insurance. (See Chapter X *infra.*)

One should not leave the topic of insurance marketing without mentioning the subject of group insurance—insurance normally provided automatically as a part of one's employment, with the premiums paid in whole or in part by the employer. Group insurance has had a soaring growth in the United States in the past half century. And yet this eminently sensible and efficient marketing technique has bypassed auto insurance almost completely. Says University of Illinois insurance professor Robert Mehr:

> The meteoric rise of group insurance in this country is one of the phenomena of the insurance business. The first group life insurance policy was written in 1911 by the Equitable Life Assurance Society of New York on the lives of about 125 employees of the Pantasote Leather Company. . . .
>
> From the start, nearly 60 years ago, group life insurance has grown and prospered so that today about $500 billion is in force in the United States covering the lives of more than 75 million people under nearly 300,000 group policies. . . .
>
> Group life insurance represents more than 36 per cent of all life insurance in force in the United States. This compares with about 20 per cent at midcentury.
>
> Phenomenal as has been the growth of group life insurance, its current growth is not so marked as that of group health insurance . . . .

At the close of World War II, the total annual group premium in the United States was about $200 million. At the present time, it is about $6.2 billion. Group health insurance premiums represent about 67 per cent of all health insurance premiums written in the United States. This compares to about 50 per cent at midcentury.[32]

Approximately 68 million Americans are insured under group life insurance plans in the United States and 119 million have group health insurance.[33]

On the other hand, according to Professor Bernard Webb, writing in 1969, "Group merchandising of automobile insurance . . . is still practically nonexistent in the United States." Even under the most generous definition of group merchandising of insurance, which includes any plans where payment for auto insurance is made by payroll deduction with or without employer contribution, "approximately one-half of one per cent of . . . private passenger auto insurance is written under collective plans."[34]

Why should this stunning contrast exist? Auto insurance stands with life insurance and health insurance in the list of the top three categories of insurance. Group sales of insurance, more than any other device, have meant the spread of efficient, inexpensive, sound insurance coverage to masses of people in the United States. Especially pertinent to millions of motorists squeezed out of the auto insurance market is that group insurance has meant that millions of persons who might well have been otherwise ineligible for life or health insurance have been able to get coverage promptly, readily and reliably through group insurance. According to a standard text on insurance, "Group insurance has . . . extended protection to a large number of uninsurable people who cannot qualify for individual insurance because of health or hazardous occupation."[35] Why, then, should the advantages of group sales be largely unavailable in the sale of auto insurance? The lack of the best marketing technique for reaching mass markets is all the more ironic in the case of auto insurance since it is the only form of insurance generally *required* to be carried by the populace. In every state of the union, auto insurance is either a prerequisite to registering one's car or strongly encouraged by the imposition of stiff penalties in its absence once an accident occurs.[36] Life insurance is nowhere required, nor is health insurance; so that the only coverage required to be carried is unavailable under the best marketing technique.

The reason for the unavailability of group auto insurance is a deeply disturbing one: Auto insurance agents in the United States have succeeded in state after state in getting passed laws and regulations in effect *outlawing* group auto insurance.[37] Supposedly, these laws are based on the premise that it is somehow unfair to people outside groups that people inside groups have the benefit of a cheaper means of merchandising—largely through the elimination of high sales commissions charged to individual purchasers by insurance agents. Commonly this fee comes to around 15 per cent of the sales price for selling a product to a purchaser required by law to buy it. Two of the country's leading insurance authorities have labeled the underpinning of such restrictive rules as "silly"[38] and "absurd."[39] Such a theory of discrimination has not been thought generally applicable to group life or group accident and health insurance, and there is no more reason to apply it to group auto insurance. In fact, the only people hurt by group sales of auto insurance are the agents who lose their commissions on individual sales. And it is their interest—and their interest alone—which is protected by such laws. Not long ago, University of Wisconsin Law Dean Spencer Kimball, the country's leading authority on insurance regulation, characterized the "typical American insurance code [of laws as] a rubbish heap without parallel in the law-making of modern man,"[40] and went on subsequently to state that nowhere is the inadequacy of insurance laws "more evident than in the restrictions placed on" group auto insurance.[41] In other words, Kimball cites anti-group auto insurance laws as just about the worst of all laws among the worst of all laws!

Anti-group auto insurance rules, now prevailing in some 35 states, are but another example of the desire of many small businessmen—despite all their praises of the virtues of competition—to protect themselves from competition. Indeed anti-group auto insurance laws perhaps illustrate this desire best of all in showing that small businessmen will not blink at resorting to legislation to protect the most naked featherbedding. Recently, too, insurance agents have renewed their battle to reinforce and extend stricter laws forbidding group auto insurance. In response to the agents' past and present efforts, Senator Philip Hart (D. Mich.) has proposed federal legislation that would outlaw state laws restricting group auto insurance.[42] As Dean Kimball and Insurance Commissioner Herbert Dennenberg of Pennsylvania (formerly professor of insurance at the Wharton School of the University of Pennsylvania) have stated in this regard, "the selfish interests of special groups should not be permitted to prevail against the interests of us all."[43]

It is important to note that the passage of no-fault auto insurance would greatly encourage the adoption of group auto insurance. Since no-fault insurance closely resembles accident and health coverage, it could be coordinated quickly and easily with widespread group accident and health sales. Added, then, to other advantages of no-fault insurance would be not only the greater availability of auto insurance but also a 10 to 15 per cent reduction in auto insurance premiums stemming from the more efficient merchandising of group sales.[44]

Chapter IX

No-Fault Insurance—
What and Why

There are several key aspects which guarantee the success of no-fault auto insurance, especially when compared with the miseries of fault insurance.

In the first place, no-fault insurance, by paying traffic victims automatically on the occurrence of an accident, eliminates the endless and expensive arguing over who was at fault in the accident.

Secondly, by paying only for out-of-pocket loss—and excluding payments for pain and suffering—a second prime source of argument is also eliminated. As already pointed out, other forms of no-fault insurance, including even supplemental coverages under the auto policy itself, entail delays of 10 to 40 times less than fault insurance, largely as a result of eliminating such cumbrous criteria for compensation.[1]

Another lubricating feature of the no-fault system is that one deals with one's own insurance company instead of a hostile stranger. As Daniel P. Moynihan (who is an expert on auto safety and insurance, in addition to all his other interests) has put it, the proponents of no-fault insurance "are right in the all-important perception as to what it is Americans are good at. We are good at maintaining business relationships once a basis for mutual self-interest is established. [No-fault insurance] . . . would establish one."[2] Professor Alfred Conard of the University of Michigan Law School has pointed out that one of the improvements stemming from no-fault insurance "will be a diminution in the shameless efforts of claimants to claim too much and of insurers to pay too little in accident settlements. This kind of conduct has always been much more flagrant in [fault] liability insurance than in first-party insurance [whereby one claims against one's own insurance company], because the claimant and the insurance company in [fault] liability insurance are strangers to each other, who hope never to meet again. In first-party insurance, they are doing business together, and both have good reason to conduct themselves honestly and fairly."[3]

The virtues of an insurance scheme whereby one deals with his own insurance company (called, as Professor Conard indicates, "first-party" insurance) was confirmed recently by a survey conducted by Consumers Union among 130,121 individuals who had experience processing auto claims. A particular source of interest was the precise comparison of experience under first-party claims (composed of supplementary no-fault coverage sold by insurance companies as optional items under the automobile policy), as opposed to claims under fault insurance. Consumers Union found much more satisfaction under no-fault first-party claims as opposed to fault claims. For example, "Almost all respondents were pleased with the way claims [submitted to their own company] were handled; 94 per cent thought the company took no more than a reasonable time to settle, and 92 per cent felt they were treated courteously." By way of contrast, *Consumer Reports* stated, "Our findings hint at the hardships endured by some accident victims while insurance adjustors [from the other driver's company] tried to knock down the size of the [fault] claim. The wait was too long for 19 per cent of the claimants reporting, and far too long for an additional 18 per cent of them."[4]

Whether a fault claim is to be paid is shrouded in irrational considerations turning on the much greater likelihood of litigation arising from such claims. Thus an "Adjustor's Work Book" for Allstate Insurance Company (the insurance subsidiary of Sears Roebuck and the nation's second largest auto insurance company) starts out by saying, "One of the essential items to be completed early in an investigation [is] . . . a full and adequate description of the person we are dealing with, whether claimant, insured or witness . . . . Part of our appraisal of a case filed is the impression the individual might make before a jury." The adjustor is instructed to watch for such characteristics as whether you:

¶ Click your teeth
¶ Crack your knuckles
¶ Scratch a lot
¶ Have a head that is flat on top
¶ Have yellow teeth
¶ Have dirty fingernails
¶ Have manicured fingernails
¶ Use "perfumes or lotions"
¶ Have a voice pitch "resembl[ing] that of the opposite sex"
¶ Use "uncommon words"

¶ "Frequent pool rooms, . . . race tracks, . . . 5-and-10 cent stores, . . . bars, art galleries, libraries, hotel lobbies, . . . burlesque shows, courtrooms or houses of ill fame."[5]

The Ohio Casualty Group of Hamilton, Ohio, advises its adjustors to get a claimant alone when it comes to signing a release. Says its guidebook, "Claimants who can be isolated from helpful friends and relatives at settlement time are not only more susceptible to settlement, but are somewhat less difficult to deal with."[6]

Only under fault claims would such tactics be generally employed and such often silly or vicious irrelevancies be the subject of such obsessive inquiry.

Is it any wonder that studies show the deep disenchantment of many who go through the auto insurance claim grinder? Professor Conard and his colleagues in the Michigan study have recorded some of the anguished responses of those twice victimized—once by their injuries, and again by the fault system's "treatment" of their injuries.

> "They were trying to humiliate me for a quick settlement."
>
> "If I had been financially able, I would have held out longer."
>
> "It was too long to wait for a settlement. It seems like insurance companies prolong cases too long."
>
> "It was pretty miserable—justice isn't for the little man. I've . . . had enough of courts. If you have . . . [a] sharp lawyer, you're all set."
>
> "The settlement was unfair, but the lawyer said take it or you might get nothing."
>
> "[My lawyer] wanted me to say something that wasn't true. I wouldn't tell a lie for nobody."[7]

Another advantage of the no-fault plans would be the elimination of duplicate payments. No longer would an auto insurance company—ostrich-like—pay out, regardless of whether other forms of insurance had, in fact, already taken care of the loss. Generally speaking, under no-fault plans, once a person is paid for his loss by, for example, Blue Cross or sick leave, he would not be paid all over again by auto insurance. Given the ever-rising tide of availability of benefits from sources other than auto insurance, this is absolutely essential for two interrelated reasons: to help control skyrocketing insurance costs, and to discourage corrupting overutilization of insured services (such as a doctor's treatment), whereby the patient can make an easy profit. (See Chapter IV.)

Trial lawyers often object to preventing people from collecting insurance from two or more policies for the same loss. Says American Trial Lawyers' spokesman David Sargent, "Let's consider the analogy of life insurance. One man chooses to buy a $10,000 policy; and, when he dies, his estate is paid $10,000. But his neighbor buys two $10,000 policies and he dies. We don't say to his estate, 'You are only entitled to $10,000.' The holder of these policies bought and paid for the additional coverage."[8]

But the fatal fallacy in this analogy to life insurance is that, generally speaking, there is no need to worry very much about overutilization there. The penalty for collecting on life insurance is already, after all, quite severe. (Even so, insurers will not allow you to overinsure your life to the point that you will be tempted to suicide.) And, of course, in the area of fire insurance we have long prevented people from overinsuring their loss, on the universally accepted premise that this creates too strong a temptation to burn one's own property.

Auto insurance—along with other insurance covering medical expenses and wage loss—can be viewed as standing somewhere between life insurance and fire insurance in the degree to which it tempts one to invoke the insured event illegitimately. It is true that the penalty in collecting on auto insurance is not normally so severe as collecting on life insurance. But, at the same time, it may be more daunting than collecting on fire insurance, in that one has to get involved in an auto accident with its normally attendant risks of personal injury, if not always death. But the further complication is that once you are involved in an auto accident, you can *then* control invoking the insured event by, for example, missing extra work (and thereby collecting payment from sick leave as well as other insurance) and making extra trips to the doctor (and thereby collecting payment from health insurance, as well as other insurance). Actually, once the accident has occurred, the risks and pains of invoking the insured event are far less under auto insurance than under fire insurance. You don't have to destroy your own property; and such things as a few extra trips to the doctor, unlike setting a fire, entail little or no chance of being detected.

Of course, it is precisely these temptations to illegitimately invoke the insured event—coupled with the fact that auto insurance then pays a multiple of that invoked loss to compensate for pain and suffering—which have led to so much of the corruption and waste of the present fault system. (See Chapter IV.)

The dimensions of this problem of duplicate payments are particularly acute because of the burgeoning forms of no-fault insurance, such as group health insurance coverage, Medicare, etc., available to traffic victims. (See Chapter IV.) The need to dovetail and coordinate auto insurance with other forms of insurance is all the more acute, in light of the apparent impending enactment of some kind of national health insurance in the foreseeable future—not to speak of more remote, but nonetheless realistic, proposals for similar large scale wage replacement plans under national auspices.

Curiously, it is the unions, whose members stand to gain the most from the elimination of duplicate payments, who have often resisted elimination of duplicate payments the most. Typical of union response, for example, were these statements from a full-page ad—run in all major Massachusetts newspapers—sponsored by a regional Teamster group opposing no-fault insurance when such insurance first seemed likely to pass the Massachusetts legislature:

> Under the [No-Fault] . . . Plan, if you are out of work because you were in an auto accident, you must FIRST use up your own hard-earned UNION OR

> HEALTH AND WELFARE BENEFITS AND SICK
> LEAVE or any other lost time insurance you have paid
> for—or earned as a result of collective bargaining—BE-
> FORE you are entitled to *anything* for lost earnings . . . .
>
> Under the [No-Fault] . . . Plan, you must first USE
> UP YOUR OWN UNION HEALTH AND WEL-
> FARE BENEFITS—or Blue Cross-Blue Shield or
> Medicare, Medicaid or any other medical pay insurance
> you carry and *have paid for*—before the [No-Fault] . . .
> Plan pays you anything for medical or hospital expenses
> . . . .[9]

What this overlooks, of course, is that the auto insurance
premiums of the union members would be substantially reduced
in cost, since other forms of insurance would become the primary
source of payment. (It also overlooks that, under such no-
fault auto insurance, payments would be made when they are
really needed—when other forms of insurance have run out.)
This would mean that union members—who have increasingly
been finding it hard to buy and maintain auto insurance at reasonable prices—would be that much more attractive as auto
insurance risks and could buy insurance at concomitantly lower
prices. What the Teamsters' stand also overlooks is that having
insurance from two or three sources covering a given accident
is a very bad investment of every premium dollar spent for such
extra coverage. One is, in effect, gambling that one will have an
accident and thereby get paid two or three times one's loss. But
how bad an investment—or gamble—this is can be seen when
one realizes that an insurance company, in offering insurance,
has bet that it has charged enough so that it can not only pay for
an insured's loss, but also pay for the company's own overhead
and still earn a profit. And insurance companies are *very* professionally expert at setting the odds in their own favor—as they
ought to be, if we are to avoid an insolvent insurance system.
Thus, in the long run—and we are all going to be buying auto
insurance for about as long as we live—very few of us are going
to make any money on insurance. Now this "bad gamble" of
buying a single insurance policy is worth it when the insurance

money will be there to meet a real need, such as out-of-pocket loss after an accident. But when insurance will only be paying a kind of windfall, it becomes a discouraging gamble indeed. The "house's cut" on every extra insurance policy is simply too great to make it a reasonable use of money. Far better to take that money we are spending on extra insurance and spend it on something else—some other fringe benefit, for example, or in more take-home pay. Then, if you really like to gamble, you could gamble comparatively smartly—like on the horses or in Las Vegas. There, the odds against you are undoubtedly bad— but they are probably a lot better than betting on making money by collecting on any given insurance policy. And there, gambling is at least fun. Or if it isn't really fun you are seeking in your gambling, Wall Street or, say, real estate, will at least give you a shot at sharing in the profit of investment, something insurance —except for variable annuities—can scarcely boast of doing.

Another way of thinking about all this is to realize that, when a realistic person gambles against professionals, to the extent that he hopes to win, he hopes to be one of the lucky few. More precisely, to the extent he really hopes to win (as opposed to just having fun at the track or the roulette wheel), he hopes to get in—win—and get out. He knows that the longer he stays on, the more likely he will lose any of his winnings. But, as pointed out, we all buy insurance all our lives. So we can't hit the jackpot there and then leave with our winnings. We can't get in— win—and get out.

Now investing—as opposed to straight gambling—does mean taking advantage of the long run. There you are realistically betting that, in the long run, the money you spend will multiply if the enterprise you bet on prospers. (And, even to the extent people do get in and get out in so-called short term trading with quick purchases and sales, they are betting on the correctness of their guesses about the long run.) But, for the premium payer, insurance doesn't involve investing. It is true the insurance company invests your insurance premium dollar, but it doesn't let you share in the huge profits it makes on any shrewd investment. You go on paying the same premium for the same benefit quite apart from how well the company does investing your dollar. (While a so-called mutual company may vary your dividend depending, in part, on its investment experience, any benefit so conferred is likely to be very small compared to the very large amounts of money to be made from investing.)

So there are only two ways of viewing multiple insurance policies applicable to the same accident: either as a gamble or an investment. And either way, multiple insurance policies give you a rotten return on your money.

The disaster of using your money in the hope of collecting under several insurance policies is all the more disastrous when you realize that, under today's fault insurance system, all of us are *required* to make such use of our money. Few, if any, of us are in a position today to eliminate one of the two (or more) coverages applicable to an auto accident. Auto insurance, which mandates duplicate payment, is compulsory in fact or in effect in every state. Similarly, the no-fault health and accident insurance which most of us carry and which, similarly, most often calls for payment regardless of whether other insurance (such as auto) might also be payable, is usually a fringe benefit of our employment and cannot be dropped by us. In addition, even if it were dispensable, we wouldn't dream of dropping it just because auto insurance might duplicate it, since (a) we can never know whether auto insurance will be paid to us after an auto accident, given the vicissitudes of payment dependent on who was at fault; and, (b) even if we were sure of being paid from auto insurance, accident and health insurance covers so many other contingencies, such as sickness, non-auto accidents, pregnancy, etc., that the fact that it might be duplicated after an auto accident is scarcely a good reason for dropping it.

So most of us are required to make this wasteful and expensive gamble of having several insurance sources possibly applicable to an auto accident, like it or not. In fact, the majority of the public apparently would rather *not* make the gamble. Under a poll conducted by the University of Illinois Survey Research Laboratory, when the general public was asked whether it would prefer to buy auto insurance that would not duplicate payments from, say, Blue Cross but would cost correspondingly less, 54 per cent responded in favor of no duplication.[10] The only surprising thing was that as many as 46 per cent would seem to prefer more expensive insurance providing duplicate payment. This is especially surprising in light of the fact that the high cost of auto insurance was found in the same poll to be the biggest source of irritation stemming from auto insurance. But, as a practical matter, despite the preference of such a significant minority for duplicate coverage, it is best to have a rule, like the one under most no-fault insurance plans, that, far from compelling people to *have* duplicate coverage, compels them to *forego* duplicate coverage. Otherwise, the temptation to profit by over-utilizing the insured service (by repeated trips to the doctor, for example)—to rig the odds of the gamble in one's own favor, if you will—is too great. This is especially true when "the house" being cheated is such a vital social institution as insuring against injury.

Insurance, when you stop to think about it, is dependent for its stability and integrity on having the risk such that "when you win, you lose."* In other words, in order for payment to be made, you have to die, or have your property burn, or get sick or be in an accident. But, with multiple insurance policies covering the same accident, you are in a position to win without losing, by staying away from work or by those multiple trips to the doctor, after which you collect twice, or three times or maybe more from the multiple policies. As a result, the essence of insurance—the randomness of the insured event—is gone. Now people can control with impunity when and how much insurance will be paid to them, without real illegality or much threat of detection. No insurance mechanism can long survive exposure to that kind of pervasive manipulation without disastrous consequences.

Sometimes insurance companies arrange it so that the solution to the problem of multiple insurance policies applicable to

---

* An exception is an annuity, where you begin to be paid after living beyond a certain age.

a given loss is to allow an insurance company, which has paid under a policy, to claim for reimbursement (or partial reimbursement) against another insurance company, also obligated to pay for the same loss. Thereby, it is argued, at least the person paid from insurance doesn't collect twice or more. But the flaw in that arrangement is that, once an efficient loss-bearer like an insurance company has paid for a loss it collected premiums to bear, it is wasteful in the extreme to re-shift that loss all over again to another insurance company. Shifting loss, entailing as it does paper work, adjusters, arbitrators and maybe attorneys, is expensive. And, when we premium payers have paid an insurance company to shift it once (from us to them), we shouldn't have to bear the expense (ultimately passed on to us) of having it shifted all over again to still another insurance company. In other words, once one insurance company has assumed the loss, let it lie. Better to have a clearly defined rule dictating which one of the possibly applicable insurance policies will pay for the loss, and let that be an end to it. That is what most no-fault plans would—and should—provide.

To return to the topic of compelling people to carry expensive coverage they may not want, this is, in essence, what also happens under the fault system with reference to payment for pain and suffering. Under fault insurance, everyone is compelled to carry insurance that pays compensation to others he carelessly injures, including compensation for pain and suffering. Thus no one has a chance to forego carrying pain and suffering insurance, because obviously we can't allow people to choose *not* to pay others. So each of us must carry this expensive insurance to pay others—and have it available to us from others—like it or not. It is significant, however, that never has any form of voluntary no-fault insurance—such as accident and health, or fire insurance or burglary insurance—been written to cover the insured's own pain and suffering. As Professor Conard has pointed out, "did you ever hear of anyone voluntarily buying insurance against pain and suffering? Everybody I know would rather keep his premium money and bear his suffering without balm. If no one in his right mind would voluntarily buy insurance against pain and suffering, it is silly to require everyone to buy it compulsorily."[11]

Actually Professor Conard may be wrong in asserting that no one would *voluntarily* buy coverage for pain and suffering. A recent poll conducted at the University of Illinois indicates that 62 per cent of those who were paid from traffic accidents felt the insurance system should be changed to allow motorists to buy optional coverage for their own pain and suffering, payable after an accident regardless of who was at fault. (Only 33 per cent felt that payment for pain and suffering should be restricted, as it is under the present fault system, to being paid by those at fault to those free from fault.) And 57 per cent indicated they would buy it.[12] Of course Conard may be right in that, when motorists see what pain and suffering coverage will actually cost, they may very well forego buying it. But many no-fault plans would at least give the *option* of buying coverage for one's own pain and suffering, while ending the folly of *forcing* everyone to buy it for others.

Chapter X

Lower Price—
Higher Value

A big advantage stemming from no-fault auto insurance is a more intelligent and balanced weighing of the risks of potential insureds. This would eliminate much of the harshness and unfairness to many who are presently classified unfairly as bad risks. One of the biggest causes of the present marketing crisis for many in obtaining auto insurance today is that your insurance company, in rating you, only takes account of whether you are likely to be involved in an accident. It does not take account of what you would be paid once an accident occurs. This is so because your insurance company will pay not you, but the unknown person you may injure in a future accident. As a result, those who are considered more likely to have accidents—for example, the young, the old, the military, the ghetto dweller (who has to drive under congested conditions)—are charged very high rates, despite the fact that when they are in accidents, their losses are comparatively small. They suffer less wage loss compared to others, for example. Under present auto insurance, it is as though everyone was charged for fire insurance solely on the basis of how likely it was that a fire would start on his property, with no consideration being given to the value of the house. Thus, under auto insurance, the poor have to pay into the insurance pool the same or more than the rich, even though they stand to draw much less than the rich from the pool. But with no-fault insurance, payable only to the extent of one's out-of-pocket loss, all of a sudden today's poor risks would at least get credit for the advantageous aspect of his risks—that his losses are likely to be smaller than others. Take the elderly, for example, who find it so hard to get auto insurance now. Under no-fault insurance, the elderly person will probably be covered for his medical expenses by Medicare; also, he won't lose work because he is likely to be retired and covered by a pension. Thus, he becomes in many ways an attractive risk. And the same is true of others who are bad risks under today's fault system. That no-fault insurance would greatly alleviate the worst pressures restricting today's auto insurance market is confirmed by two insurance industry sources. Nationwide Insurance Companies (the nation's fifth largest auto insurance company), in recently switching its opposition to no-fault insurance, made the following point: "The public should find that . . . insurance . . . under the [No-Fault] Plan is substantially more available to it than is . . . [fault insurance] . . . . This would be true because under the Plan more applicants will be desirable to insurance companies than is now the case. Examples of the more acceptable risks are the youth, the elderly, and the serviceman. There will likely be a narrower spread in premium rates than exists today. It is expected that under a first-party [no-fault] system, the spread of rates between adult and youthful drivers—and between metropolitan and non-metropolitan areas—will be less."[1] Similarly, T. Lawrence Jones of the American Insurance Association, in speaking of how no-fault insurance will ease the marketing crunch, has stated:

> In the first place, underwriting standards [by which the risks of potential insureds are judged] will be formed more specifically according to the policyholder's driving record and personal need than they are today. More rational judgments can be made because the potential loss will be known to the insurance company at the time of application for a policy . . . .

> The greatest boon to less restrictive underwriting standards would result from the elimination of the [fault] . . . system itself, which would also eliminate the concern of underwriters that certain occupational groups will be poor witnesses or be uncooperative in the settlement of a claim against them.

> This will greatly improve the availability of auto insurance for people whose driving record is otherwise acceptable.

> We would also expect the number of people in the assigned risk pools to decrease.[2]

Another potential advantage of no-fault insurance would be in the area of automobile safety and repairability. Under fault insurance, your insurance company finds it difficult, if not impossible, to rate your car according to the quality of its safety equipment, such as padded dashboards, collapsible steering wheels, windshields more likely to yield on impact, etc. Such equipment, after all, protects you and the occupants of your car; but your insurance company, under the fault system, does not pay you or the occupants of your car but rather the occupants of the other car in the accident. But, once we shift to a first-party no-fault system, your own insurance company will be paying you and the occupants of your car and so it will be able to rate your car according to its injury-proof and damage-proof features.

Already, the availability of widespread no-fault insurance covering damaged cars is being used to encourage less fragile automobiles. At the present time about 60 to 70 per cent of all cars on the road are covered by so-called collision insurance— supplementary no-fault insurance by which a motorist covers damage to his own car from his own insurance company, regardless of who is at fault in the accident. (The widespread availability under the auto insurance policy of complete no-fault coverage for damage to cars, as opposed to the paucity of such coverage for injury to people, may very well be an outgrowth of the insistence of banks and other leading institutions, who finance cars bought on time, that their interest be covered in the event of accidents. Not for such smart money any reliance on a fault system!) Just as Detroit has long been notorious for building needlessly unsafe cars, so it has been equally guilty of building needlessly fragile ones. An insurance industry study found, for example, that when 1971 model vehicles were crashed into a concrete barrier at only 5 miles per hour, the average damage was $332. (For 1970 models it was $216.)[3] Bumpers are so bad on American cars that, according to Edward Daniels, claims manager for the automobile club of Michigan's insurance unit, some of them can be bent "with a hard kick"![4] (There is a method to Detroit's madness in all this. Detroit—and its dealers —make huge profits on repairs and the sale of replacement parts. Arthur Mertz, vice president of the National Association of Independent Insurers, has reported that his association has computed the costs of parts necessary to completely assemble a 1967 Chevrolet Impala with a list price of $3500. The parts, bought separately, would cost $7500, with the labor costing another $7500.[5] This reflects, among other things, the near monopoly position of the seller. Initially in buying a car, you can buy a Chevy, Ford or Plymouth; but once you have bought, say, a Plymouth, you can purchase many replacement parts only from Plymouth. This is especially true of the "crash parts" (the ones most likely to be damaged in a collision), which are chiefly sheet metal sections and usually available only from the original manufacturer.[6] This may help explain why the price of replacement parts for a new Plymouth rose 22 per cent between 1965 and mid-1969, while the price of a new Plymouth rose only 11 per cent.[7])

Note that such a rating system, based on injury and damage-proof features, could only be developed when the insurance company pays its own insured and therefore knows in advance what it will be paying for. When coverages for injury to persons are provided by no-fault insurance similar to that covering damage to cars, potential damage to people as well as to cars can be taken into account in rating a car. This might well constitute the most important breakthrough of all for auto safety. It could dwarf even the effect of federal regulation of the design of the car, with all its dangers of having the effectiveness of regulations diluted by the enormous influence of the auto industry. This undermining of the regulatory process by the industries supposedly being regulated is certainly what has happened with many other regulatory agencies, such as the Federal Trade Commission and the Interstate Commerce Commission. But an independent, economic force of the size of the insurance industry might well be a match for Detroit's more irresponsibly unsafe tendencies. At the least, it would probably be an effective supplement to government safety regulation.

Perhaps the most significant advantage of all under no-fault auto insurance will be its lower price. It now seems indisputable, on the basis of information from a variety of sources and actuarial studies, that no-fault auto insurance can be designed to pay many more people at substantially less cost. That this is so stems from the prodigious waste of the present system. By eliminating or cutting down on the lavish resources presently expended in (1) arguing over who and how much is to be paid, (2) paying for pain and suffering and (3) duplicating payment from other sources such as Blue Cross, enough can be saved not only to pay all those not presently paid (more than half of all traffic victims) but to cut auto insurance premiums very significantly.

But the key to no-fault auto insurance reform that cuts costs and makes sense is the *elimination* of the waste of the fault system.

And here we reach an issue of real bite.

Increasingly, trial lawyers who have been bitterly opposed to a substitution of no-fault insurance for fault insurance (see Chapter XI *infra*) have been acknowledging that the present fault system works badly indeed. Thus, Craig Spangenberg of Cleveland, in his capacity as an official spokesman for the American Trial Lawyers, testified before the Consumer Subcommittee of the U. S. Senate Commerce Committee:

> There can be no doubt that an impartial, broad-scale study of all elements of the [existing motor vehicle accident compensation system] . . . is needed, and needed now. Automobile insurance is becoming a national headache . . . . [It is] a system which is not working well.[8]

And, more particularly, the trial lawyers are acknowledging that the biggest failure of the present fault system is its failure to compensate many traffic victims. Thus Jacob Fuchsberg, former president of the American Trial Lawyers Association, proposes reform whereby "there would be no one injured [in a traffic accident] who would not receive some money toward his expenses."[9] Fuchsberg then proposes measures that would add greatly to the costs of the present system by making insurance payment available to all those not now being paid, but which would in no way reduce the waste and inefficiency in the manner of paying those already paid. Substantially the same criticism can be levelled at the proposals of the American Bar Association's Special Committee on Automobile Accident Reparation, which also suggests making payment available to all traffic victims, without seriously altering the right of those already being paid.[10] To a lesser, but still substantial, extent, the same is true of recent proposals by two insurance trade organizations, the National Association of Independent Insurers and the American Mutual Insurance Alliance.[11] In essence, what is being advocated by the trial bar is, in the words of Louis Davidson, another prominent member of the American Trial Lawyers Association, "a system of nonfault automobile insurance . . . where nothing is taken from the public but rather everyone has at least what he had under the [fault] . . . system, with some getting more."[12] That, of course, must inevitably cost much more than today's insurance. Trial lawyers airily dismiss such added costs. Says Mr. Fuchsberg, "We can afford them, as we can mass air travel systems, mass housing programs, mass highways, the stratoplane and other things that only limited imagination has prevented us from reaching out for in the past."[13]

But the question of such added costs deserves much more careful scrutiny than the lawyers are ready to give it. We have already pointed out the prodigious problems stemming from the cost/price squeeze which, in turn, results from the steeply rising cost of automobile insurance. Perhaps it should not surprise us that lawyers propose reforms that simply add to these already prodigious costs (and, not so incidentally, to the already massive fees that lawyers collect). But an already overburdened public can scarcely view such reform with equanimity, especially when the present system is so fat with wasteful cost and excess payment.

Indeed, the folly of the kind of reform proposed by lawyers and many in the insurance industry can best be illustrated this way: Today, under auto insurance, I am called on by law to insure myself for paying your losses, if I am at fault; and you are called on by law to insure yourself for paying my losses, if you are at fault. But "who is at fault" is so unpredictable that for years insurance companies have offered the option of some no-fault coverages, whereby I can insure payment to myself and my family regardless of fault and you can likewise insure yourself and your family regardless of fault. But these supplemental no-fault coverages (usually payable for car damage and limited medical expenses) in no way diminish the need for—or payment under—fault insurance payable to the occupants of the other car.

And now, as we see, trial lawyers and many insurance executives are advocating as a solution to the ills of auto insurance more and more supplemental no-fault insurance. But as such coverage—along with burgeoning accident and health and social security coverages—increases, as more and more I insure myself and you insure yourself, each regardless of fault, why do we need to duplicate that no-fault insurance with liability insurance based on fault? The question is especially pertinent when fault insurance is so wasteful, paying much more for lawyers and insurance overhead than for benefits to you and me. *In other words, as more and more you cover yourself for your loss, regardless of who was at fault, and I cover myself for my loss, regardless of who was at fault, why do we need to sue each other over who was at fault? Who benefits from all those suits over who was at fault except lawyers and insurance companies?*

What truly meaningful reform entails, then, is going much further with no-fault coverage by amending the law so that it no longer calls for me to insure you and you to insure me under an unworkable (fault) coverage. Rather, each of us will insure himself under a workable (no-fault) coverage, with each of us then being in a position to forget about claims based on fault.

All this has been demonstrated in a speech by Bradford Smith, then the president of the Insurance Company of North America. Smith, in a stunningly candid self-indictment of his own industry, spoke as follows:

> What alternatives are offered to a motorist under the present law? If he distrusts his chances of recovery under the [fault] . . . system and wants to be positively assured of recovery, he can buy [no-fault] . . . insurance which is readily available and will compensate him promptly and equitably without regard to legal liability. The difficulty is that the customer cannot substitute such a direct benefits [no-fault] contract for the [fault] . . . contract. For complete protection he must purchase both the [no-fault] . . . policy and the [fault] . . . policy.

> Thus, [no-fault] . . . insurance, as a solution, is impractical unless the law is changed to eliminate liability under the [fault] . . . system. To the public, purchasing [no-fault insurance] . . . policies and being required to also purchase a [fault] policy for the benefit of others and having others required to purchase [fault] policies

for his benefit in the event of legal liability is illogical, inconvenient, and unnecessarily expensive.

But, up until now, that is the only alternative we have offered to simple reliance on the [fault] . . . system for recovery of loss due to automobile accidents; and our only explanation has been that it is true that our system involves a duplication of expenses, but there is also a duplication of benefits. If a claimant is successful in his [fault claim], . . . he will recover this judgment in addition to whatever he recovers from his [no-fault] benefits contract. The public might well charge that the industry has developed a system requiring a motorist to buy twice as much insurance as he needs, so that in the event he is injured he may recover twice as many benefits as he needs.

Yes, that sounds preposterous, but that is, in effect, the present position.

So long as the premium for this duplicate coverage is a matter of a dollar or two, a policyholder might accept this proposition and look upon it like the football pool, ignoring insofar as possible the fact that he is the football. But when the premiums are substantial and grow larger in response to rising hospital costs, medical costs, automobile repair costs, and legal costs, he rejects this proposition. He can hardly be expected to be interested in paying double insurance premiums. Given the choice, it seems clear that he would prefer to pay the single premium and forego any double recovery in return for the elimination of duplication of cost.[14]

All this explains why truly worthy no-fault plans are those which prescribe a *switch* from fault to no-fault insurance. It also explains why proposals from the bar and segments of the insurance industry advocating that, for the great mass of accidents, both fault and no-fault claims be available should be viewed most sceptically by the public.

The first no-fault proposal to receive widespread attention recently was advanced by Professor Robert E. Keeton of the Harvard Law School and myself in 1966.[15] Under the so-called Keeton-O'Connell Basic Protection plan, every motorist would no longer be required to buy fault insurance covering others up to $10,000 (the usual limit in most states today). Rather, he would be required to buy no-fault insurance up to $10,000 payable to himself, his family, occupants of his car and pedestrians injured by him. This insurance would be payable without regard to who was at fault in the accident and would cover out-of-pocket loss (mainly wage loss and medical bills) to the extent they were not already covered by some other source. No payment would be made for pain and suffering. In turn, because everyone would now be insured by his own company for his own loss up to $10,000, everyone would waive his fault claim against others, roughly within the same range of coverage. As a result, for the great mass of smaller and medium size claims (where the waste of the fault system is greatest), no-fault claims would replace fault claims. In effect, a trade would be imposed by law. In return for giving up one's claim for a possibly large settlement, including compensation for pain and suffering as well as for out-of-pocket loss but dependent on proving the responsibility for the accident based on fault, the traffic victim would be assured of automatic compensation for all his out-of-pocket loss regardless of who is at fault in the accident.

In 1968, the American Insurance Association (AIA), a trade association composed of some 165 stock companies writing approximately one third of all auto insurance in the United States, stunned the insurance world by abandoning the insurance industry's monolithic and bitter opposition to no-fault insurance. AIA proposed no-fault insurance going even further than the Keeton-O'Connell plan. Under the AIA plan, *all* fault claims would be abolished and substituted for them would be no-fault claims for out-of-pocket loss, regardless of the size of the claim.[16] A year later, in 1969, Governor Nelson Rockefeller of New York State, acting on the recommendation of the superintendent of the New York State Insurance Department, Richard Stewart, advanced a similar proposal.[17]

At the other end of the no-fault spectrum, in 1970 the Massachusetts legislature passed what has been termed a "mini Keeton-O'Connell bill," calling for payment of up to $2,000 of out-of-pocket loss without regard to fault, but eliminating fault claims only for claims where medical loss does not exceed $500.[18]

Also in 1970, Senator Philip Hart (D, Mich.) proposed a federal bill that would require states to amend their laws to provide no-fault benefits for medical expenses and $30,000 of wage loss, with a corresponding elimination of fault claims unless the victim suffered "catastrophic harm" (including permanent disability or disfigurement).[19]

Which no-fault approach is best?

With the possible exception of the Massachusetts bill, any of the proposals mentioned can be unhesitatingly recommended over the present system. And even the Massachusetts bill—with all its compromises and ambiguities—is turning out to be a definite improvement over the present fault system, so bad is the fault system. The danger of the Massachusetts bill is that the fault claims are preserved in so many cases that there is a chance that, sooner or later, they will increase to the point where we will approach that perilous situation of having both fault and no-fault claims applicable to the great mass of smaller and medium size claims, with the corresponding risks of corruption and skyrocketing costs.

After all, at today's medical costs, by putting a person in a hospital for a few days and running a battery of tests, the $500 Massachusetts ceiling required before fault claims can be brought can readily be breached. Given the long history of lawyers, doctors and victims exaggerating traffic claims for their profit, such a plan offers thin protection against the evils of the present fault system.

And indeed, so-called no-fault proposals from many in the insurance industry—while apparently based on compromise—are even worse than the weak Massachusetts law. The National Association of Independent Insurers and the American Mutual Insurance Alliance—two of the principal trade organizations of insurance companies representing companies that write well over half of all auto insurance within the United States—have long been bitterly opposed to no-fault insurance. But they have both recently proposed bills now being widely introduced before state legislatures. The bills call for no-fault payments up to around $8000 for medical bills and wage loss, but would also allow fault claims to be brought within the same range of coverage. Damages for pain and suffering in such fault claims would be limited to one-half of the amount of medical bills if those bills were less than $500 and to an amount equal to the medical bills if they were over $500. In cases of very serious injury (death, permanent disability, etc.), there would be no limit on payments for pain and suffering. In all cases, any no-fault auto insurance payments would be allowed to duplicate most payments made from other no-fault coverages, such as Blue Cross or sick leave.[20]*

There are at least two fatal flaws in such a proposal. Note that in *every* case fault claims are preserved, retaining the possibility of lawyers and adjusters fighting over who is at fault in every accident. Secondly, there is still the temptation in every case to pad on medical bills, to duplicate payment already made and to increase payment for pain and suffering. So the nuisance value and waste of small claims—the cancer of the present system—are retained, albeit with the jackpot cut down somewhat. But note that those segments of the insurance industry proposing this reform, if they succeed in selling their plan or variations of it to the public, will have succeeded in putting over a system they like best—a system whereby they get to sell everyone two policies covering every accident instead of one: one policy for fault insurance and the other one for no-fault insurance. The same old sour wine.

It is significant that this business of having both fault and no-fault claims applicable to every accident, large or small, directly contravenes the standards for no-fault insurance proposed recently by the Department of Transportation. Once substantial no-fault insurance is instituted, said the Department of

---

* Illinois recently enacted a version of this plan. See note at p. 121 *infra.*

Transportation, "no person should recover for [pain and suffering under a fault claim] . . . unless he establishes that he suffered permanent [injury] . . . or that he incurred personal medical expenses . . . *in excess of a rather high dollar threshold* [emphasis supplied]."[21]* The proposals by the two insurance trade organizations have no threshold at all.

But, in accordance with the DOT standards, the no-fault plans which preserve fault claims only in very major cases (such as the Keeton-O'Connell and Hart plans) do not preserve the nuisance claims. There is little fear of padding medical bills, etc., in very serious cases because such cases are so very serious there is no need to pad. On the contrary, the main worry there is that insurance sources and sick leave will run out before real demands are met.

But, given the uncertainties and unfairness of the fault system, why should it be preserved in major cases? In other words, which is better, the New York and AIA approach of completely abandoning fault claims or the Keeton-O'Connell or Hart approach of eliminating most but not all fault claims? Perhaps the principal stumbling block to the New York-AIA approach is cost. Although the proponents of the AIA and New York proposals have predicted substantial cost savings even under their unlimited coverage, the costs of covering catastrophic loss could be staggering. For example, Professor Conard and his colleagues estimated in their Michigan study that the three per cent of traffic victims who suffer out-of-pocket loss of $10,000 or more account for 57 per cent of all out-of-pocket loss suffered by all traffic victims.[22] Similarly, the gross underestimations of the costs of Medicare and Medicaid have tended to make skeptics of us all concerning optimistic actuarial estimates of the cost of relatively unlimited insurance coverages. American society, after all, has never faced up to the cruel financial problems imposed on its citizenry by catastrophic illness or injury. Our European cousins cannot understand why we all tolerate living under the sword of Damocles of financial ruin which long term disability

---

* The Department of Transportation criteria for auto insurance reform are fully set forth in Appendix IV *infra*.

or ailment can impose on almost all of us. But on what basis do we carve out traffic accidents and force everyone to cover only that loss when it becomes catastrophic? Keep in mind that in forcing everyone to insure for $10,000 of no-fault benefits for traffic loss, we are not changing much in the way of the amount of required insurance, since everyone is already called on to carry that amount—albeit in fault insurance. But requiring everyone to buy not only different but perhaps much more costly insurance covering only auto accidents is something else again.*

There is a second problem, in addition to cost, presented by a *total* abolition of fault claims and substitution of no-fault claims reimbursing only out-of-pocket loss. This is the problem of the victim with permanent disfigurement or other damage, whose out-of-pocket loss is very low but whose psychic loss is very high. To speak brutally, it costs very little (say, $700) to sew up a stump and provide an artificial leg. In addition, for many in a white collar or professional category, there would be no significant reduction in income from the loss of a leg. Thus the bargain of eliminating the possibility of damage for psychic loss in higher amounts in return for certainty of payment in lesser amounts might well be unacceptabe to such an individual and to society generally. For this reason as well, then, the Keeton-O'Connell Basic Protection and the Hart plans of no-fault insurance preserve fault claims in such cases of terrible loss.

But if the costs of an open-ended, unlimited no-fault bill are in doubt, no longer can it really be denied that a somewhat limited no-fault bill of the Keeton-O'Connell Basic Protection type would cost *substantially* less than present fault insurance, while at the same time assuring payment for *substantially* more people.

Frank Harwayne, an internationally prominent actuary, has estimated that, if the Keeton-O'Connell plan were enacted in Michigan, it would assure payment, by a conservative estimate, to some 55 per cent more people than are paid under fault in-

---

* For a more extensive discussion of whether there should be a complete or only a partial abolition of fault claims—and for a compromise proposal between the two approaches—see Appendix III *infra*.

surance, while cutting a typical premium covering personal injury losses by about 25 per cent.[23] Harwayne had earlier estimated savings on a similar scale for New York State.[24] And, despite the bitter opposition of many in the insurance industry to the Keeton-O'Connell plan, not one single casualty actuary employed in the insurance industry has seen fit to publicly challenge Harwayne's predictions of such savings. Indeed one industry actuary who analyzed Harwayne's study in detail— Richard Wolfrum of Liberty Mutual—suggested that "the total possible reductions [in costs from the Keeton-O'Connell plan] are substantial to the point of being shocking . . . ."[25]

These comments foreshadow rather closely the comments of Massachusetts Insurance Commissioner C. Eugene Farnham on the experience under the Massachusetts "mini-no-fault" bill shortly after it went into effect. Based on the drastic reduction in personal injury claims filed with the no-fault system in effect, Commissioner Farnham stated, ". . . it is staggering. There is no question about it. . . . [W]hen you relate the decline in claims to possible savings in the future, it is just incredible."[26]

That the Massachusetts law was inevitably going to cut insurance costs, at least initially, was foretold by the rate-setting process contemporaneous with the bill's enactment. Prior to January 1, 1971, the effective date of the Massachusetts bill, Massachusetts auto insurance rates had been frozen by law since 1967. Everyone conceded that rates were due to go up by at least about 30 per cent, in the normal course of events, beginning in 1971. Instead, with the enactment of the mini-no-fault bill, rates were *cut* 15 per cent, with the insurance companies making no protest. (And since they did not protest[27] a cut of 15 per cent, that probably means rates could have been cut even more.)

If a modest no-fault bill of the Massachusetts variety can result in such savings, the savings from a truly adequate no-fault bill will obviously be that much more impressive.

So convincing has the evidence become in favor of no-fault insurance that it has produced—to his credit—a dramatic turnabout in the view of Secretary of Transportation John A. Volpe. When Volpe was Governor of Massachusetts, he vigorously opposed the Keeton-O'Connell no-fault plan. In 1967, after the Keeton-O'Connell bill had passed the Massachusetts House, then Governor Volpe stated that "more likely than not" he would veto the bill if it passed the Senate and called it a "step in the wrong direction."[28] But in late 1970, with the benefit of the completed DOT study before him, Volpe had changed his mind: He was reported to have told a meeting of the DOT Auto Insurance Advisory Study Committee, "I might say that I have . . . learned . . . about the problem of compensation and auto accident losses during the last two years. I learned a little bit about it as governor of Massachusetts. If I knew then what I know now—as a matter of fact . . . I think the Keeton-O'Connell plan might be on the books now. But we didn't know all those things in those days, and the boys didn't want any compromises."[29] By the spring of 1971, so much of a convert had Volpe become that apparently he urged the Nixon Administration to *require* the states to adopt no-fault insurance. Instead, as we shall see, the Nixon Administration requested the Congress to pass a resolution urging the states to enact no-fault insurance.[30] (See Chapter XI *infra.*)*

---

* As this book is being printed, Florida has enacted a modest no-fault law, somewhat more extensive than that in Massachusetts in providing more no-fault benefits ($5000) and in eliminating fault claims for pain and suffering unless medical bills exceed $1000. (As to the Florida law's no-fault provisions concerning property damage, see the note at p. 160, Appendix I *infra.*) Delaware has enacted a worse law providing $10,000 in no-fault benefits but not abolishing the fault claim for pain and suffering in any case. Oregon has enacted an even worse law providing no-fault benefits of $3000 for medical bills and $6000 for wage loss but not abolishing any fault claims for pain and suffering. Illinois has enacted a bad law providing for no-fault benefits of $2000 for medical bills and about $7800 for wage loss, but allowing fault claims in every case. See text supporting the note at p. 117.

Chapter XI

Defending the Indefensible

With all its faults, how is the fault system defended?

The answer is—passionately.

And the more the evidence accumulates on all sides on the unworkability of the fault system, the more the trial bar and many insurance executives adopt a siege mentality, calling for more and more loyalty to the beleaguered cause. Since 1966, an ever growing range of major news media has examined the fault system and pointed up its horrendous shortcomings. The list includes publications covering a varied spectrum—including *The New Republic, The New York Times, The Wall Street Journal, Time, Life, Fortune, Forbes, U. S. News & World Report* and even the column of William Buckley (no radical, he!). On what other issue would *that* group agree? In the face of this mounting tide of criticism, the attitude of the bar is illustrated by a press report of a meeting of the New Jersey Bar Association supposedly devoted in part to a discussion of no-fault insurance. According to the *Newark Star-Ledger,* "[Attending lawyers] denounced the [no-fault] . . . plan in a stormy conclave that at times bordered at near hysteria, rendering virtually useless any attempts to rationally evaluate the pros and cons of this proposed reform."[1]

Similarly, State Farm, the nation's largest auto insurance company, in its attempt to defend the fault system, conducted, in its words, "what may well be the most massive public opinion poll ever untertaken by private industry." It asked its approximately 11 million policyholders whether they agreed with this proposition:

> The driver who causes an accident, or his insurance company, should pay for the losses of other people in the accident.

Not surprisingly, of course, around 90 per cent of those responding answered "Yes" to this very simplistic, one-sided presentation of the issue of no-fault insurance.[2] The proposition, as put by State Farm, obviously suggests little of the real trade involved in a switch from fault to no-fault insurance: that trade involves certainty of payment for out-of-pocket losses under no-fault insurance versus a chance at payment not only for out-of-pocket losses but for pain and suffering as well, based on who was at fault, under fault insurance.[3] (It is significant that when a balanced question was put to the general public by the University of Illinois Survey Research Laboratory, clearly setting forth the pros and cons of both fault and no-fault insurance, 71 per cent of those responding favored no-fault insurance, with 29 per cent opposed.)[4] But, unashamed of the blatantly partisan nature of its survey, State Farm proceeded to trumpet its trumped up results in full-page advertisements in 60 leading papers throughout the country, including *The New York Times, The Chicago Tribune* and *The Los Angeles Times,* as well as in three page advertisements in *Time, Newsweek* and *U. S. News & World Report.*[5]

How effective the combined opposition to no-fault insurance of the trial bar and many in the insurance industry is may be suggested by a report from *The New York Times*: "[No-fault automobile reform] . . . has run into a stone wall in state legislatures across the country. . . . In state after state, the plan has been defeated or bottled up in committees, often through the efforts of powerful lobbies of lawyers' groups and insurance companies, both of which are heavily represented among members of state legislatures."[6]

Even the White House apparently caves in before the prodigious pressures of insurance lobbies. According to former Assistant Secretary of Transportation Richard Barber, a scholarly and highly respected lawyer and economist presently with the National Academy of Sciences, Secretary of Transportation John Volpe had approved the DOT recommendations to the White House of a "progressive, specific program" for a federal requirement of no-fault insurance. But, according to Barber, in a series of White House conferences in which insurance industry officials participated, the Department of Transportation "was forced not to retreat, but into a near rout." The result, according to Barber, was a "White House-dictated approach . . . pale, anemic, and lacking in substance," whereby the Administration recommended only a resolution declaring it to be "sense of Congress" that the states should enact no-fault legislation. Said Mr. Barber, "The unprogressive, unresponsive forces in the insurance industry . . . won a major victory in the White House."[7]

Trial lawyers and many insurance executives insist that what they are defending under the fault auto insurance system is not their fees or premiums but a basic pillar of morality—and even religion—with vast ethical significance for our whole society. In rallying to the defense of the fault auto insurance system, a report of the American Bar Association's Section on Insurance, Negligence, and Compensation Law warned that dilution of the fault principle would mean dilution of "the religious belief that each of us is responsible to his God for his own conduct." The report went on to suggest "that morality and the free enterprise system could be injured if the present [fault] system was modified."[8]

The president of one New York county bar association, in speaking against the no-fault system before a New York joint legislative committee on insurance, stated, "Gentlemen, I beg of you, don't repeal the Ten Commandments by enacting a no-fault plan!"[9] Craig Spangenberg, one of the leading defenders of the fault system as it applies to auto accidents in the American Trial Lawyers, the organization of claimants' attorneys, has said:

> In America today, we enjoy a procedure which has evolved over centuries of human experience, and has withstood the ultimate test of time . . . . A man who recklessly inflicts pain, disfigurement, and disability upon his neighbor ought to answer for his wrong, and the innocent victim ought to be made whole.
>
> The concept of fault is as old as human experience. The belief that liability should follow fault is as ancient, and as valid, as the belief that summer follows spring.[10]

In the first place, to imply—or state—that the fault principle has come down undiluted from time immemorial in the common law is to misread history rather egregiously. The principle of liability based on fault really stems in the United States from about 1850 with the case of Brown v. Kendall.[11] And, since its heyday in the late 19th century, it has been steadily eroded in area after area of the law, often at the urging of the same personal injury lawyers who seek to engrave it in stone for auto accidents. In the area of products liability, for example, plaintiffs' lawyers have eloquently argued against any requirement that a manufacturer must be negligent before he is held liable for a defect in his product. In other words no matter how blameless the manufacturer—no matter how much the injury resulting from the use of his product is beyond his control—the plaintiffs'

lawyers are maintaining, with ever increasing success in jurisdiction after jurisdiction, that the manufacturer be made to pay.[12]
They have also long successfully maintained that the negligence
of the injured party should not bar his claim in such cases.[13] Of
course, it is true that, in products liability cases, the eminently
litigable issue of whether the product is defective is left for the
lawyers, even if the issue of negligence is abandoned.[14] But note
that *morals* have nothing to do with it. The plaintiffs' bar seems
not so much interested in the moral question of making a man
pay for his wrong as in preserving complicated litigable issues,
quite apart from moral considerations. And from those litigable
issues, not so coincidentally, they profit hugely. This is not to
say that all trial lawyers consciously think through these matters
so crassly. But, consciously or unconsciously, the effect is the
same.

Secondly, how can one talk with moralistic fervor about the
wrongdoer "answering for his wrong" when one's wrong in a
traffic accident, if wrong there be, usually consists of a momen-
tary motoring slip of the type that all of us are guilty of again
and again, and when the "wrongdoer" is not only allowed but
required to pass the payment for his wrong along to an insurance
pool?

On the first point, we hand over swift machines weighing
two tons apiece, each with the power of hundreds of horses, for
use on crowded roads, to the gamut of our society—the young,
the old, the harassed and the physiologically immature. Obviously this exacts an inevitable and massive actuarial toll of
injury and death, quite apart from any "moral shortcoming" on
anyone's part.

All this raises a point of considerable philosophical importance. In his bestseller, *The Greening of America,* Yale Law
Professor Charles Reich describes traditional approaches to traffic accidents as typical of what he calls Consciousness I mentality
—"appropriate to the 19th century society of small towns, face-
to-face relationships, and individual economic enterprise." Consciousness I, he writes, "insisted on seeing the ills of industrialism
not as what they were but as moral problems. If a given number

of automobiles are crowded onto a highway, there will be a predictable number of accidents. The moral approach tries to deal with this as a question of individual driver responsibility. It stresses safe driving and criminal penalties. Yet reduction of the accident rate is almost entirely a problem in engineering."[15]

Indeed, the decline in auto injuries and deaths in 1970—the most significant ever—has been attributed by sophisticated experts mainly to engineering advances. Even more important than better roads, say the experts, is that since 1966, with the passage of federal legislation, cars have come equipped with safety advances such as seatbelts and shoulder harnesses, collapsible steering columns, less dangerous windshield glass and redesigned dashboards to reduce the chance the driver or passenger will be injured by striking hard or sharp objects. Such engineering improvements are now cited as the root cause in reducing the highway toll.[16]

And if it makes little sense to focus primarily on individual driver error to achieve safety, even less does it make sense to do so to distribute losses through insurance, where our primary goal should be to pay—not to deny payment—for the inevitably large losses stemming from massive highway travel. For the purposes of both safety *and* insurance, we must look at highway travel in the macrocosm—and focus primarily on lessening loss by widely applicable engineering devices and distributing losses by widely applicable insurance devices.

As a corollary of all this, another of the new DOT studies, entitled *Causation, Culpability and Deterrence in Highway Crashes,* has emphasized how little human culpability, in any controllable sense, is involved in the driver's part in traffic accidents. Defining culpability as "synonymous with individual responsibility, negligence, driver error, or fault," the report concludes that "wherever crash investigation has been of high quality, it has implicated as causal factors numerous variables that are clearly beyond the driver's control—e.g., environmental factors for which he is clearly not responsible or organismic factors of which he is unaware or which he cannot modify."[17]

The American Bar Association's Special Committee on Automobile Accident Reparations recently attempted to refute the proposition that fault is (a) hard to determine or (b) should not serve as the criterion for deciding who should be paid. According to the committee, an examination of typical auto insurance claim files reveals in most cases readily identifiable evidence of fault. It cites as the classic instance where fault is "clearly determinable" the rear-end collision, since in such an accident, according to the committee, almost always and automatically the driver of the car striking the rear of another car is to be blamed.[18] But, in fact, even in this supposedly simple type of case, is fault readily determinable? According to one engineering study, such rear-end collisions become "inevitable under certain circumstances."[19] In a typical traffic pattern,

> the . . . lead car decelerates and then accelerates back to his original speed. You notice that, say, the second driver puts on his brakes and decelerates but at a little later time because there is a time-lag. His distance with respect to the first car oscillates. The next car decelerates still later, and you can see that this deceleration pulse happens later and later as you go down the line of cars, and the amplitude grows until . . . metal is being bent! . . .

The severely congested nature of modern, urban "stop and start" traffic should make the foregoing painfully realistic to most drivers today. Another point should be noted, however. A driver attempting to maintain an adequate distance between cars to ensure his safety during traffic acceleration and deceleration would likely find this impossible. Gaps left open between cars, deliberately or inadvertently, on multiple lane roads are quickly filled in by drivers from the other lane. And in streets with only a single lane in each direction, cars entering from side streets or pulling away from the curb tend to fill gaps left in the traffic flow.

At least one implication of . . . research regarding the assessment of "fault" is that while the driver factor may be asserted as being responsible in rear-end collisions, the individual can hardly be shown to be "at fault" in the sense of being morally culpable for running into the rear of someone else's car under truly congested traffic conditions.[20]

Another DOT study, entitled *Driver Behavior and Accident Involvement: Implications for Tort Liability,* concludes that most drivers are often "guilty" of driver error. A certain magnitude of driver error is "representive of the general behavior of the general average of drivers and must be considered as normal. . . ." Put another way, says the study, "a significant gap exists between the standard of behavior required by the negligence law and the average behavior normally exhibited by most drivers."[21]

Perhaps the best illustration of the inevitability of accidents under almost any conditions occurs regularly at the General Motors Proving Grounds where carefully trained drivers are in carefully maintained cars on carefully engineered roads. Despite professional drivers operating under optimal conditions, accidents persist.[22]

As a result of these and other findings, a DOT study recommends efforts for traffic safety be aimed, in order of priority, at (1) the crashworthiness of vehicles, (2) emergency health care services for traffic victims, (3) better roads and (4) "lastly, changing driver behavior"; and those efforts, emphasizes the study, must be different from the simplistic efforts based, for example, on civil law suits extant today.[23]

All this is not to deny any individual responsibility for negligent driving. It is to recognize that faulty driving cannot be viewed in isolation from the vast social forces surrounding it. It is also to recognize that, especially in the case of automobile accidents, a moralistic approach with emphasis on an individual person's performance can be a hugely wasteful and unrealistic focus. This is especially true of automobile accidents because, as suggested, the intervention of immense pools of insurance has so peculiarly undermined the validity of focusing on the individual lapse. After all, having people "answer for their wrongs" by having an insurance company pay in their stead is about as morally effective as allowing people to hire substitutes to serve jail sentences.

Note, too, that no-fault insurance does not abrogate criminal responsibility for reckless driving, or administrative sanctions such as the loss of a driver's license. In addition, to the extent that one thinks that safety can be induced through varying a person's insurance rates depending on his driving record, that can be done under either fault or no-fault insurance. Workmen's compensation premiums, although payable on a no-fault basis, vary with the premium payer's safety record. Indeed, in large measure the so-called merit rating systems for rewarding good and punishing bad drivers, by varying their insurance premiums under the present fault system, are in fact usually based not on fault but upon simple accident involvement, regardless of fault.

The point is that, when we inject insurance into the legal system on the massive scale that we have with auto insurance, it no longer makes sense, in the words of Yale Law Professor Fleming James, to think in terms of liability "based on fault in the sense that made it originally seem so fair and gave [the system] . . . so strong a moral [base] . . . ."[24] No longer does the system in fact make the wrongdoer pay for the injuries caused by his wrong. Rather, the system imposes responsibility for the so-called wrong on innocent persons—all those who contributed to the pool of insurance, including the injured party. So when Jones sues Smith after a traffic accident, he is suing not only Smith but also *himself* and all who pay insurance premiums.

Similarly, if the talk of morality of forcing wrongdoers to pay for their wrongs is unrealistic under the present fault insurance system, so, by the same token, is the talk of the immorality of paying wrongdoers under a no-fault system equally unrealistic. Once we begin thinking in terms of insurance, we see (or we should see) that every form of insurance *except* liability insurance pays wrongdoers: Life insurance, accident and health insurance, social insurance, fire insurance and even the medical payments and collision coverage under the automobile policy itself. Indeed, a large motivation of all of us in buying insurance is to protect ourselves and our family against our own lapses.

Of course trial lawyers, despite their arguments to the contrary, recognize that there is really nothing immoral in paying negligent drivers for their losses. Trial lawyers themselves, as we have seen, urge more and more that no-fault payments be made available to traffic victims. (See Chapter X *supra.*) But then they shift and insist that the liability of the "wrongdoer" should not be lessened in the process of making such payments. But that gets us back to the futility of punishing people by having their insurance companies pay on their behalf, and the further folly of having suits to determine payment based on fault, when most if not all the loss is already covered by no-fault insurance. (See Chapter X *supra.*)

It is the myopia of the trial bar and of many in the insurance industry in harking back to inapplicable morality and in refusing to recognize the broader implications of insurance for accident law that encourages them to defend so passionately an indefensible system.

The truly ironic feature of all this is that, although all the excesses and failings of the fault system are supposed to be endured as a price paid for individual justice—as a price for tailoring payments to the true deserts of each individual—the system ends up failing perhaps worst of all in those very terms. According to the New York Insurance Department study: "In general, the highly abstract standard of liability called 'fault' and the indeterminate measure of damages called . . . 'pain and suffering' offer rich rewards to the claimant who will lie, the attorney who will inflame, the adjustor who will chisel and the insurance company which will stall or intimidate."[25] As Daniel Patrick Moynihan has put it, "Automobile accident litigation has become a 20th century equivalent of Dickens' Court of Chancery, eating up the pittance of widows and orphans, a vale from which few return with their respect for justice undiminished."[26]

In their impassioned defense of the fault system, trial lawyers most often save their biggest rhetorical guns for the immorality of the way no-fault insurance treats the drinking driver. They point with outrage to the situation where the drunk driver is involved in an accident; if the drunk is badly hurt, with large medical bills and wage losses, they cry, "He will stand to receive large benefits from the no-fault insurance pool; and at the same time he will be free from liability."

What about this hypothetical case which, judging by its emphasis by trial lawyers, is the ultimate in the chamber of horrors supposedly stemming from the introduction of no-fault automobile insurance?

It is time the problems of dealing with the drinking driver were discussed without the fatuous fulminations commonly dominating such discussions. Researchers are increasingly dividing drinking drivers into two categories—the problem drinker and the social drinker. Researchers insist too that not only are drinkers disproportionately involved in all accidents entailing serious injury and death but also, as to those drinking accidents, the problem drinkers are very disproportionately involved again.[27] Roughly speaking, the research seems to suggest that about one-half of all fatalities involve drinking drivers, and at least one-half of that one-half involves problem drinkers.[28]

Consider the problem drinker. What countermeasures are likely to deter him from driving while drunk? Will the prospect of being held liable months or years after the event, and thereby having his insurance company pay damages on his behalf, deter him from drinking? Conversely, will the prospect of not being paid damages from someone else, months or years after the accident, deter him? To ask the question is to answer it. If all the immediate misery the problem drinker causes himself and his family does not deter him from his dangerous drinking, to suggest that such remote and hypothetical possibilities will affect his behavior is ludicrous.

There are probably few adults in America who have not personally dealt, at one time or another, at one level of intimacy or another, with an alcoholic—whether a spouse, or cousin, or co-worker or companion. Can anyone of us recall any more tragic or intractable problem—the endless disgraces and humiliations, the endless resolutions to reform, the endless, sad, broken resolutions? Alcoholism is so frustrating both for individuals and society that psychiatrists, accustomed on the whole to dealing with comparatively intractable illness, find alcoholics "more difficult and often much more difficult to treat" than others.[29] About all we seem to know about alcoholism is that we don't know much about it—except that those afflicted are very sick, both physically and emotionally. And probably the last way a civilized society ought to treat the sick is to deny them insurance payments when they further injure themselves. And in overwhelming measure we do not do so: *only* fault liability insurance payments are denied to the drinker today. He is paid from all other forms of insurance, from life insurance, accident and health insurance and fire insurance through medical payment and collision insurance under the automobile policy itself. So to castigate no-fault auto insurance for making payments to the alcoholic driver is scarcely a very powerful, or perhaps even humane, argument.[30]

That leaves the social drinker. There are, of course, thorny problems of separating the serious from the social drinker, even for the purpose of general definition, not to speak of the greater difficulty of doing so for the treatment of specific individuals. But, passing that, how much sense does it make to deny the social drinker involved in an accident insurance money to pay for his wage loss and medical expense? Once again, most forms of insurance do not do so. And furthermore, insurance payments should not be thus denied. We are a society whose mores, like it or not, call for drinking and driving. Few adults are not part of social groups where drinking and driving mix. It may be that through Draconian punishments we can alter these mores, but that is doubtful at best. In order to do so, we must overcome firmly entrenched and pervasive attitudes. The last massive effort of American society to alter the law and attitudes toward drinking—Prohibition—hardly augurs well for such an undertaking. At the present time, too, the extent to which juries refuse to criminally convict drinking drivers on the grounds that "There but for the grace of God go I . . ." is common knowledge to every prosecutor and policeman. And these are the same jurors about whom trial lawyers wax so eloquent as the embodiment of community standards and wisdom. Aren't these jurors, who throughout the country and for so long have balked at punishing the social drinker involved in an accident, trying to tell us something concerning how "immoral" drinking driver offenses are? Aren't they recognizing how innocent—relatively speaking—is the conduct of the social drinker who drives, such that the conscience of the community—the jury—often refuses to impose criminal sanctions on him? And if jurors, whose instincts trial lawyers trust so deeply and hold so precious, balk at punishing drinking drivers in the relatively few and egregious cases prosecutors think suitable for criminal trial, how sensible is it for those same trial lawyers to insist on a scheme that will punish all social drinkers involved in accidents by refusing to pay their medical bills and wage loss? The main result of such a tactic, after all, is to cast the bulk of the burden on the even more innocent families of such drivers. Surely, too, the social drinker who is not deterred by the possibility of injury to himself and his passengers or the loss of his driver's license or criminal sanctions is, like the problem drinker, not likely to be deterred by the outcome of a possible insurance claim months or years later.

The best thinking on traffic safety today would put the lowest priority on trying to change the driver. And it would put the lowest priority in trying to change the driver on trying to change the drinking driver; and it would put the lowest priority in trying to change the drinking driver on trying to change the drinking driver through threats concerning insurance claims.[31] And so trial lawyers, in emphasizing as they continually do the supposedly detrimental effect on traffic safety of no-fault insurance in its treatment of the drinking driver, are emphasizing the lowest item of priority on the lowest item of priority on the lowest item of priority.[32]

And on this topic of "punishing" or deterring negligence, except for an occasional nominal fine, criminal law does not often deem careless driving worthy of much punishment; it ordinarily takes reckless driving to invoke the criminal law in any serious way. And yet the fault insurance system "punishes" merely careless driving by denying the accident victim any payment for his loss—which may well run into tens of thousands of dollars! No criminal court would ever consider such "punishment" as appropriate.

Even for the occasional act of reckless driving, the criminal courts would not be likely to punish beyond a fine of several hundred dollars. But the fault liability law "punishes" once again by the Draconian penalty of denying all insurance payments, no matter how enormous the amount.

Why should the civil law, which is, at most, only indirectly concerned with punishment, so severely punish careless or reckless conduct when other forms of insurance do not punish at all, and when even the criminal law, which is primarily concerned with punishment, would either punish not at all or much less severely?

Worst of all, perhaps, is the effect on our whole legal system of all these auto accident suits. Our legal system is on the verge of breakdown (some would say it *has* broken down) trying to handle the criminal and civil cases it now faces. According to a recent study by *The New York Times:*

> Congestion is strangling the courts in big cities throughout the country and is turning justice into a commodity that Americans regularly find illusive, capricious and uncertain.

> Every day the court backlogs leave innocent men in the jails and guilty ones on the streets. Witnesses and victims wait hours for cases that are never called. The claims and causes of the injured remain unheard.

> The delays are long and the effects are lasting, not only for the poor, the black, and the young, but also for the rich, the white, and the old, the business man, the motorist, and the consumer.

> Beyond the routine wholesale delays, gross overloading cripples the courts in dealing incisively with

the broad problem of urban violence that is becoming
a ranking priority at all levels of government.

. . .

The cases and people stack up. In New York, for
example, the blame for the [recent] jail riots . . . was
placed largely on notorious delays that kept more than
40 per cent of the inmates waiting a year or more to
be tried.[33]*

And the worst is yet to come. The civil liberties decisions
of recent years have imparted rights to criminal defendants
which, while invaluable to them and arguably to society, are
extremely taxing in the complex issues they present in countless
cases before the courts. Similarly, the civil rights decisions of
recent years have opened the courts to many new litigants,
including the poor, the black, the juvenile offender, the prisoner,
the mentally incompetent, the draftee, the student, etc. If, in
the past, the law seemed too often to be employed by the
dominant forces in society against the poor and powerless, now
the latter are increasingly given the opportunity to use the
courts to redress their wrongs, just as others always have done.
And all of us, rich and poor and neither, are beginning to invoke
the courts in a rising era of "social litigation," supplementing
the social legislation of the past, in broader suits to protect our
environment and ourselves as citizens and consumers, especially

---

* Although papers like *The Times*, emphasize the role of delay in causing the riots, delay, while unquestionably a cause, can be advantageous to
a criminal defendant just as it is to civil defendants, like insurance companies, for some of the same reasons. According to a recent study of a
New York criminal defense lawyer working for the Legal Aid Society,
"During the riots, inmates' demands for less crowding, better food, ex-
termination of rats and vermin were supported even by the hostage guards.
But their demands for speedy trials, though they found strong support
in the press, were less sincere. Virtually every prisoner in the Tombs
[jail] is guilty, either of the crime charged or of some lesser but connected
crime. He knows that he will either plead guilty or be convicted in a trial,
and that he will serve time. He knows, too, that delays will help his case.
Witnesses disappear, cops' memories fade, complainants lose their desire
for vengeance. As prosecutors see their cases decaying, they lower and
lower the pleas [they will accept]. Meanwhile, time served in the Tombs
before sentencing counts as part of the sentence." (Mills, "I Have Nothing
to Do with Justice," LIFE, March 12, 1971, pp. 57, 65-66.)

through so-called class actions suits. In addition, more and more social and political issues—not only integration, for example, but war—are going to the courts. Professor Maurice Rosenberg, probably the country's leading authority on judicial administration, in 1965 contributed to a book called *The Courts, The Public, and The Law Explosion.*[34] Recently Rosenberg said, "My views have changed since 1965 to the extent that what we called a law explosion then looks like a pop by comparison with what we have now."[35]

Recently, author Jeremy Main, reviewing the most promising proposals for reforming our courts, including those pertaining to the law applicable to wills, divorce, and drug addiction, stated, "All these reforms would be overshadowed if the courts were relieved of their single greatest burden: the automobile."[36] A recent study by the Federal Judicial Center for the Department of Transportation estimated that nationally 17 per cent of all judge time in both civil and criminal matters is taken up with auto accident cases. That estimate is probably low.[37] On the civil side, typically 50 to 80 per cent of the jury docket is taken up with auto cases.[38]

Two recent speeches by Chief Justice Warren E. Burger of the United States Supreme Court clearly indicate his belief that, unless auto accident cases are removed from the courts, our judges and juries cannot possibly handle the crucially important criminal and new civil suits on their dockets.[39] It is unthinkable that critically significant litigation in our society —both civil and criminal—must be slighted, or even ignored, while we spend our precious legal and judicial resources trying to decide who went through stop signs five years earlier in order to prevent most people injured in auto accidents from being paid from auto insurance.

The answer of the trial bar to the impact of auto cases on court congestion is (1) to deny it exists, (2) to insist that, even if it does exist, it exists only in major metropolitan areas and (3) to insist that the answer to it is to appoint more judges. To deny that auto cases contribute to court congestion is to deny what overwhelming evidence has long demonstrated.[40] To attempt to dismiss it on the grounds that it exists only in major metropolitan areas is to slight a massive and growing part of our populace. And to suggest that the solution is the appointment of more judges is to fly in the face of wisdom and experience. Perhaps one of the few areas where Chief Justice Earl Warren agrees with Chief Justice Warren Earl Burger is in their repeated assertions of the futility of simply appointing more judges as a solution to the problem of court congestion.[41] Similarly, President Nixon, in addressing himself to the problems of court congestion, recently dismissed this solution: "If we limit ourselves to calling for more judges . . . operating in the same system, we will produce more backlogs, more delays, [and] more litigation. . . ."[42]

Part of the problem is that many of the approximately 95 per cent of the cases presently settled are settled *out* of court because of the delay *in* court—litigants cannot or will not wait for trial. But if delay is cut or removed, many of the cases now being settled will be willing to move up to trial, thus wiping out any saving in delay! Finally, even if more judges were the answer to court congestion, it is doubtful the public should be asked to pay the high cost of judges unless they will be wisely used—and trying auto accident cases in the face of other desperate needs for our legal and judicial system is scarcely a wise investment. Mayor John Lindsay has estimated that the annual cost to New York City for each judge is $250,000, once the costs of a courtroom and supporting personnel are included.[43] In urging the appointment of more judges to solve the problems of court congestion and delay engendered by auto cases, we see one more example of the trial lawyers' characteristic indifference to profligate expenditure by others for little if any gain, except for lawyers themselves.

Chapter XII

Where from Here?

Lawyers are opposed to no-fault insurance because they sense that the need for lawyers will largely disappear in auto claims under no-fault insurance. No-fault insurance has indeed been called "no-lawyer insurance."[1]

But why are so many in the insurance industry opposed to no-fault insurance? One answer is that far from all of them are opposed. But, even with the conversion of many insurance companies and executives to the no-fault idea, many, if not most, in the insurance industry still oppose it or advocate it only as a rather minimum supplement to fault insurance. Why?

Partly it is because the insurance industry is, by nature, a very conservative industry—and, in many ways, it ought to be. One of the biggest "assets" of an insurance company is its bank of actuarial data based on what has happened in the past—by which it can predict what will probably happen in the future. If the rules under which an insurance company pays out money change drastically, obviously the value of its actuarial data is undercut. And, with the unknowns greatly increased, an insurance company is that much more uneasy about what risks it can insure and at what price.

Another reason many insurance companies fear no-fault insurance stems from the resemblance of no-fault auto insurance to accident and health insurance. Many companies have relatively little experience writing accident and health insurance, especially on a group basis as a fringe benefit of employment. This includes the so-called direct writers, such as Allstate, State Farm and Government Employers, along with other mutual companies, such as Kemper. These are the same companies who have gained more and more of the market since World War II. (See Chapter VII *supra*.) Conversely, the companies which have lost the most business have been the old line stock insurance companies, such as Aetna or Travelers, which also insure a great deal of accident and health coverage, especially on a group basis. Companies like Allstate and State Farm have greatly feared that, since no-fault insurance is so much like accident and health insurance (payable by your own company without reference to who was at fault in the accident) and thus amenable to being written as part of group coverage (see Chapter VIII *supra*), the companies more experienced in group accident and health insurance will regain much of the market they have lost in recent years, once no-fault automobile insurance becomes a reality.

A third factor often said to explain the opposition of some insurance companies to no-fault insurance lies in the fact that for years insurance companies have relied increasingly, not on their insurance business to keep them profitable, but rather on their income from investments. Some insurance executives, it is argued, are not interested in insurance that will cut costs—and premiums—thereby reducing the amount of money companies have to invest.

Another reason for the resistance of so many in the insurance industry to a sensible idea like no-fault insurance is related to the first factor given: an innate conservatism. But it is the less defensible side of that factor. It has to do with a lack of imagination and a corresponding lack of both innovative management and receptivity to new ideas generally. "As a rule," admits Charles K. Cox, president of the Insurance Company of North America, "the insurance business has been pretty sleepy."[2] There are several reasons for this. Low pay is one of them. Says H. J. Maidenberg, consumer columnist for *The New York Times,* "Secondary management salaries in the traditionally low paying insurance field are set either to repel aggressive, bright executives, or to force many in the industry to leave."[3] Working in a highly regulated industry may be another cause of torpor in the insurance industry. "Let's face it," says a member of the New York Insurance Department staff, "this is a hothouse industry, just like the railroads. Nearly every time it wants to make a move it has to get approval from us. This is not the sort of atmosphere which bright young men thrive in."[4]

Many in the insurance industry have also resisted no-fault insurance on the ground that it would lead, they say, to a federally run and owned insurance system. Says James Kemper, Jr., president of the Kemper Insurance Companies, speaking of the Keeton-O'Connell no-fault plan, "The surest road to federal regulation *and* federal automobile insurance is the [Keeton-O'Connell] . . . plan. . . . [The Keeton-O'Connell] . . . plan, a compulsory accident insurance system which . . . largely eliminates the need of determining fault, is primarily a system for dispensing benefits, and therefore a natural precursor to a complete takeover of this segment of the private sector by the federal government. . . . [I]t is a matter of cause and effect: [no-fault insurance] . . . leading irresistibly to federal insurance."[5] There are several answers to this. In the first place, there has been simplified no-fault criterion for payment of claims in many forms of insurance for generations without governmental takeover. Federal takeover certainly did not follow, for example, in the case of workmen's compensation, a no-fault coverage. Certainly the wide variety of other forms of no-fault insurance—such as accident and health coverage and fire insurance—has not led "irresistibly" to their being taken over by the federal government. Secondly, the reason for government takeover of any line of insurance seems to be not so much the ease of payment but whether private insurance is performing adequately in selling and servicing the market. For example, Medicare (medical insurance for the aged under Social Security) came into being because private insurance companies were not providing adequate medical insurance for the elderly. Similarly, both federal crop and flood insurance came about because of the inadequacy of privately offered insurance. As an additional example, federal reinsurance to cover property in the inner city was an outgrowth of the inadequacy of the private market and indeed occurred at the invitation of the insurance industry.

Insurance executives also seem to fear that if a good no-fault bill were passed, which (like the New York or the Keeton-O'Connell bill) makes auto insurance payable only after accident and health insurance and, say, sick leave are exhausted, there would not be enough loss to cover above these other forms of coverage to sustain the vast empire that is casualty insurance. But, as a practical matter, the great, crying need for casualty insurance today is to cover the large losses not being covered. In an age of burgeoning technology, large and horrible losses from the malfunctioning of technology are inevitably going to continue to afflict many in our society. Indeed, already a major problem of casualty insurance is not that there are not enough risks to cover but that there is not enough insurance "capacity" to cover the risks already created. Witness the problems, for example, of getting sufficient coverage on jumbo jet aircraft. Even in a traditional area like auto insurance, it is the large losses that are not covered. The typical traffic victim who is permanently and totally disabled sustains an average loss of $76,000, but receives compensation of only $12,000 from auto liability insurance.[6] And the number of people recovering—and their percentage of loss covered by payment—is unquestionably much smaller in other areas of loss, such as those stemming from malfunctioning manufactured products[7] or, say, accidents in the course of medical care.

Thus, the casualty insurance industry need not fear that spreading forms of health insurance, for example, are going to obliterate the need for a private casualty insurance market. On the contrary, that need—in all its variety and variations—is just now being really perceived for the first time. Take the issue of national health insurance. Many lawyers and insurance executives state that impending national health insurance—whether publicly funded as suggested by Senator Edward Kennedy, or privately funded as suggested by President Nixon—will swallow up the problem of auto insurance and make moot all our current dispute over a separate fault or no-fault system of auto insurance.

But no system of national health insurance will destroy the need for—and the need for reforming—a separate system of auto insurance. It is true that national health insurance would meet most of the medical needs of traffic victims. But medical bills are only a relatively small part of the loss stemming from traffic accidents. Forty-six per cent of compensable losses stemming from traffic accidents is from property damage: Of the remaining 54 per cent of compensable loss applicable to personal injury, only 12 per cent is for medical expenses, with 40 per cent for wage loss (and 2 per cent for "other expenses").[8] Thus, even national health insurance, of whatever kind or whatever dimension, will take care of only a small fraction of the total losses stemming from auto accidents. Nor is that likely ever to change. There is no serious proposal for including wage loss within national insurance or Social Security at the present time. And, with the fantastically high costs that national health insurance is likely to impose,[9] it will be a long time before any national insurance or social security system is going to be extended to cover wage loss as well. Even if and when a system of national insurance is thus extended, the pattern of social insurance in Europe would indicate that only modest levels of income will be covered—up to, say, $150 a week or so—leaving much, if not most, wage loss uncovered for many.[10] And it is surely doubtful that any national insurance or Social Security system will ever be extended to property damage. So a separate and vast system of auto insurance is going to be with us for as long as we can foresee. It behooves us, then, to make sense out of that insurance—by replacing, in substantial measure, fault claims with no-fault claims—in the coverage applicable not only to medical expenses but also to wage loss and property damage.*

A related question sometimes asked here is why reform of the fault system for compensating injury should be limited to auto accidents. How about falls in the home or injuries from manufactured products or medical malpractice claims? There are several reasons for limiting no-fault insurance—at least at the outset—to auto accidents. Automobiles are clearly the most dangerous instrumentalities with which we all deal on an everyday basis, and the damage they do to persons and property reflects this. Secondly, automobiles are both so widespread and so dangerous that we already have a system whereby almost everyone has an insurance policy covering auto accidents. It is true that those policies, in the past, have called for an insurance company to pay someone else based on the insured person's fault; but, because everyone has a policy, it is relatively easy to switch over to no-fault insurance by changing each policy to cover the losses of the insured person himself, without reference to who was at fault. But take the case of someone who burns his hand on a stove. Are we to say he is automatically to be paid for that injury, without regard to anyone's fault? Who is to pay it? To force stove manufacturers to pay everyone injured by stoves would be a tremendous change and increase in their legal liability. And, if the stove manufacturer is not to pay, note that, unlike the case with auto accidents, the injured person

---

*For means of extending a sensible comprehensive system of no-fault insurance to property damage, see Appendix I *infra*.

would not have a separate insurance policy covering stove injuries. He may have accident and health insurance covering some payment for all kinds of illness and injury, but payment from that source doesn't entail any change in the common law and certainly doesn't entail a no-fault insurance system as we have been discussing it. Such a no-fault insurance system involves, as we have seen, a switch from fault to no-fault insurance. But with stove injuries—and injuries from all kinds of manufactured products, as well as, for example, from medical malpractice—there really isn't a vast pool of insurance now extant capable of paying for all injuries regardless of fault. On the other hand, we *do* have, at least for a great range of losses in auto accidents, a pool of insurance now extant capable of paying for all injuries regardless of fault. But the only insurance applicable to injuries from manufactured products today covers accidents where the product is defective. And proving that the product is indeed defective is about as complicated as proving that the manufacturer was at fault in the way he produced his product. Indeed, in most cases, the two are really synonymous. So difficult is it to prove that there was fault or a defect in the production of a typical manufactured product, what with the need for complicated engineering testimony, etc., that only a small fraction—probably less than five per cent—of injuries from manufactured products are presently compensated. In sum, outside of automobile accidents, we don't have a legal and insurance system readily transposable to no-fault insurance.

Of course, we could do what has been suggested in New Zealand—cover all injuries under Social Security on a no-fault basis.[11] But that gets us back to the point made earlier that just absorbing medical costs under Social Security or national health insurance in the United States is going to be sufficiently costly that adding on expensive coverage for all wage loss from all injuries is going to be a long time coming. Similarly, as previously suggested, if and when we do that, we are going to leave a lot of loss uncovered by Social Security, as has happened in Europe. That loss will have to be met, if at all, by some kind of separate insurance system applicable to the activity causing the accident. In other words, reimbursing all the wage loss ever to accrue in the future of a young man disabled permanently or for a long term by a power tool or even a stove is never going to be covered by Social Security; and the question becomes under what circumstances, if at all, does the manufacturer of the power tool or stove pay for the bulk of the loss not covered by Social Security?* In addition, even if we could cover all losses from all injuries under Social Security, economists specializing in loss allocation tell us it is unwise to have all injuries, from whatever source, paid for out of a big, undifferentiated pool of insurance: Rather, a given activity or industry should be made to pay for the particular damage it does. Otherwise, there is less incentive to keep that activity or industry safe. Isn't the incentive to produce a safe product greatly lessened if persons injured by your product are paid exclusively from general tax revenues? And then the question becomes whether that separate insurance system for a given activity or industry should be a no-fault system, and *that* question gets us back to the problems we have just discussed about whether it is feasible to have a separate system of no-fault insurance applicable to injuries from stoves, for example.

In short, going beyond auto accidents for no-fault insurance gets us into *very* uncharted seas *very* quickly. All the more reason, then, to start with auto accidents where we are ready for it, where we can see where we are going and where we can make judgments about whether it is feasible to extend it to other areas.

Who is to accomplish this change to no-fault insurance, federal or state government? For historical, if not very logical, reasons, insurance has always remained primarily the bailiwick of state governments in the United States. Obviously, a business as large and as pervasively interstate in character as insurance might logically be a concern of the federal government. On the

---

* Some—but by no means complete—compensation is available under Social Security today for the person totally disabled for twelve months or longer, after a six-month waiting period. But such compensation is not made to the person partially disabled or totally disabled for less than 12 months. See 42 U. S. Code Sec. 423.

other hand, it is *not* true that only a federal solution to auto insurance is feasible, given the heavily interstate nature of the problem. We have long lived with varying state law applicable to auto accidents: Some states, for example, have had rules of contributory negligence as opposed to comparative negligence, while others have not (see Chapter II *supra*); some states bar most claims by passengers against their host drivers, while others do not. Many other examples of varying rules applicable to auto accidents could be cited. Also, we have achieved comprehensive and consistent reform of legal areas as pervasively interstate as banking and commercial contracts through state-by-state action. So the interstate complications of varying state law need not force us to a single, unitary federal reform in the area of automobile accidents.

But state inaction may.

Even many liberals in recent years have begun to question the wisdom of more and more federal solutions to more and more problems in a country as vast and as variegated as ours. On the other hand, the ills of auto insurance clearly illustrate the main reason Washington has preempted attempted solutions at so many problems: state inaction. Given state inaction on auto insurance—and the dominance of state legislatures by insurance and lawyer lobbies—federal action may well be necessary. It may be necessary not only to get any no-fault bill passed, but also to right the wrongs of watered down no-fault bills, which the states are pressured into passing by those same lawyer or insurance lobbies as an inadequate concession to the need for reform.* Things have long passed the stage of crisis in automobile insurance, and either tier of government—state or federal—which is prepared to pass a sensible, effective no-fault bill should be encouraged to do so.**

One suggested compromise is a combination of state and federal action whereby the federal government would promulgate

---

* For some examples, see note at page 121 *supra*.
** For a description of an optional bill where motorists would be given the option of choosing either fault or no-fault insurance, in order to allow no-fault insurance to demonstrate its effectiveness by competing with the status quo, see Appendix II *infra*.

general standards of no-fault insurance, which the states would be mandated to follow—with each state working out its own specific legislation.[12]

In one way, it is stunning that it has taken us so long to change our intolerably bad auto insurance system. On the other hand, it is not so surprising. As Daniel Patrick Moynihan stated in a speech in 1967 at the University of Illinois on "Changes for Automobile Claims?":

> Many of the essential issues concerning "Changes for Automobile Claims" were raised in 1932 in the *Report by the Committee to Study Compensation for Automobile Accidents,* published by the Columbia University Council for Research in the Social Sciences. This was a civilized country in 1932 and there were a lot of automobiles around. The committee came out very explicitly on behalf of scrapping the concept of [fault] . . . liability in automobile accidents in favor of a non-fault . . . solution for such accidents. That was 35 years ago. And yet the proposal which the researchers at Columbia University so confidently recommended to a rational nation made no impression whatsoever . . . . Things do not change that simply.
>
> The undeniable fact seems to be that built into the American system is a predisposition to keep things as they are in this and other respects. Anybody would be ill-advised to suppose that the American society changes very rapidly when it shows itself able to resist for so long such proposals for reform. Remember that one of the things that really matters about this country is that this is an extremely stable country. There are no more than nine nations in the United Nations today whose government has persisted without change since 1914. We are one of them. We live in a society established in the eighteenth century, with the second oldest written constitution in the world. We are one of the most stable on-going societies on earth. This is a thought not hard to contemplate on the Illinois Prairie and one which

should make anyone who foresees great transformations a little humble.[13]

Some idea of how stable a country we are is indeed conveyed by the difficulty of changing something as *relatively* small and as *absolutely* bad as our auto insurance system. Despite all the clamor from right and left for basic changes in America, we are unlikely to see fundamental change, not to speak of fundamental upheaval, in our society. C. P. Snow has put it this way:

> The worry I have met here and there among Americans is a fear of revolution. This is totally unrealistic, perhaps the most self-destructive of American worries. The underlying structures—as the young call them—of American society are immensely strong. By structures, I mean the institutions that the radicals get cross about. Industry, the trade unions, the whole administrative apparatus. These structures are far stronger than either those who support them or those who hate them can easily believe. They will remain so for the foreseeable future.
>
> . . . I would be prepared to make a bet, though I shan't be there to collect, that by the year 2000, the essential framework of [the United States] . . . will be remarkably similar to what it is today.
>
> The basic structures are impregnably strong.[14]

But of course the secret of long range stability is change. Any stable society is stable because it *can* change when necessary. Indeed, the United States has had a remarkable capacity for change, as Gunnar Myrdal has noted: "Take Reconstruction and the moving away from it, take Prohibition and abandoning it, take the example of Americans entering World War II as extreme isolationists and ending it as extreme interventionists. I know of no nation in the world that can change its fundamental attitudes so rapidly as America."[15]

Nowhere, except perhaps in matters of war and race, is change more necessary than in the way we view and use technology. And the ultimate technology in our society—the engine

that runs us all—is the automobile. D. P. Moynihan has had
something to say on this too, as it pertains to auto insurance:

> . . . [T]he problem of automobile insurance must be
> seen as simply one of several social costs of the auto-
> mobile. Not to see it first in this context is to miss its
> meaning. . . . These problems [of auto insurance] are
> characteristic of a larger problem of American life today
> —namely, the aftereffects of the introduction of tech-
> nology. We are a society—a capitalist society—wherein
> persons who successfully introduce new technology reap
> very high rewards. By the same token, our society is
> not very much restrained by the less attractive second,
> third, and fourth order of effects stemming from new
> technology. We put all the incentive on the plus or
> minus of the first order. That means we are a very in-
> novative society; that means people are always thinking
> up things; that means people are getting rich returns
> for being inventive and for taking risks. It also means
> that some years later it can turn out that those pills
> make babies turn blue, or everybody's got cancer, or
> those cars kill a lot of people, or the courts get clogged
> with automobile claims. All these are the second,
> third, and fourth order of effects which we are not
> very good at controlling. Air pollution is certainly one
> of the most common examples.
>
> In another society—not one I would particularly
> want to live in, but many people have opted for it—
> whenever someone comes along with a new idea, they
> say, "what are the second, third, fourth and fifth order
> of effects?" And if these latter don't look very promis-
> ing, one is not allowed to undertake the first one. A dull way
> of life. American life, on the other hand, is full of
> chances, full of rewards. It's very exciting, because you
> never know what's going to happen next, even whether
> or not you're going to be killed. But the fact is that we
> are beginning to see that we are going to have to be a
> little more orderly. We are going to have to begin to

ask, what are the second, third, and fourth order of effects of proposed changes?

One of the tertiary effects of the automobile has been this tremendous problem of insurance, which, in turn, involves problems that manifest themselves in costs; not only in direct costs to individuals, but in social costs. A good example is the effect of automobile insurance on our legal system, which turns out to be very seriously affected. Somehow, those who are trying to deal with the automobile from another world, such as insurance, are going to have to understand that they are dealing with a prototypical problem of our society—how to deal with the effects of technology, in this case the automobile.[16]

What with the pervasive presence and effects of the automobile and the dominant place it has in our society in so many ways—economically, culturally, socially, atmospherically, legally—General Eisenhower might just as reasonably have warned us of the insidious and invidious effects of the automobile-industrial complex as of the military-industrial complex. Our economy is much more dependent, after all, on the auto and its satellite industries than on the military and its satellite industries, immense as the latter may be. In both cases, the vast interlocking interests of multifarious industries—taking advantage of a craving for mobility in the one case and for security in the other—spawn enterprises—whether roads or wars—that take on a senseless, destructive life of their own. Just as whether we learn to control the military-industrial complex has worldwide repercussions, so how we deal with the aftereffects of this particular piece of technology—the automobile—is of crucial importance not only for ourselves, but also for the rest of the world. Everywhere else on the globe, it would seem, other nations cannot wait to exceed our excesses with the automobile. Go to Yugoslavia—go to Israel—go to any burgeoning country—if you would see new dimensions in the destructive effects of the automobile.

At long last we in America are beginning—and only beginning, and only with faltering gestures, it is true—to cope with the automobile: To make it safer; to make it cleaner; to make it more efficient; to provide alternatives; and to assure payment of the toll in injuries and damage which it inevitably exacts. On this last point, we reach a sub-issue of awesome dimensions itself: The viability of our legal system. Once again it is D. P. Moynihan who has summed it up:

> [I]n considering this whole area [of auto accident compensation], we ought at all times to be thinking of one really important issue—much more important than profits, much more important than private enterprise, much more important than the self-esteem of professors: and that is the functioning of our legal system. We are dealing here with one of the central aspects of sovereignty, one of the fundamental bases of social stability. The perception of the larger society that justice is being done is sacred. And justice is possible only when it is done quickly and reflects the community sense of what is right and what is wrong. This transcends the issue of government regulation or non-regulation, transcends the issue of how you distribute or don't distribute the wealth, transcends the issue of whether or not certain groups are discriminated against or not discriminated against. This has to do with the stability of our society. We are dealing, then, with something fundamental, and if those concerned with automobile claims cannot produce solutions that preserve the viability of the American legal system, then they fail. And not just they fail—after all, none of us matters that much—America fails, and that does matter. That is what is at issue here. The present system of automobile insurance is preventing the American legal system from functioning properly, and no more solemn issue could be put before the American citizenry. . . .
>
>   . . . In the resolution of this issue—in what is likely to be a fairly conspicuous arena—the reputation and

the standards of . . . the American bar are at stake. If the bar cannot do anything but proceed with the squalid concerns that have characterized its dealing with this issue for the last twenty years, then the bar is sicker than anyone knows, and we are in deeper trouble than we know.[17]

And so, as with the whole issue of the aftereffects of technology, the way we treat the automobile accident is a fundamental touchstone of how well our society—and perhaps the world—can adapt justice to the needs of the modern day. Just as the way we treat the automobile accident is a revealing omen of our capacity to cope with technology, so the way we treat the automobile accident is a revealing omen of our capacity to adapt justice to the needs of modern man. The law's job is—and always has been—to bridge the need for fairness to each fellow with the broader needs of society for a rule applying to most fellows. The wisdom of all law—and especially the common law—is based on the assumption that we cannot start each case afresh. We need rules. And rules, by definition, seek to fit the needs of any particular case into the broader perspective of similar cases. Accommodating those two interests is agonizingly difficult work. The more the rules are tailored to the individual, the more difficult it becomes for society to administer them. In the course of coping with this dilemma, our system of justice is breaking down with what might be called legal overkill in area after area of the law—from automobile accidents to divorce, to real estate, to probate, to tax, to commercial contracts, etc. In all these and other areas, we are strangling ourselves with rules and procedures which, with myopic perversity, are supposed to serve the needs of the individual client, while, in fact, they throw up so many points of confusion, contention and controversy that both the client and society are ill-served by their legal system and their lawyers. The lawyers end up—unwittingly perhaps—largely serving themselves. In other words, we end up with the worst of both worlds; we have rules that are so cumbersome that *neither* the individual nor society is served.

Law suits, after all, are a civilized society's way of conducting private warfare. When important and irreconcilable differences persist, a civilized man is called on to say, not "I will kill you," nor even "I will strike you," but "I will sue you." But law suits—like all forms of warfare—can be a cruelly wasteful business. If there is one thing we Americans should have learned in recent years it is that wars undertaken for any but the most essential causes can be disastrous. On a lesser—but still devastating—scale, we have been resorting to warfare, and threats of warfare, as the key element in settling millions of auto insurance claims every year.

Nothing is worse than unnecessary wars.

No one can have an answer for all areas of the law and their bootless complexity. When John Frank, a brilliant practitioner, attempted to outline, in area after area of the law, means of reducing what he called needlessly complex "decision points,"[18] eminent expert after eminent expert exclaimed: "Not in *my* area! In *my* area, all this complexity is immutable."[19] Maybe they are right. But if they are right individually, they are wrong collectively. Because, as Frank pointed out, our legal system cannot go on the way it is.

At least in one area we know the way out. We can simplify and better auto insurance at a stroke by no-fault insurance. It is true that thereby we will no longer be focusing on each of millions of traffic accidents to dissect the deserts of the conduct of each driver. In the end, that is what the trial lawyers—and many insurance executives—protest so bitterly. What they fail to see—with ineffable blindness—is that all that dissecting has long since ceased to be worth the candle, except to them. The law of auto accidents is the ultimate example of the law's need in many areas for more expeditious, less fussy rules; rules, which by nature of their expedition, actually become fairer than the savage inefficiencies of the common law applicable to auto accidents. In adopting no-fault insurance, not only will we redeem one vast area of the law—that applicable to auto accidents—but maybe we can learn something about groping our way towards sanity in other areas as well.

Epilogue

One keeps coming back to the question of why a system so indefensible as the fault system for auto insurance should be defended so passionately and effectively.

Keep in mind that, on the whole, we certainly are not dealing, in the case of the defenders of the present system, with evil men. On the contrary, the overwhelming number of lawyers and insurance personnel who defend the horrendous fault/auto insurance system are as sensitive and intelligent as most men. Although many harsh things have been said in this book about lawyers and the extent of corruption in the present system, overwhelmingly it is the *system* which is to blame for the short-comings of auto insurance, and not the men who run it. Given the system, except for some egregious excesses in urban areas with respect to chasing and padding claims, most lawyers and insurance personnel—along with victims and doctors—behave about as you would expect most men to behave under the same temptations and pressures.

But, just as doctors have for years passionately defended our manifestly inadequate system of health care delivery, so lawyers defend our manifestly inadequate system of auto insurance. In both cases, the system seems on the verge of breakdown; but the individual practitioner, whether medical or legal—working comfortably and profitably within the system—is puzzled by the attack on both the system and himself. He finds himself working hard and helping many people on a case-by-case basis. So immersed is he in the system that he fails to step back and see the system—whether medical or legal—in larger perspective, with all its inadequacies for many individuals and for society.

We have learned a lot about the vulnerability of professionals in recent years: If automobile accident claims are too important to be left to the lawyers and medicine too important to be left to the doctors, so also have we had brought home to us the truth of the old saw that war is too important to be left to the generals. And we have gained a new insight: That technology is too important to be left to the technicians. Recognizing these truths is by no means the culmination of a solution to these problems. On the contrary, it means only the beginning of a solution, as all of us undertake some hard thinking for the experts about their expertise.

The only thing ultimately harder than doing that will be not doing it.

Appendix I

Provisions for Property Damage[1]

By Robert E. Keeton* and Jeffrey O'Connell

Extending the Keeton-O'Connell plan's Basic Protection no-fault insurance—which is compulsory—to vehicular damage would deprive the car owner of the option he now has to do without insurance against damage to his own car. A motorist's choice whether or not to obtain insurance against damage to his own car can be viewed as almost exclusively his own business. But a motorist's decision as to insurance covering personal injury is a very different one because it is so much more likely to involve substantial interests of other people, as well as interests of society in general.

A very substantial percentage of all car owners—over one-third in many states—choose not to carry the no-fault coverage now available for damage to their own vehicles (collision coverage). A person with an older car is especially likely to make this choice. He may consider it cheaper to cover the risk of damage to such a car himself, thus avoiding the relatively high cost of collision insurance on a relatively low-value car. Persons electing not to carry collision coverage may also be influenced by the fact that they could take as an income tax deduction

---

* Professor of Law, Harvard University.

casualty losses of this type. This motivation may be even stronger for the affluent owner of a car of high value than for the less affluent owner of a used car of low value. Thus, our decision not to include damage to one's own vehicle in the compulsory Basic Protection insurance is based on the undesirability, as well as the impracticality, of trying to force each car owner to insure against damage to his own vehicle. Including damage to vehicles in the overall plan on an optional basis under so-called Vehicle Protection Insurance, as described below, avoids these difficulties.[2]

By way of explaining Vehicle Protection Insurance, it may be stated at the outset that most of the various proposals for a new system of property damage insurance (including the American Insurance Association and New York Insurance Department proposals, as well as ours), have one common element. Each would require every insured motorist to carry property damage liability insurance for any residual liability for damage to the property of others that remains under the new system. The proposals differ, however, with respect to the options available for coverage of damage to the policyholder's own car.

According to an earlier proposal of Property Damage Dual Option coverage under the Keeton-O'Connell plan, the car owner would have had the option of carrying either no-fault insurance under which a tort claim for damage to his car was precluded, or fault insurance under which he could recover for damage to his own car only if he could prove that he had a valid fault claim against some other person.[3]

The American Insurance Association[4] and the New York Insurance Department[5] proposed, instead, that the car owner have the option of no-fault insurance or *no* insurance; all tort actions for damage to vehicles would be abolished. Thus, they would have eliminated the second option under Property Damage Dual Option coverage (the option of retaining one's right to sue under a fault claim) and would have added instead an option of noncoverage. In other words, a motorist could choose to cover himself for damage to his car by no-fault insurance or he could choose not to be covered for such damage at all; but under no circumstances would he have a claim for damage to his own car based on the fault of a third party.

In essence, the new Vehicle Protection Insurance proposal makes available all three of these options. First, if the policyholder wants no-fault protection for damage to his own car, he can obtain it, and at a cost somewhat lower than he now pays for coverage for damage to his own car and the cars of others. The amount he pays for these purposes at present includes the total cost of his no-fault collision coverage on his own car and all but a very small fraction of what he pays for property damage fault liability coverage. (The small fraction is that part of the latter coverage applying to damage to property other than cars —such as damage to a fence or a building.) The saving results from a motorist's having to carry only one coverage applicable to car damage (a no-fault coverage on his own car), whereas formerly two coverages were needed (no-fault coverage on his own car and fault coverage for damage to the cars of others).

The second option would be available to the motorist who wants protection for damage to his car only in case he has a good fault claim against another person. He can obtain this protection at virtually no change in cost from what is paid under the present system by a person carrying property damage fault liability but not collision coverage. Under Vehicle Protection Insurance, one's own insurer would make this payment, even though it is based on the fault liability of a third party.[6] Finally, because under the proposed Vehicle Protection Insurance all benefits, including those based on fault, for damage to the policyholder's car are payable by his own insurance company, a motorist could be allowed the option of dispensing with all claims for damage to his own car while remaining free of liability for damage he might negligently cause to cars of others. If a motorist elects this option, thereby reducing his insurance protection, he saves both the collision premium and that major portion of the property damage fault liability premium attributable to damage to cars. This third option can also be seen as a full-deductible, and it is so described in the provision drafted for inclusion in a statute.[7]

We recommend the new Vehicle Protection Insurance as a solution to many of the difficulties that plague automobile insurance for damage to cars. *

---

* Florida's new no-fault law provides for a version of this kind of triple option for property damage. For damage to cars under $550, all traditional fault claims are abolished. Instead, for such loss a motorist can choose to cover damage to his own car by insurance, payable by his own company, based on either a fault or no-fault criterion or he can choose to have no coverage of any kind applicable to his car. For damages over $550, traditional fault claims against the other motorist are preserved either for a motorist himself or under subrogation by his insurance company, which has paid him on either a fault or no-fault basis. The deductible is a "vanishing" deductible, in that once the threshold is exceeded—i.e., once damages reach $551 or more—one can collect not only the damages over $550 but also those under it. (But won't the low figure of $550 plus the vanishing deductible sorely tempt motorists or their insurance companies to induce auto repair shops to pad bills to exceed $550?)

Appendix II

An Optional No-Fault System [1]

By Robert E. Keeton[*] and Jeffrey O'Connell

To a great degree, reform of the automobile claims system has foundered on the fear of government officials that the predictions of increased benefits and lower costs under a no-fault insurance system may not work out in practice. Reporting to the Senate Commerce Committee on the results of the Department of Transportation study, Secretary of Transportation Volpe described the problem as follows:

There are many ideas, and a large number of proposals which have been advanced over the years [concerning the problem of motor vehicle accident compensation], but each presents sizable problems. Further, there is no significant basis of experience for assessing the relative strengths and weaknesses of new approaches. While the present system has its obvious faults, we should not hastily move to a system merely because it is new. Caution, common sense and consideration of sound public policy demand that we carefully assess

[*] Professor of Law, Harvard University.

the full range of alternatives and move gradually in the direction of reform, checking actual experience as we proceed.[2]

Is reform possible beyond a scaled-down no-fault plan, such as that enacted in Massachusetts, without making what some would fear to be an irrevocable commitment to the no-fault concept of insurance? Perhaps the answer lies in optional, rather than compulsory, no-fault insurance plans.

Under a compulsory plan,[3] motorists are required to have no-fault insurance coverage as a prerequisite to registering an automobile. If the no-fault insurance system—and its concomitant exclusion of tort actions—was as extensive as under, say, the Keeton-O'Connell Basic Protection Plan, all but a very small percentage of the personal injury claims arising from automobile accidents would be handled entirely under this new no-fault insurance.

Under an optional no-fault insurance plan,[4] each liability insurance policyholder would have a wider choice than under either the present fault system or a compulsory no-fault system. He could choose a package that included no-fault insurance and liability insurance coverage beyond the scope of no-fault coverage. Alternatively, he could continue to carry only the kinds of coverage he now carries under the fault system.

We believe that a compulsory plan is better, by an edge. Among other advantages, it is simpler to explain and to administer because it requires every motorist in the state to have the new coverage. Also, of course, by encompassing all motorists under the new no-fault coverage, it distributes the advantages of no-fault insurance to everyone and, concomitantly, eliminates that much more of the waste inherent in the fault system.

On the other hand, an optional plan has the great advantage of giving the individual the freedom to choose the kind of insurance he prefers. The several surveys of public reaction to a no-fault system, though susceptible of varying interpretations, have at least demonstrated that a substantial number of people favor no-fault insurance, as well as that a significant number are apparently willing to live with the present fault system.[5] Given this apparent division of opinion, perhaps it makes good sense to allow each motorist to choose what form of coverage he desires.

To the government official who is asked possibly to stake his political future on automobile insurance reform, an optional system offers a chance to place the issue before the public through a marketplace referendum. In this connection, Franklin Marryott, former vice-president and general counsel of the Liberty Mutual Insurance Company and long a thoughtful leader of the casualty insurance industry, has urged that any changes in the current automobile insurance system

> should, and as a practical matter must, be gradual and should involve a high degree of continuity with the past.
>
>   . . . .
>
> . . . [C]hange should [also] be such that it leaves an avenue of retreat if it turns out that serious error has been made. The commitment must not be irrevocable.[6]

It has always been our opinion that the Basic Protection Plan—by combining no-fault and fault coverage and thereby preserving substantially the mechanism of the present fault system—meets these criteria. But an optional plan goes even further in this direction; indeed, that is both the strength and the weakness of the optional plan. In general, though, it may make sense in our society to structure reform proposals whenever feasible in such a way as to allow the freedom and flexibility permitted by practical, competitive experimentation. If the no-fault system is efficient and effective, an overwhelming number of persons will probably opt for its coverage. On the other hand, it is at least conceivable that the no-fault system may long continue in robust competition with the fault system, or may even wither and die as a result of that competition. In any case, reform will have had a trial during which it will have been forced to demonstrate its effectiveness in open competition with the status quo. It may be appropriate at this point, therefore, to consider in some detail a modification that we now offer as an alternative to our proposed Basic Protection statute.[7]

Under this proposal, existing liability insurance statutes, which either require or strongly encourage the purchase of fault liability insurance, would remain in effect. But each Bodily Liability insurance policyholder would be offered the option of electing Basic Protection insurance, which would replace liability insurance and fault claims within the low-to-medium range of losses. When thereafter injured in an automobile accident, a motorist who had elected Basic Protection coverage would be entitled to have his net out-of-pocket losses up to $10,000 reimbursed by his own insurance company, without regard to who was at fault in the accident. Within specified limits, he would have elected to give up his rights to negligence claims against other drivers. Ordinarily the policyholder's election would apply to all the members of his household. The election would bar fault claims to the extent of the first $5,000 of pain and suffering damages and the first $10,000 of other damages, such as wage losses and medical expenses.

Under the optional system, if two Basic Protection insureds collide, each would be paid by his own Basic Protection insurer, and each would have given up his negligence claim against the other to the extent of the Basic Protection exemptions. On the other hand, if two liability insurance policyholders collide, each would have a potential negligence claim against the other, exactly as under the present negligence system. Finally, if a motorist who has elected Basic Protection collides with a motorist who has chosen liability insurance, the Basic Protection insured would be paid by his insurance company regardless of who was negligent and would have given up his negligence claim to the extent of the Basic Protection exemption. The liability insurance policyholder, on the other hand, would retain his negligence claim against the Basic Protection insured (whose insurance policy would cover that liability).

This last situation, unless otherwise corrected, would result in a built-in disincentive to buy no-fault coverage, since the motorist who opts for Basic Protection would give up his negligence claims and yet would be forced to cover not only himself (under no-fault coverage) but also those opting for fault coverage who could collect against him under the negligence system. Consequently, means must be found to assure that the savings resulting from the surrender of fault claims by the no-fault insureds accrue to themselves. In response to the need for a corrective mechanism, the proposed statute requires that the Basic Protection policyholder's company, together with other companies writing automobile liability insurance in the state, participate in a pool, or some other similar arrangement established by the companies with the approval of the Commissioner of Insurance. The proposed statute guarantees that, through the pool, not only will cost savings resulting from the surrender of a Basic Protection policyholder's negligence claims go to his own company rather than the other driver's company, but also that his company will pass along to him, in the form of reduced premium charges, a fair share of all such cost savings.[8] With these savings, the average Basic Protection policyholder could buy the combined package of Bodily Injury Liability insurance and Basic Protection insurance at less cost than he now pays, or would pay under the new system, for Bodily Injury Liability insurance alone. The savings for the Basic Protection policyholder are further increased because he would no longer need Medical Payments and Uninsured Motorist coverages, since they are included within Basic Protection.

Similarly, each Property Damage Liability insurance policyholder would be offered the option of electing Vehicle Protection insurance[9] to accompany his liability insurance. A person electing this coverage would be entitled to reimbursement from his insurer for damage to his own car, without regard to who was at fault in the accident—a benefit comparable to that now received under Collision insurance policies. He would also give up his rights to negligence claims against other insured drivers who cause damage to his car. Here too, through the pool, his insurer would be credited with the cost savings resulting from the surrender of his negligence claims; and in turn he would receive, in the form of a reduced premium, a fair share of all such cost savings. Thus, his combined premium for Property Damage Liability insurance and Vehicle Protection insurance would be lower than the combined premium for Property Damage Liability insurance and Collision insurance.

If a motorist still preferred to be covered under the present system (for example, because he wanted the opportunity to sue for pain and suffering damages even in small cases), he could simply decline these new optional coverages (Basic Protection and Vehicle Protection). He could still also carry, if he so desired, Medical Payments, Uninsured Motorist, and Collision coverages, along with his Liability coverage.

The person electing to buy Basic Protection insurance along with his Liability insurance would also have the opportunity to buy some additional no-fault coverages, referred to as Added Protection insurance. These coverages fall into two groups. The first would provide coverage for net economic losses beyond those covered by the $10,000 of Basic Protection coverage. The other group would provide General Compensation insurance to pay benefits for such items as pain, suffering, physical impairment and inconvenience. The proposed statute authorizes a wide variety of such optional coverages, subject to approval by the Commissioner of Insurance. For example, it authorizes an optional coverage that would pay benefits amounting in a particular case to the largest of the following: (1) a stated percentage of loss, (2) a stated sum per month for total disability or a percentage of that sum proportionate to partial disability or (3) an amount stated in a schedule for specified types of injuries. These added coverages, we emphasize, are optional. They allow a person to have benefits for pain and suffering associated with minor injuries if he wants to and is willing to pay fair insurance rates for those benefits. But they also leave him free to choose to forego such benefits and to pay correspondingly lower insurance rates.

The pool that is used to make certain that the right insurers and policyholders receive credit for the savings of Basic Protection is an insurance arrangement the details of which will admittedly be technical.[10] Fortunately, however, the ordinary policyholder does not need to understand its technical features in order to benefit from its operation. And, although the proposed statute would provide for flexibility as to the form of the pool, it would also make the pool's operations subject to supervision by the Commissioner of Insurance and his actuarial staff.

It is helpful to an understanding of the pool to compare its function to that of re-insurance. The risk re-insured against is the chance that a particular company in a particular year will incur double costs from a disproportionate number of certain kinds of accidents, since some accidents, as we have seen, will cause a company to incur double costs; that is, the company may have to pay Basic Protection benefits to its insured and may also have to defend a negligence claim brought against its insured because the person with whom he collided had elected not to carry Basic Protection. In other cases a company will escape the costs of an accident entirely. Ordinarily, an insurer would pay nothing to either party in the accident when, for example, its own policyholder had elected to carry only liability insurance and the person with whom he collided had elected Basic Protection and was thereby precluded from making a negligence claim.

In still other accidents, there would be no double-or-nothing problem. For example, as suggested earlier, whenever two Basic Protection policyholders collided, each company would pay Basic Protection benefits to its own insured and would have the benefit of the surrender of the other driver's negligence claims. Similarly, whenever two liability-only policyholders collided, each company would be in the same position in which it is under the present liability system, i.e., faced with the prospect of paying the other driver if, but only if, the requisite proof concerning negligence is available.

One way the pool might work, for illustration, would be to provide that some companies contribute to the pool, and other companies receive from the pool, payments calculated under the following formula:

(average claim cost)* × (claim frequency)** × (number of Liability-Only policyholders above or below average).***

Thus, if Company A has 50,000 Bodily Injury Liability insurance policyholders and the statewide average, for all insurers, of such policyholders who elect Basic Protection is 60 per cent, then with average distribution Company A would have 30,000 Basic Protection policyholders and 20,000 Liability-Only policyholders. If Company A actually has 33,000 and 17,000, respectively, then its "number of Liability-Only policyholders below average" is 3,000 and it receives from the pool a payment in an amount calculated as follows:

(average claim cost) × (claim frequency) × 3,000.

If, on the other hand, Company A has 26,000 and 24,000 respectively, then its "number of Liability-Only policyholders above average" is 4,000 and it pays to the pool an amount calculated as follows:

(average claim cost) × (claim frequency) × 4,000.

As indicated earlier, given the evils of the present fault system—especially as it applies to small and medium-sized claims—we are inclined to recommend that a compulsory no-fault automobile insurance system apply to such claims. But we suggest that a voluntary system may well be a way of breaking the logjam now blocking reform. And an optional system has many independent virtues apart from the pragmatic consideration that it may open the political channels for effective reform.

---

* "Average claim cost," as used here, means the average amount paid in disposition of an automobile Bodily Injury Liability insurance claim under minimum limits Bodily Injury Liability insurance coverage, together with an average cost of administration and overhead attributable to one such claim.

** "Claim frequency," as used here, means the number of claims made per insured car (a fraction) under minimum limits Bodily Injury Liability insurance coverage (adjusted to take account of the claims precluded).

*** "Liability-Only policyholders" are those policyholders who carry Bodily Injury Liability insurance but do not elect to carry Basic Protection insurance.

Appendix III

Complete or Partial

Abolition of Fault Claims?[1]

By Robert E. Keeton* and Jeffrey O'Connell

Perhaps the most distinctive feature of the previously proposed Keeton-O'Connell Basic Protection Plan[2] is that it dovetails fault and no-fault compensation through the use of its *partial* tort exemption. The two key ideas of Basic Protection are: first, to provide no-fault coverage for all out-of-pocket economic losses up to a selected limit, the amount suggested being $10,000; and, second, as a corollary, to eliminate all tort actions based on negligence except those for losses above the no-fault benefits and for pain and suffering in cases of severe injury.[3] The Basic Protection Plan, then, would require every motorist to insure himself for out-of-pocket losses up to $10,000, and, in turn, would exempt him from tort liability to others roughly within the same range of coverage. The precise form of partial tort exemption we have suggested is one that would eliminate claims based on negligence unless the damages, as assessed under tort standards, were higher than $5,000 for pain and suffering or higher than the $10,000 limit of no-fault benefits for all other items, including medical expenses and lost wages.[4]

---

* Professor of Law, Harvard University.

The American Insurance Association (AIA) Plan,[5] the New York Insurance Department Plan,[6] and the variation on the AIA Plan developed by Minnesota State Senator Davies,[7] all propose that the basic no-fault coverage for economic losses have no overall limit—neither at the level we proposed ($10,000) nor at any other level. The New York Plan also rejects internal limits, though both the AIA and Davies Plans include such limits; for example, both of the latter plans include a limit of $750 per month for wage loss.[8] In turn, both the AIA and New York Plans also propose almost total abolition of tort liability for damages arising out of automobile accidents.[9]

Objections to extending the basic no-fault coverage without limit are based on considerations of both cost and equity. Plainly, coverage without limit for accidental losses is socially desirable and should be made available if it can be provided at a cost that is both reasonable and equitably distributed. But we believe it is less than clear that these conditions can be fulfilled under a "no-limit" plan.

First, is it possible to provide no-fault coverage for all economic loss at a cost low enough to make it feasible to require every motor vehicle owner to pay a fair share of that cost as a prerequisite to registering his vehicle (or to require every driver to pay a fair share as a prerequisite to obtaining his driver's license)? If so, problems of equity among traffic victims with respect to benefits for *economic* loss at least (passing for the moment the issue of payment for pain and suffering) are avoided. If, in contrast, the cost is so high that such an arrangement is not feasible for motorists, then a choice must be made as to what economic losses resulting from traffic accidents will go uncompensated. Problems of equity among victims come immediately to the fore as the choices among the many possible exceptions from full coverage are considered. In other words, in determining the extent to which losses are to be reimbursed through required insurance coverage one must face a cost-equity dilemma.

To whatever extent provisions for compensation fall short of assuring every victim *full* compensation at least

for out-of-pocket loss, the system fails to assure distribution of loss—that is, it fails to spread it among a
large group and instead leaves it to be borne by an individual. To this extent, the system must still confront
the argument that as between just two individuals—
an innocent victim and a blameworthy driver—it seems
unfair to make the victim bear the loss. To escape this
argument and its basic appeal to one's sense of what is
fair, a pure no-fault system must come at least very
close to compensating fully for out-of-pocket loss.[10]

The New York Plan does purport to come close to completely
reimbursing out-of-pocket loss. The AIA Plan, however, is more
vulnerable because of its internal limits, particularly the limit
of $750 per month for wage loss.[11] But, in either case, the ques-
tion remains whether (even assuming the equity of the amount
and distribution of the no-fault payments) the cost of the payments can fairly and reasonably be exacted from the premium-
paying public. Although cost estimates of the New York and
AIA studies have predicted substantial savings, these projections
have been vigorously attacked as underestimating the cost of
providing lifetime or indefinitely extended benefits for out-of-
pocket loss.[12] We ourselves are uneasy as to whether allowance
has been made in these estimates for all cost factors (including
inflation, among others)[13] involved, for example, in providing
lifetime compensation to victims suffering serious and permanent
injury. Can the AIA and New York estimates be reconciled with
the estimate of Professor Conard and his colleagues that the
three per cent of traffic victims who incur out-of-pocket losses
of $10,000 or more account for 57 per cent of the aggregate
out-of-pocket loss suffered by all traffic victims?[14] Note too that
some of the findings reported by the Department of Transportation in 1970 emphasize how little even of his out-of-pocket loss
is now paid to the seriously injured victim through automobile
insurance—and, indeed, apparently from all sources. According
to the recent Department of Transportation study, only $2.5
billion of the $5.1 billion in compensable out-of-pocket losses
resulting from those automobile accidents occurring in 1967

that involved deaths and serious injuries were repaid from all
types of insurance. Automobile insurance itself accounted for
less than $1.1 billion of the repayments, with the other compen-
sation coming from health and accident and other insurance.[15]
Moreover, we have long known that serious injury or prolonged
illness can cause even the relatively affluent to face financial
disaster.[16] Finally, the gross underestimation of the costs of
Medicare and Medicaid have—perhaps rightly—made all of us a
little skeptical of actuarial predictions of the costs of relatively
open-ended insurance plans. Is it not fair to conclude, then, that
to pay the remaining out-of-pocket losses above those now paid
from one source or another may involve very large sums indeed,
compared to what is now being paid from automobile insurance?

Keeping in mind the cost-equity dilemma, one must note
also that this analysis has thus far taken no account of general
damages, including payment for pain and suffering. Since a
significant number of automobile accidents involve an innocent
victim and a blameworthy driver, many will argue in virtually
all contexts, and perhaps others will argue in at least some
contexts, that equity requires an award of general damages, including "compensation" for pain and suffering, as well as reimbursement for out-of-pocket loss. This argument gains force as
the severity of injury increases; it has special force in relation
to cases of permanent disfigurement involving severe injury but
relatively low out-of-pocket loss.[17] Many victims, for example,
sustain minimal out-of-pocket losses but very severe psychic
losses (e.g., the amputee with a desk job or the grossly dis-
figured person whose earnings are not affected by disfigurement).
For these victims, and for society generally, the bargain of
eliminating the possibility of general damages in higher amounts
in return for certainty of payment in lesser amounts may be
unacceptable.

Thus the cost-equity dilemma poses two questions: first,
can we afford to pay for all out-of-pocket loss? And second,
even if we can, should we force on *all* victims the bargain of
assured and relatively full compensation for out-of-pocket loss
at the price of abandoning all tort claims?

The Basic Protection Plan answers this cost-equity dilemma by preserving the tort action for severe injury cases. The Plan thereby does at least a little more, and probably a great deal more, for the severely injured victim than the fault system does for him. In all probability it will pay him, net of attorney's fees, at least as much as the fault system pays, but offers the advantage of paying $10,000 of that sum without delay, as no-fault benefits, while he pursues his fault claim for additional benefits.

The AIA Plan (including the Minnesota variation) and the New York Plan offer such a victim more in no-fault benefits since those plans have no overall limit on such benefits. But they offer much less in total benefits than the Basic Protection Plan offers to such a severely injured victim who has a good claim in tort against a solvent, or well-insured, blameworthy driver. In this respect—and with respect to their overall cost— we submit that the AIA Plan and New York Plan may not offer a satisfactory answer to the cost-equity dilemma. In other words, not only may those proposals fail to hold costs down to feasible levels, but also, in trying to do so, they treat inequitably some severely injured victims who are very deserving of more favorable treatment by the reparation system.

Perhaps the ideal answer to the cost-equity dilemma in these circumstances, preferable to both the AIA and New York proposals and the original Basic Protection Plan, is: (1) to provide by compulsory insurance a basic level of no-fault insurance for out-of-pocket losses of all victims, (2) to offer optional no-fault coverage for additional out-of-pocket losses without limit and (3) to provide that tort actions will be preserved for losses above the limit of the compulsory coverage, unless the victim has elected to carry the unlimited no-fault coverage that would correspondingly preclude his tort claim in full.[18] Thus, each motorist would be required to insure himself (and passengers in his car, including his family, as well as pedestrians injured by him) for basic out-of-pocket losses, with a corresponding elimination of tort claims by all motorists against each other within the range of this basic coverage. In addition, those motorists who want to be assured of relatively unlimited payment for their out-of-pocket losses at the cost of giving up their tort claims for unlimited damages, including pain and suffering, could do so. No one, however, would be forced to do so. If it should develop in practice that unlimited no-fault coverage for out-of-pocket losses would be no more expensive than the AIA and New York cost studies indicate, most car owners would probably elect the full coverage because of its attractively low cost and because the advantage of such full protection for out-of-pocket loss would outweigh the disadvantages of giving up claims for general damages such as pain and suffering. Those who also want coverage for psychic loss would be able to use part of the savings to buy optional no-fault coverage providing it.[19] If, on the other hand, the New York and AIA cost estimates prove to be too optimistic, more motorists would make a different cost-benefit calculation and would reject the optional coverage. In short, we suggest that it may be better to let this cost-equity issue work itself out in the market place than to try to resolve it in the legislature.

We therefore suggest a modification of our proposed Basic Protection Insurance Act to offer this optional no-fault coverage without limit.[20]

Despite our reservations about the costs of open-ended plans, the New York and AIA studies do indicate that coverage for no-fault benefits, and even full coverage without limit, can be offered at a cost much lower than we had previously supposed possible. This different perspective on costs may also justify the reassessment of another related issue. In our original proposal, we recommended that no-fault insurance up to $10,000 be compulsory and that liability insurance for losses outside the tort coverage should be optional, adding that it would seem

> wiser to use whatever dollars the motorist is required to pay in premiums for compulsory insurance to support basic protection coverage alone. If it were proposed to a legislature that $10,000 of basic protection coverage be compulsory and an additional $5,000 of tort liability coverage also be compulsory, we would recommend instead raising compulsory basic protection to $15,000.[21]

We pointed out, however, that in the event of disagreement with our assessment of the relative advantages of adding more no-fault coverage or instead adding a basic level of liability coverage to the compulsory package, it would be a simple matter to modify the draft statute to so provide.[22] Since no-fault insurance costs generally are lower than we originally anticipated, and since the Harwayne and AIA studies consider explicitly the cost of a first level of liability insurance coverage under a Basic Protection system[23] and find it to be very low indeed, we believe it to be both feasible and sensible to include a basic amount of liability insurance in the compulsory package. We would recommend at least $10,000. Among the advantages gained by this arrangement are that Basic Protection policyholders would have coverage for the costs of defense against liability claims;[24] and both they and their potential tort victims would have the benefit of so-called residual liability insurance protection to cover, for example, accidents that occur while driving in a state that has not enacted a Basic Protection system.

Appendix IV

Motor Vehicle Crash Losses

and

Their Compensation

in the

United States

A Report to the Congress and the President

March 1971

By

John A. Volpe

Secretary of Transportation

Excerpts from pp. iii, iv, vii-ix, 94-146 from the Summary Report of the U. S. Department of Transportation Auto Insurance and Compensation Study.

[Table of Contents to Appendix IV]

	Page*
Preface	179

* * * *

F.	Summary of the findings	180
	1. Limited Scope of the Auto Accident Liability Reparations System	180
	2. Rational Allocation of Compensation Resources	180
	3. Cost Efficiency of the Auto Accident Liability Reparations System	181
	4. Timing of Compensation Benefits	181
	5. Rehabilitation of Accident Victims	182
	6. Property Damage	182
	7. Strains on Insurance Institutions	183
	8. Impact on Other Public Institutions	184
	9. Highway Safety and Crash Loss Minimization	184

Part III.	Alternatives to the Automobile Accident Tort Liability System	185
A.	Conceptual Considerations and Options	186
	1. The Legal Rule	186
	2. The Role of Insurance	188
	3. Kinds of Losses to Be Compensated	189
	4. Private vs. Social Insurance	191
	5. Compulsory vs. Voluntary Approaches	193
	6. Insurance and the Loss Minimization Objective	193

* Adapted for this Appendix.

B. Basic Alternatives   195
    1. "Do Nothing Significantly Different"   195
    2. "Improve the Present Reparations System"   196
    3. "Evolutionary Reform, Type I"   199
    4. "Evolutionary Reform, Type II"   201
    5. "Total No-Fault"   204
    6. "Government Insurance"   206

Part IV. Recommendations for Change   208
   A. Toward a Better Compensation System   208
    1. Basic Reliance on First-Party Insurance   209
    2. Availability of Benefits to All Accident Victims 209
    3. Coordination of Benefits   210
    4. Maximum Choice   210
    5. A Privately-Operated System   210
    6. Maximum Opportunity for Rehabilitation   211
    7. Minimal Use of Adversary Procedures   211
   B. A Specific Recommendation   212
    1. Compulsory First-Party Benefits   213
    2. Required Medical Benefits   213
    3. Income Loss Protection   214
    4. Lost Service Benefits   214
    5. Property Damage   215
    6. Elimination of Action for Damages   215
   C. Cost of Insurance   216
   D. Implementation   217
   E. The Expected Results   220

Preface

Public Law 90-313, a Joint Resolution of the Congress, authorized the Secretary of Transportation to conduct a comprehensive study and investigation of the existing compensation system for auto accident losses.

The Joint Resolution recorded four specific Congressional findings which substantially guided the conduct of the study and the scope of its concern. These included:

. . . suffering and loss of life resulting from motor vehicle accidents and the consequent social and economic dislocations are critical national problems.

. . . there is growing evidence that the existing system of compensation is inequitable, inadequate and insufficient and is unresponsive to existing social, economic, and technological conditions.

. . . there is needed a fundamental reevaluation of such system, including a review of the role and effectiveness of insurance and the existing law governing liability.

. . . meaningful analysis requires the collection and evaluation of data not presently available such as the actual economic impact of motor vehicle injuries, the relief available both from public and private sources, and the role and effectiveness of rehabilitation.

The perspective of the study, then, was a national one, concerned with the nationwide system of auto accident compensation and its performance, rather than the problems peculiar to one state or region. By implication, the study was asked to address whether, in fact, the system was "inequitable, inadequate and insufficient and . . . unresponsive." Moreover, the study was specifically referred to "insurance" and the "law governing liability" as the subjects to be investigated.

. . .

The Department sponsored several major and minor research projects. Much of the output of these projects has been published over the past year in a series of research reports. The principal findings are briefly summarized in this report.

* * * * *

F. Summary of the Findings

A review of the detailed factual findings of the Study's research and those of other research lead to a number of summary conclusions about the operation of the present system.

1. Limited Scope of the Auto Accident Liability Reparations System

One major shortcoming of the auto accident liability system stems not from the way it performs but rather from its intended scope of operation, i.e., . . . only those who can prove that others were at fault while they were without fault in an accident have a legal right to recover their losses. Today, our society need not settle for a reparations system that deliberately excludes large numbers of victims from its protection or that gives clearly inadequate levels of protection to those who need it most. With only 45 percent of those killed or seriously injured in auto accidents benefiting in any way from the tort [or fault] liability insurance system and one out of every ten of such victims receiving *nothing* from *any* system of reparations, the coverage of the present compensation mechanism is seriously deficient.

2. Rational Allocation of Compensation Resources

The present tort liability reparations system allocates benefits very unevenly among the limited number of victims that it purports to serve. The victim with large economic losses, who generally also suffers more severe intangible losses, has a far poorer chance of being fully compensated under the tort system for his economic loss, much less any intangible loss, than does the victim with only minor injuries. As has been seen, only about half of the total compensable economic losses of seriously or fatally injured victims are compensated from any reparations systems. For those whose economic losses were more than $25,000, only about a third was usually recovered. Those with relatively small economic losses, by contrast, fared much better; if they recovered from tort and had losses less than $500, their recovery averaged four and a half times actual economic loss. Despite the popular view that large settlements for automobile accident personal injuries are common, they are, in fact, still a statistical rarity when viewed in the context of the entire population and its losses.

3. Cost Efficiency of the Auto Accident Liability Reparations System

The automobile accident tort liability insurance system would appear to possess the highly dubious distinction of having probably the highest cost/benefit ratio of any major compensation system currently in operation in this country. As has been shown, for every dollar of net benefits that it provides to victims, it consumes about a dollar. As it presently operates, the system absorbs vast amounts of resources, primarily in performing the functions of marketing insurance policies and settling claims. The measurable costs of these two functions alone approach in general magnitude all net benefits received by auto accident victims through the tort liability system.

Claims settlement, of course, is complicated by the adversary nature of the tort liability system. The possibility of greater efficiency in some areas, such as sales expense, has been thwarted by local laws and regulatory rules that arbitrarily curb the introduction of potentially more economical approaches, such as group auto insurance.

4. Timing of Compensation Benefits

The tort liability insurance system tends to deliver benefits without regard to the victim's need, in some cases paying too late and in others too soon. Three different investigations by the Department have demonstrated that despite commendable efforts by the insurance industry to introduce "advance" or partial payment techniques, the system is still, in the main, quite slow in providing benefit payments. The system pays most slowly in cases where the need for timely payment would appear to be greatest, i.e., in cases of permanent impairment and disfigurement. Moreover, the system can operate to discourage early rehabilitative efforts and places a premium upon their deferment beyond the time when they could be most effective.

5. Rehabilitation of Accident Victims

Closely related to the problem of delay in the payment of benefits is that of lost opportunities to minimize very large personal injury losses by the timely use of comprehensive rehabilitation programs for seriously injured accident victims. A disappointingly low utilization of rehabilitation by such victims was revealed in one survey, even when it was recommended to the victim.

Admittedly, rehabilitation under certain other loss-shifting regimes, notably workmen's compensation, has also been disappointing. However, this has been largely due to the overconcentration of these programs on reducing their own costs, i.e., on returning the injured person to work *as soon as possible* in order that the compensation system be able to reduce benefit payments. While vocational rehabilitation does benefit both the insurer and the victim, truly effective rehabilitation must deal with all of the victim's handicaps, including not only those affecting his work performance, but those affecting his non-work activities as well.

To achieve the maximum potential benefits from the rehabilitation process, the relationship between private insurance benefits and the various rehabilitation agencies, including local, state and national agencies, must be consciously and explicitly coordinated and made to be mutually supportive.

6. Property Damage

The Department's study of the auto accident compensation system focused principally on the bodily injured victim. This priority seemed appropriate for several reasons. First, people are more important than property. Second, the most serious accident losses are associated with people, not property. Third, the present compensation system is doing much better today with property losses than it is with people losses. Fourth, the problems of personal injury losses are far more complicated than those of property losses. Fifth, the principal problems afflicting the compensation of property damage losses are either also present in compensating personal injury losses, or are externalities such as vehicle design or repair costs.

Nevertheless, property damage losses are important; they are very large in dollar value and they affect far more people than injury losses. In recent years the cost of repairing vehicles has risen sharply with a consequent rise in the cost of insuring for that repair. Experts, many of them within the insurance industry, have rightly traced part of this rise to the designs of the vehicles themselves. Unfortunately, there is no way for liability insurance to distinguish between damage-resistant vehicles and fragile vehicles, or between very expensive vehicles and those of less value, because the liability insurer cannot know what kind of a vehicle its insured will negligently strike.

Rating systems for collision insurance have only very recently begun to take any consideration of the vehicle's damageability. Now that the vehicle's contribution to crash losses is widely recognized and being increasingly considered by the insurance community, some countervailing pressure on vehicle manufacturers to design more crashworthy and damage-resistant automobiles may be in the offing.

7. Strains on Insurance Institutions

The accumulated problems of the tort liability auto insurance system are now making an undeniable impact on the insurance industry itself. Underwriting profits have turned to underwriting losses for many, if not most, companies. Several analyses have indicated that some capital has already been withdrawn from the business of insurance, with a consequent diminution of its ability to offer protection. If such a trend were to persist or accelerate, it would present a social problem of very serious proportions.

Auto insurance today is becoming more and more difficult for many drivers to buy in the voluntary insurance market.

Between 1966 and 1969, the number of motorists having to obtain their insurance through assigned risk plans grew from 2.6 million to 3.2 million, or 23 percent. [National Association of Independent Insurers, *Chart Analysis of Automobile Insurance (Assigned Risk) Plans.*] One of the Department's studies estimated that 8 to 10 percent of all drivers were in the "hard-to-place" insurance market in 1968; and recent months have witnessed a further tightening of the auto insurance market, with some major companies either refusing or severely limiting any new business. This development comes at a time when consumers' requirements for automobile insurance protection are increasing if only because of rising medical and auto repair costs.

8. Impact on Other Public Institutions

Automobile accident disputes are a major contributory factor to the present problems of the nation's judiciary, even as a multitude of other demands threaten to overburden and, thereby, undermine its effectiveness. Automobile accidents contribute more than 200,000 cases a year to the nation's court load and absorb more than 17 percent of the country's total judicial resources.

The motor vehicle accident tort liability insurance system also has exerted great strains on the existing system of State insurance regulation. It is not coincidental that the burgeoning problem of insurer insolvencies has been concentrated among specialty auto insurers serving the high-risk market. The resulting difficulties created by these insolvencies for consumers, regulators and the insurance institution in general, have proved so resistant to solution that they have led to proposals for a greater centralization of regulatory control, thereby threatening local initiative and freedom in insurance regulation.

9. Highway Safety and Crash Loss Minimization

Highway safety research and technology is demonstrably moving from an art to a science. However, the tort liability system has served, albeit not intentionally, to impede the development of this science in many ways. It discourages openness and frankness and encourages deceit on the part of participants about what happened before, during and after crashes. With the effectiveness of safety programs depending upon a scientifically sound understanding of the causes of highway crashes, insured drivers are now routinely instructed by their insurance companies to speak to no one other than the police, and even then to admit nothing, lest their cases be prejudiced. Injured victims are similarly cautioned by their attorneys to avoid disclosure.

With its single-minded preoccupation with driver error or negligence as the determinant of the compensation decision, the tort liability system ignores all other contributing factors to crash losses, such as the vehicle and the roadway. Cars that are poorly designed to resist damages and to protect occupants from injury can turn what should have been a minor crash into a large loss or even a serious tragedy. Yet the tort liability insurance premium does not and cannot reflect the value of the car's protective attributes in any way because the third-party's vehicle is unknown until after an accident has occurred.

* * * * *

In summary, the existing system ill serves the accident victim, the insuring public and society. It is inefficient, overly costly, incomplete and slow. It allocates benefits poorly, discourages rehabilitation and overburdens the courts and the legal system. Both on the record of its performance and on the logic of its operation, it does little if anything to minimize crash losses.

Part III. Alternatives to the Automobile Accident Tort Liability System

The automobile accident reparations system can be viewed as consisting of two main components: the "reparations component," i.e., the basic legal and procedural rules governing reparations and the "insurance component," especially as it relates to, and buttresses, the "reparations component." The latter comprises not simply insurance itself, but also the compulsory insurance and compensation laws, assigned risk plans, mandatory policy provisions, etc. This dichotomy should be kept in mind in viewing the public policy alternatives with regard to the automobile accident reparations system.

Over the years, the reparations system has not lacked for would-be reformers. Its complexity, both in theory and in operation, has permitted great individuality in the framing of reform proposals, whose number has burgeoned, especially in the last decade. They range from minor adjustments to comprehensive programs for fundamental change. Some attempt to achieve improvement through the insurance component, some through the reparations component, and some through both. Some see the problems arising outside the reparations system and seek changes in other institutions or regimes, e.g., court administration, car design, driver licensing and training, traffic law enforcement, etc. A few are patently nostrums; most are serious, well thought out, often imaginative proposals. No attempt will be made here either to summarize or analyze even the major plans now being widely studied.

A. Conceptual Considerations and Options

There is, in fact, a vast and largely unmanageable number of combinations possible among the various reform alternatives on such important considerations as: (1) the legal rule governing reparations, (2) the role of insurance, (3) the kinds of losses to be compensated, (4) private vs. social insurance, (5) compulsory vs. voluntary approaches, and (6) the insurance/loss minimization objective. In order to illustrate the breadth of choice possible, some of the principal alternatives in each of these areas will be briefly described without attempting to examine how all alternatives in one area might interact with all those in another or make judgments about them. Subsequently, the advantages and disadvantages of the major choices for change also will be described.

1. The Legal Rule.

The prevailing legal rule regarding automobile accident losses is, of course, that of tort liability under which the innocent victim is legally entitled to recover all of his losses, tangible and intangible, from the wrongdoer if he can prove that the latter was at fault and it is not established that he was himself at fault. While many other advantages are now claimed for this rule (e.g., fairness, vindication, deterrence, etc.), its basic original social purpose (before the advent of insurance) was to shift the burden of loss from the innocent victim to the wrongdoer. Some of the available options are:

a. Substitute a comparative negligence rule for that of contributory negligence. Under the comparative negligence rule most widely advocated for general adoption, the claimant would be barred from recovery only if his negligence equaled or exceeded that of the defendant; for a lesser degree of negligence, his recovery would be reduced to such extent as it contributed to causing the accident.

b. Substitute an absolute liability rule by which the driver/owner of any vehicle would be automatically responsible for any damage to others in an accident, *regardless* of whether he, another driver, or anybody was "at fault" or negligent. Justification would rest on the assumption that the motor vehicle is an "inherently dangerous" object and that driving is an "inherently dangerous" activity, and as such, the driver/owner should be absolutely responsible for any damages.

c. Abolish tort liability in automobile crashes, with each driver/owner accepting responsibility for some or all losses sustained by pedestrians and by occupants of his own vehicle in return for which he would enjoy immunity from suit for those losses.

d. Replace jury trial judgment of some or all liability claims with compulsory arbitration.

e. Adopt a "direct action" statute under which the claimant is permitted to bring action directly against another motorist's liability insurer.

2. The Role of Insurance.

Today, there are essentially four types of insurance serving the automobile victim; two are oriented specifically to the automobile accident, and two are general insurances.

Under most State financial responsibility laws, automobile liability insurance is virtually compulsory, in practice if not in theory. From the policyholder's perspective, auto liability insurance is designed to protect his assets in the event he is found at fault in an accident; from the public's perspective, compulsory liability insurance is intended to assure that the innocent accident victim will have a source from which to recover and, thus, would not become a burden on the State because of his uncompensated losses.

Uninsured motorist insurance is a related form of coverage, generally required to be provided or offered to the purchaser of liability insurance to protect him against "guilty" third parties who are uninsured, or insured by an insurer that subsequently becomes insolvent.

The first-party automobile insurance coverages—medical payments, comprehensive, and collision—are essentially voluntary. Collision and comprehensive insurance, however, are usually required when the purchase of a car is financed.

General private insurance—life, accident and health, disability income, etc.—provides an important source of compensation for the auto accident victim, albeit sometimes redundantly where there is also a tort recovery.

Social insurance—social security disability, Medicaid, veterans' benefits, etc.—are also important sources of recovery for the accident victim, but they too contribute to the problem of duplicative recovery.

Besides the coordination of benefits problems created by this plethora of possible recovery sources, there is the question of the desirability of "internalizing" auto accident costs, i.e., "making motoring pay its own way" rather than shifting the burden of accident losses to general or social insurance programs. In addition, there is the question of limits and deductibles, i.e., whether a private, competitive insurance system should attempt to deal with small losses, or whether it is well-equipped to deal on a large scale with catastrophic losses to individuals.

Some of the options in this area are:

a. Abolish the collateral source rule under the fault system in order to preclude the plaintiff from claiming damages with respect to expenses recovered from other sources, or, alternatively, allow the defendant to show that the plaintiff has recovered such expenses from other sources.

b. Make all auto insurance first-party insurance that is primary (or alternatively, excess) to all other insurance coverage or primary (or excess) to benefits provided by other compensation systems.

c. Make first-party auto insurance mandatory with respect to bodily injury loss (hospital/medical expense, disability income) but voluntary with respect to property damage, collision, etc. Preclude by statute or rule recovery under tort for any losses mandatorily covered by first-party auto insurance.

d. Provide for reasonable deductibles under a first-party system to avoid the excessive transaction costs of handling small claims.

e. Make recovery unlimited under compulsory coverages, at least for tangible economic losses.

f. Permit insurers to limit their liability, subject to minimum statutory limits of liability.

3. Kinds of Losses to be Compensated.

Under tort liability rules, intangible as well as tangible (i.e., economic) losses are legally recoverable. Liability insurance tries to respond to this goal, at least in theory, subject to the limits of liability contained in the policy or required by the applicable statute. As previously noted, intangible losses include those losses not susceptible to objective measurement in dollars, e.g., pain and suffering (the "ouch"), mental or emotional disturbance, bereavement over the loss of a loved one, inconvenience, annoyance, and loss of vocational or social opportunity incident to loss of limb, sight or function or because of disfigurement. Because there is no objective way to put a price on these losses, the price is established under the tort system either through bargaining or, where agreement is impossible, through decision by a jury.

A first-party insurance system that eliminated or limited the right to recovery for pain and suffering and similar intangible losses might reduce the expense part of the insurance dollar by eliminating the bargaining or litigation inherent in attempting to evaluate intangible damages and by eliminating the other transaction costs involved.

Additionally, under a first-party system, the insurance consumer would enjoy the contractual right to recover benefits from the insurer whom he has chosen and to whom he has paid his premium. In contrast, under the present system, the injured party has no rights whatsoever against the wrongdoer's insurer unless he obtains a judgment against the wrongdoer.

There is also the question of whose losses a specialized auto insurance system should compensate. The innocent victim falling within the tort liability system has the right, in theory if not in practice, to recover all his losses. Victims of many other kinds of accidents can recover only certain types of losses (e.g., they cannot recover their intangible losses), and then only if they have voluntarily chosen and been able to insure themselves in advance. This is true no matter what their need, no matter how slight or unintentional their negligence. Moreover, the main impact of a wrongdoer's negligence can and often does fall uncompensated on wholly innocent parties, e.g., on the survivors of a fatally injured but negligent driver. Should the compensation system, especially one supported by the premium payments of all drivers, make this harsh distinction between victims whose relative contributions to the cause of the accident may be slight, if perhaps indistinguishable?

Major options in this area area:

a. Abolish any legal right to compensation for intangible damages in auto accident cases.

b. Abolish the right to be compensated for pain and suffering, inconvenience, discomfort, grief, emotional loss of a loved one, etc., but retain the right to recovery for loss of sight, limb, major function, permanent serious disfigurement or impairment, etc.

c. Establish a schedule of damages for specified types of intangible loss, e.g., $5,000 for loss of limb or $10,000 for loss of sight.

d. Permit intangible damage insurance to be sold on a voluntary basis, if insurers can work out satisfactory methods and procedures.

e. Permit all victims except those who intentionally injure themselves, or are grossly negligent, etc., to have equal rights to compensation according to their needs.

f. Replace contributory negligence with a comparative negligence rule.

4. Private vs. Social Insurance.

The automobile insurance and compensation system today is a private institution, subject, however, to regulation in the public interest. It is regulated not only by insurance and motor vehicle regulatory authorities, but also by the courts which interpret statutes and review legal doctrines in the light of a public policy favoring compensation of innocent accident victims. Although financial responsibility and compulsory insurance laws have made the possession of liability insurance virtually obligatory, the choice of one's insurer and the amount of one's protection (above minimum limits) is still largely a voluntary matter for the majority of good drivers. Some commentators have suggested that the problems of our private auto accident compensation system are so great and apparently so resistant to solution, and that the public's interest in their solution is also so great, that only a governmentally managed insurance approach promises a truly fair, efficient and comprehensive system. Financing for a social insurance auto accident compensation mechanism could be achieved through general tax revenues, taxes on motor vehicles or fuel, or scheduled fees for drivers/owners.

A key facet of this issue concerns the "residual" auto insurance market for those motorists who are unable to obtain liability insurance in the voluntary market and are forced to obtain it from assigned risk plans or high-risk insurers at significantly higher rates. Such difficulty in obtaining coverage and the high cost of buying it in the "residual" market usually falls heaviest on those already economically and socially disadvantaged. Regardless of what form auto insurance takes (i.e., fault or no-fault, first-party or third-party), as long as insurers are free to reject marginal applicants, some motorists will be unable to buy coverage in the voluntary market.

Some of the principal alternatives in this area are:

a. Shift the compensation of some auto accident losses (costs)—e.g., medical, rehabilitation, income maintenance, but not property or intangible losses—or all auto accident losses to a governmentally directed social insurance approach, perhaps employing private carriers on a fee basis to service the system (a la Medicare).

b. Have the government become an "insurer of last resort," either itself insuring such residual risks at rates less than the actuarial rates or subsidizing such risks by paying or guaranteeing private insurers the difference between the actuarial rates and the fully compensatory rates.

c. Require private insurers to accept all applicants, perhaps with the aid of some reinsurance institution such as that used in Canada.

d. Replace the private automobile insurance system with a governmentally owned and operated automobile insurance mechanism, the funds of which would be raised through the contributions of drivers and owners.

5. Compulsory vs. Voluntary Approaches.

State statutes have rendered minimum limits of auto liability insurance virtually compulsory for the average driver. However, the absence of any compulsion to insure one's own losses and the relatively low minimum liability insurance limits have left very large amounts of loss uncovered by auto insurance, or indeed by any type of insurance. Moreover, even with financial responsibility laws, substantial numbers of motorists are not insured for liability while many others are without effective coverage for particular accidents because of coverage gaps or breaches of policy provisions by the insured.

The major alternatives here are:

a. Establish a nationwide, universal, compulsory insurance system based on tort liability, requiring high limits and making the insurer's liability absolute so that the victim's claim cannot be defeated because of policy defenses.

b. Establish a nationwide, universal, compulsory insurance system based on a first-party concept, requiring high limits but maximizing the area of voluntary choice through the introduction of deductibles applicable to the named insured and those within his control (e.g., members of the household) and, perhaps, to others (e.g., uninsured guest passengers or pedestrians).

c. Maximize the area of voluntary choice with respect to all insurance coverage (most logically by making everyone responsible for his own losses).

6. Insurance and the Loss Minimization Objective.

If the first link in any accident causation chain is driver error or negligence, modern accident theory has increasingly pointed to the vehicle as being the principal determinant of whether or not there will be loss and if so what its nature and severity will be. Liability law and auto insurance rating schemes focus almost entirely on the driver, his behavior, his driving exposure, his potential as a defendant in a liability suit and the estimated likelihood of his accident involvement. The ability of the vehicle to protect either itself or its occupants in a collision is not, indeed cannot be, included in liability insurance rating plans because the insurer cannot know who the victim will be or in what kind of vehicle he may be riding.

By contrast, in a first-party system not only would an insurer know in advance what kind of owner/driver it was insuring, but, in addition, it would know what kind of car the insured was driving or occupying, what protective or safety devices it incorporated, whether it was overpowered for its size and weight, whether it was overly or needlessly susceptible to major damage from minor impact, etc.

The deterrent effect of legal liability for negligent driving as a loss minimizing measure is often advanced as an attribute of the tort liability rule (i.e., since the rule holds that a person is responsible for damage directly resulting from his negligence). However, whatever force this threat may once have had, it would seem that insurance has essentially nullified it by allowing drivers to shift the costs of their accidents to the rest of the insuring population. Thus, while the fiction of punishment of the guilty driver remains in the law, the economics of insurance has freed him from its reality. Precisely what effect this fiction of tort liability "punishment" has on the diligence of law enforcement agencies in implementing traffic regulations designed to punish negligent drivers is not clear; but it is clear that the great majority of accident-involved drivers who might be considered negligent in a tort sense are not fined or punished under our traffic laws. If society does want "guilty" drivers to be "punished," and if the threat of "punishment" is judged to deter negligent driving, then perhaps renewed emphasis should be given to the direct punishment of accident-causing drivers.

Some alternatives in this area would be:

a. Place auto insurance on a first-party basis and permit or insist that insurers consider the loss prevention capabilities of the vehicles they insure.

b. Establish national standards for driving conduct and for the imposition of penalties for driving violations (such as fines, mandatory revocation or suspension of license, compulsory rehabilitative treatment for the alcoholic driver, etc.), and let the compensation system do what it can do best, i.e., compensate victims for their losses.

B. Basic Alternatives

While not reflecting the many nuances and subtleties of the various specific detailed reform plans that have been offered, the range of basic alternatives can be seen in the six described briefly below:

1. "Do Nothing Significantly Different"

An obvious option, in fact the one currently being followed, is to do nothing significantly different in connection with either the "reparations component" or the "insurance component" of the automobile accident reparations system. Justification for this approach might rest on such grounds as:

a. The cost problem of insurance will recede as a public issue as inflationary tendencies abate and as loss costs are controlled by the cumulating effects of safety measures and pressure on car designers.

b. The insurance availability problem will improve as inflation slows and rate levels become more satisfactory.

c. The number of people affected by compensation problems is not large even now; and with the growing tendency of drivers to buy high limits of liability insurance and the growing availability of benefits for all victims from non-auto insurance sources, it will become even less of a problem in the future.

    d. The tort liability rule should not be disturbed for any but the most compelling reason, and the present problems of auto insurance do not constitute such a reason.

Advantages of the "Do Nothing" Option

This option, at least superficially, is not without some appealing advantages. For example,

    a. It is easy.

    b. It would involve no precipitate economic dislocations or shifts in competitive advantage for the business participants in the system.

    c. In the near term, its results are fairly predictable.

    d. No new governmental initiatives would be required.

Disadvantages of the "Do Nothing" Option

The disadvantages of this option are both numerous and obvious. The principal ones are:

    a. It ignores a serious public problem for which experience gives little hope of a spontaneous cure.

    b. It is difficult to reconcile with the demonstrated and growing intent of the consumer and his legislators for some kind of change.

    c. It risks the development of a crisis such that nothing short of a government takeover of the compensation responsibility would solve.

    d. It does nothing about insurance costs.

2. "Improve the Present Reparations System"

This alternative, which reflects the American Bar Association's concession that the automobile insurance and compensation system needs reform, is premised on the assumption that reform can, and should, stop short of abandonment of the tort system or other "hallowed" legal tenets such as the collateral source doctrine. (The Defense Research Institute, a research organization of insurance company lawyers, advocates that the defendant be permitted to lay before the jury the fact and amount of the plaintiff's compensation from other sources.)

The principal features of this plan may be considered under the headings: (a) judicial reform, (b) substantive-law reform, (c) insurance reform, (d) automobile insurance costs and (e) legal services.

Judicial Reform

This plan argues that the hardship and injustice resulting from court delays can be eliminated through streamlining and improving the judicial process, e.g., by providing for unified court systems with presiding judges empowered to assign other judges to best advantage. Also recommended is the provision of administrative officers to assist the court in scheduling trials and maintaining the flow of cases. Improvements in judge selection and tenure and in pre-trial and trial procedures are seen as ameliorating trial delay. While rejecting *mandatory* arbitration, voluntary waiver of jury trial and the provision of panels of judges who attract jury-waived cases would be cautiously encouraged. Efforts toward voluntary arbitration of small claims would be cautiously encouraged. Advance payments would be facilitated by statutes negating any inference of liability on account of such payment. Primary emphasis, however, is placed on increasing the number of judges, with provision made to maintain an appropriate ratio by automatically adding judges as population increases.

Substantive-law Reform

The plan, while recognizing that comparative negligence will result in more recoveries both by way of judgments and by way of settlements, recommends a Wisconsin-type comparative negligence rule. Immunities such as governments' sovereign immunity, the inter-spousal and intra-familial immunities and the immunity of charitable organizations would be eliminated. Guest passenger statutes, however, would be retained because "[t]heir repeal would have a marked upward (and apparently unacceptable) effect on insurance costs in the states having them."

[ABA *Report,* p. 87.] Statutory limitations on recovery in wrongful death cases, where measured by pecuniary loss, would be removed. In those States where the sole measure of recovery in such cases is punitive damages, statutory limits would be retained.

Insurance Reform

There would be universal, compulsory automobile liability insurance with mandatory uninsured motorist coverage, including insolvency protection. There would be no compulsory provision of non-fault benefits on a first-party basis since this is viewed as containing the seeds of the destruction of the adversary system. However, study should be given to a plan for payment of medical expenses under a "medical-pay, cross-over" scheme through which the accident victim, including the pedestrian, would receive his medical expenses, regardless of fault, under the medical payments coverage of the other party, i.e., on a third-party basis. This provision of limited mandatory benefits on a strict liability basis would not entail the extinction of the adversary system.

Automobile Insurance Costs

Principal reliance for any cost reduction would be placed on the ability of the insurance industry to find better and less costly ways of providing and distributing the current insurance product, and on more speedy and efficient ways of delivering insurance services.

Legal Services

The contingent fee system would be retained, but with the courts assuming responsibility for the examination, scheduling and supervision of contingent fees and for the discipline of attorneys who violate established rules or act unprofessionally. The courts could require the filing of information on contingent fee arrangements as well as the filing of closing statements, and they would be empowered to promulgate contingent fee schedules when appropriate. Courts would also provide for the filing and disposition of clients' complaints against attorneys.

Advantages of the "Improve the Present
Reparations System" Option

a. It would bring reparations to some victims not now
   compensated, e.g., those barred by contributory negligence or immunity doctrines.
b. Compulsory, universal insurance would prevent uninsured motorists from being able to benefit from the
   system while not contributing to it.
c. Delay occasioned by court congestion would be mitigated.

Disadvantages of the "Improve the Present
Reparations System" Option

a. It retains most of the costs inherent in any adversary
   system.
b. It does not come to grips with the needs of the
   "guilty" victim and his dependents or survivors.
c. It is more likely to increase costs than decrease them.
d. A more efficient judicial administration may increase
   the litigation burden rather than decrease it since
   more cases can be litigated, albeit faster.

3. "Evolutionary Reform, Type I"

Type I Evolutionary Reform would require a compulsory,
first-party medical and income benefit coverage as a floor for
compensable damages for all motor vehicle accident victims.
Any amounts received under this coverage would be subtracted
from any additional recovery a victim might be entitled to under
tort.

This type of proposal frequently is coupled with other measures to improve the provision of compensation under tort liability rules. The comparative negligence concept would be
adopted, providing for recovery under tort based on the degree
of fault rather than requiring the absolute absence of fault as
under contributory negligence. It would also allow insurance
companies to deduct the claimants' income tax savings in the
determination of recoverable damages. The plan also anticipates

the adoption of measures to promote the use of advance liability payments in meritorious cases.

Several features are designed to improve the cost effectiveness of the present system. These include mandatory arbitration of small claims under $3,000 so as to reduce the amount of legal and judicial effort and expense needed for the vast majority of small cases. Standards for measuring pain and suffering damages would be established. For example, one proposal contemplates paying for pain and suffering an amount equal to 50 percent of medical and income loss below $500 and 100 percent above $500. Additional amounts would be allowed in cases involving permanent disfigurement, impairment or death. Attorney fees would be regulated by law subject to modification by the courts. Stiff penalties would be provided for fraudulent claims.

Advantages of "Type I Evolutionary Reform"

a. It enables most accident victims to obtain timely compensation for their personal injuries as a matter of contract, while still leaving the tort remedy essentially unimpaired.

b. Controls on pain and suffering payments and contingent fees, and compulsory arbitration should provide some cost savings and help reduce court congestion.

c. It would provide a modest compromise with the total no-fault principle, and as such, might be considered by those who wish to so view it as an evolutionary step toward a more comprehensive no-fault system. (Some versions of the plan would allow the first-party insurer to subrogate against the other party's insurer for any first-party benefits paid. Such a system would not, of course, be a step in the direction of no-fault insurance.)

d. It would increase the cost efficiency of the system, at least modestly.

Disadvantages of "Type I Evolutionary Reform"

a. The assurance of first-party recovery might add to the tendency to litigate or hold out for larger tort settlements.

b. The low level of assured first-party benefits does not effectively treat the problem of the seriously injured victim, and there is no incentive to better rehabilitation.

c. Since it deals only with personal injury benefits, there would be no pressures on car designers through insurance rates to design less fragile cars.

d. While some costs would be purged from the system, it is unlikely that the savings would be sufficient to offset the increased costs of the additional benefits.

e. If the first-party carrier is allowed to subrogate on the basis of fault, the system will continue to incur the transaction costs of shifting the loss.

4. "Evolutionary Reform, Type II"

This proposal would predicate the basic desirability of the no-fault concept of auto accident compensation but would attempt to recognize and cope with the problems of practical implementation and public acceptance involved in a shift to a largely first-party reparations system. The principal insurance and compensation aspect of this option would be:

a. First-party automobile accident insurance covering all economic loss (medical, income, etc.) up to high levels would be compulsory, with coverage extended to the vehicle owner and all members of his household, to any person operating, occupying or using a motor vehicle with his permission and to any uninsured pedestrian struck by a motor vehicle. This insurance would cover economic loss resulting from accidental bodily injury, sickness or disease, including death, or damage to such motor vehicle sustained while in or upon, entering or alighting from a motor vehicle, or as a result of being struck, as a pedestrian, by the motor vehicle and arising out of the ownership, operation, maintenance or use of such motor vehicle.

b. A mandatory deductible would be imposed for the purpose of avoiding the inordinate expense of handling small losses; a choice of deductibles for the various coverages would be available to the insured at appropriate rates. In addition, several options could be made available to the insured with respect to the ceiling on recoverable wage loss. Rates appropriate to the ceiling selected (and hence to the insured's ability to pay) would apply.

c. Such coverage would apply only as excess over any other insurance or benefits available under any other insurance policy or benefit plan. The deductible and the concomitant rate selected by the insured would ordinarily reflect the extent to which he anticipates other coverage or benefits available to him to respond to any loss sustained by him or members of his household. (An alternative, which would recognize the fact that auto accidents frequently involve many kinds of loss, and that consequently it may be more efficient to deal with one benefit source than several, would be to make this coverage primary and let other systems bear the burden of coordinating their benefits with auto insurance. In this case, savings from the elimination of duplicate benefits would be achieved in the non-auto insurance coverages.)

d. Every owner, operator, person or organization responsible for the operation or use of an automobile insured for the first-party coverage would be immune from tort liability for the types of damages covered in the mandatory first-party insurance. Tort recovery for intangible damages would be limited to serious cases only, if at all.

e. Rate structures and rating plans would be expected or required to give consideration to the safety devices and damage-resistant features of the insured vehicle.

f. Incentives for rehabilitation would be provided, and the tort fines contemplated by the plan could be allocated to such purpose or to highway safety programs.

g. The system would be implemented in stages, on a single nationwide schedule. There would be an opportunity to review and assess the performance of the new system before proceeding to the next stage.

Advantages of "Type II Evolutionary Reform"

a. Ultimately, depending on the implementation schedule, this plan should sharply reduce litigation and accident-related court congestion.

b. The plan, at least on its logic, should permit the achievement of substantial economies in the delivery of benefits.

c. It would assure a much higher level of benefits to all victims.

d. With the assured availability of higher personal injury benefits, insurance could be made to support rehabilitation programs more effectively.

e. Insurance rates could be made to reflect the loss-causing potential of poor car design.

f. Gradual implementation would give time for institutions to adjust and for the plan to be tested and improved.

Disadvantages of "Type II Evolutionary Reform"

a. The cost savings, diminution of court burden, higher compensation levels, etc., would be postponed to the extent full implementation was delayed.

b. While a convincing case can be made that compensation for personal injury should not have to run the gauntlet [sic] of an adversary determination, the same is more difficult to make with respect to property damage to the car. This is especially true of the

"parking lot" accident or "fender-bender" where who
"caused" the accident is manifestly clear and yet the
"innocent" car owner might have to absorb a rather
high deductible.

c. During the transition to the no-fault system, there
will be some overlapping between first-party and
third-party systems that may produce diseconomies
of an unknown nature.

d. Even though they may be in a minority, some of the
public may find no-fault arrangements unacceptable.

e. The absolute costs of the system are unknowable
(Medicare will be cited), and it will be argued that
these costs will create a degree of disenchantment
that can lead only to social insurance.

5. "Total No-Fault"

This total no-fault option reflects the proposal of the American
Insurance Association (AIA) which concluded that the de-
ficiencies of the present system are traceable to the fault method
of determining eligibility for reparations and to the rule of damages which permits recovery for intangible losses without providing an objective standard for measurement. As proposed, it
held forth the prospect of a premium saving from adequate rate
levels of up to 45 percent on compulsory coverages. The principal provisions include:

a. Compulsory first-party insurance covering all economic
loss without limit (except wage loss over $750 per
month) for the vehicle owner, his family, vehicle occupants not otherwise covered and pedestrians. This
insurance would be primary for the owner and his
family and provide coverage in any motor vehicle
accident except public vehicles, in which case that
vehicle's insurance would be primary.

b. Complete immunity from any tort liability arising
from a motor vehicle accident.

c. A tax offset of 15 percent applicable to income reimbursement, subject to proof of a lower value.

d. Exclusion of payment for pain and suffering, but the inclusion of additional payment for permanent impairment or disfigurement not to exceed 50 percent of hospital and medical expenses.

e. Requiring automobile insurance to be primary (no deductions are made for duplicate payments made by health insurance, sick leave, etc.) on the theory that the motoring public should bear the cost of motor vehicle accidents and that overtime collateral benefit systems will exclude motor vehicle accidents. (The New York proposal of Governor Rockefeller would retain the basic features of the AIA plan except that it would make the compulsory no-fault coverage excess to all other benefit sources.)

f. Economic loss benefits payable as losses accrue, thereby permitting timely payments not possible for most victims under the prevailing lump-sum settlement system.

g. Residual liability coverage covering the motorist in any State or jurisdiction where tort law continues to apply.

h. An "Assigned Claims" plan to handle any cases not covered by the compulsory insurance.

i. Exclusion of benefits for damage to one's own vehicle unless collision coverage is voluntarily purchased. All motorists would have to purchase property damage coverage to pay for any damage they cause to someone else's property other than motor vehicles.

j. Exclusion of benefits for anyone who intentionally inflicts injury upon himself through the use of an automobile.

Advantages of a "Total No-Fault" System

a. System costs, court burden and delays in payment should be minimized.

b. Benefits should more closely parallel the economic needs of the victim.

c. Rehabilitation could be encouraged.

d. Maximum incentives would be placed on designers to develop safe and durable cars.

e. Premiums would accord better with ability to pay.

f. Insurers would be better able to assess the loss potential of prospective insureds.

Disadvantages of a "Total No-Fault" System

a. Depending on benefit levels, total costs might rise.

b. Intangible losses that now are compensated would go uncompensated.

c. Such a drastic change comprises many uncertainties and unknowns.

d. The respective competitive advantages of individual companies might change sharply and in unpredictable ways.

e. The change would effectively eliminate any major role for the auto accident negligence bar, and if reform did not work, that capability might be difficult to reconstitute.

f. If no-fault proved unacceptable in practice for whatever reason, the structure of the tort liability insurance system might prove incapable of reconstitution, with the only option being that of a social insurance scheme run by the government.

g. However slight, whatever value the fault system has as a deterrent to deviant driving behavior would be lost.

6. "Government Insurance"

Government-run reparations systems are now operating in Canada and Puerto Rico. This particular version is designed to provide an automatic accident compensation scheme that would guarantee a reasonable minimum of compensation for losses arising from motor vehicle accidents regardless of fault.

The plan would encompass not only personal injury (non-fault) benefits but also first-party automobile physical damage coverage and third-party liability and uninsured motorist coverage with combined limits of liability of $35,000. In short, the plan does not erase the fault system, although any tort recovery is diminished by the non-fault benefits previously received.

Insurance would be compulsory. A premium charge would be assessed with respect to the vehicle itself and another premium charge against each driver at the time of his licensing and varying with his traffic record. The system, therefore, lends not only to the equitable implementation of a safe-driver, merit rating plan, but also allows the driver to be insured rather than just the car. The registration certificate and the operator's license would constitute the insurance policy.

The compulsory insurance would be a government monopoly, but supplemental coverages could be provided by private insurers as well as by the government. The compulsory, non-fault coverage would encompass: (1) personal injury, including compensation for impairment of bodily function, weekly indemnity and a discretionary supplemental allowance for out-of-pocket expenses not otherwise reimbursed; (2) death benefits; and (3) comprehensive motor vehicle physical damage coverage, including collision. All except the death benefit would be subject to a deductible.

Under the personal injury benefits, weekly indemnity at a specified rate per week would be provided during the period of total or partial temporary disability up to a maximum of two years. Provisions would be made for payment for disability remaining after treatment measured by the degree of disability of the injured part in relation to the body as a whole. Loss of sight or hearing and disfigurement would also be covered. There would be a maximum amount payable under the disability schedule. Where death results, death benefits up to $10,000 would be payable.

Advantages of "Government Insurance"

a. There would be no "residual market" problem for "high-risk" drivers since the government monopoly would spread loss costs across the entire driving population.

b. Responsibility for driver licensing, traffic law enforcement, safety standards, etc., would rest with the same institutions responsible for dealing with motor vehicle accident loss costs.

c. Marketing costs would be reduced.

d. Standards of compensation would be more responsive to legislative intent.

Disadvantages of "Government Insurance"

a. Government insurance would require the creation of a government insurance institution of formidable proportions.

b. Experimentation and adaptation to local needs and desires would become more difficult.

c. Costs would probably rise (viz., Medicare) and benefits would be circumscribed.

d. Government insurance would lose the incentives to economy and efficiency that, in theory at least, are now provided by the private, competitive market.

Part IV. Recommendations for Change

A. Toward a Better Compensation System

Weighing all the advantages and disadvantages of the various choices available, the main outlines or principles of a better compensation system can be identified: a system that would be more efficient, offer greater flexibility and personal choice, be fairer, give greater incentives to loss reduction and do a better job, overall, of reparating victims' losses.

1. Basic Reliance on First-Party Insurance

One of the important unmet needs apparent in the experience of the existing tort liability system is for a continuing, mutually confident and cooperative relationship between the insured and his insurer. Unlike the present system where the innocent victim must deal in an adversary relationship with a strange company, a "compensation" system in which the insured evaluates and chooses his own benefit source in advance of his loss would appear to offer many advantages. It would seem to be far more effective and satisfactory if the person injured in an accident could look to his own insurer for compensation just as is now true of homeowners or health and accident insurance where benefits are forthcoming as a matter of contract rather than of fault-finding and bargaining or suit. Such a "first-party" arrangement automatically places a greater importance on the quality of service to the victim, encouraging insurance companies to compete on this basis. Victims dealing with their own insurer would be less inclined to jeopardize that relationship by way of exaggerated or fraudulent claims than they are today when dealing with "somebody else's" company.

A basically first-party system would also enable the insurer to evaluate its risk in the broadest and fairest context, since it will know who it may have to compensate, the value and protective attributes of the vehicle they will be occupying, their driving habits, exposure and record, and their probable economic needs in the event of an accident. Unsafe, overpowered or delicately designed vehicles could begin to reflect their true costs in terms of their potential for causing and sustaining accident losses.

2. Availability of Benefits to All Accident Victims

A socially responsible auto accident reparations system should guarantee basic benefits to all accident victims, except, of course, those who willfully injure themselves or others. It should cover the economic losses associated with medical expenses, income loss, funeral expenses, required replacement services and property losses, at levels designed to prevent or effectively mitigate any serious economic dislocation for the individual victim or his dependents in all but the most catastrophic cases. Supplemental benefits should be available on a voluntary basis. At the same time, drivers should be given the choice not to insure themselves against minor losses, but instead to absorb them directly and, thereby, avoid the high administrative costs that the insurance institution incurs when handling minor claims.

3. Coordination of Benefits

The respective roles of governmental and the many different private insurance systems should be clearly defined and coordinated. At present, it is possible under some circumstances for a victim to collect compensation for the same loss from several different sources. To the extent that social insurance is available, private insurance sources should be relieved of any obligation to duplicate those benefits. By the same token, benefits paid by automobile insurers under mandatory coverages should not be duplicated by other private insurance systems such as general health and accident insurance. While not as clear-cut, among reparations sources it can be logically argued that any mandatory auto insurance should be the primary benefit source.

4. Maximum Choice

The individual car owner should be given maximum choice of his insurance source. Individuals should be free to choose between a separate auto insurance policy with the required minimum mandatory coverage and other broad medical-disability plans which meet the standards for that coverage, perhaps through the addition of supplemental benefits, especially for auto accident losses. Thus, for example, one could elect to insure either through his automobile insurer or through his health and accident insurer, providing the latter offered a policy that met the standards for auto accident coverage. In this way, the consumer's insurance coverage options would be maximized.

5. A Privately Operated System

Society should continue to rely upon private enterprise to operate the auto accident compensation system, until and unless it shows itself unwilling or incapable of doing an efficient job.

To this end, the compensation system should entail a minimum of compulsion on the consumer for the purchase of private insurance. Individuals should not be compelled to buy more insurance than is necessary to prevent them from becoming a serious problem to themselves, their families or society in the case of an accident. Additional insurance coverage should be made widely available, voluntary and entirely optional on the part of the consumer.

Any different policy would clearly threaten the private nature of the system since compulsion on the citizen to buy will almost certainly lead eventually to pressure upon government to supply the service.

6. Maximum Opportunity for Rehabilitation

Although private insurance funding can and should be utilized to pay some of the rehabilitation costs and to sustain the insured's income while participating in prescribed rehabilitation programs (whether designed for vocational or other purposes), the private insurance industry is not well equipped, organized or motivated to provide rehabilitation services directly. The public agencies already in existence afford far greater promise of better future rehabilitation for auto accident victims. Support for these existing agencies should be increased at all levels of government, and consideration should be given to the possibility of requiring private auto insurance carriers to refer victims to rehabilitation routinely when the circumstances of their injuries warrant such referral.

7. Minimal Use of Adversary Procedures

Ultimately, most if not all automobile accident loss reparation should take place without the use of adversary procedures. However, in the case of compensation for intangible losses, the fault concept and the adversary system may provide a more acceptable basis than economic losses for making reparations. Even here its use should be limited to truly serious cases, i.e., those involving permanent disfigurement or impairment or, perhaps, those where medical losses exceed a fairly high threshold level.

Good reason argues that there be at least this limitation placed on the right to sue in tort for intangible damages. For example, the threat of suit in minor personal injury cases is widely recognized as the basic reason for the "overpayment" of small claims, frequently at a high multiple of the objectively measurable economic loss involved. The absolute amount of these "overpayments" is very large. On the basis of data drawn from industry claim files, it has been estimated that as much as 34 percent of *all* bodily injury liability insurance payments were for the intangible losses of non-permanently injured claimants whose measurable economic losses to date of settlement were less than $5,000. If only claimants with $2,000 or less in economic loss were counted, the amount of their "overpayments" still constituted almost a third of *all* payments to *all* claimants. As noted earlier, more than half the people questioned in the Department's public attitude survey indicated that compensation for pain and suffering should be eliminated if it would reduce insurance costs.

B. A Specific Recommendation

To explain further the kind of a system that we believe the States should now strive toward, it may be useful to describe what its ultimate configuration might look like following a suitable period of experimentation and testing. It should be emphasized that this is a goal to be achieved over time, not an action blueprint for tomorrow. Moving in stages toward such a goal would allow us to test its virtues and discover its faults, thereby giving us new knowledge that could serve to modify the goal itself. A little observation is worth a great deal of speculation, and State experience with diverse plans will provide us with that opportunity for pilot project testing which must precede massive reform.

This system, as we see it now, should be based on universal, compulsory first-party insurance for all motor vehicle owners covering all economic losses above voluntarily accepted deductibles up to reasonably high limits. Insurers should be free to offer additional insurance coverage above these limits. Victims should retain their present right to sue in tort for specified intangible losses, but the right should be restricted to the truly serious cases. Victims should not be able to sue in tort for economic losses compensated by their own insurers or voluntarily accepted as a deductible. The system should be implemented in stages at the State level. The private insurance industry should service the system, which should continue to be regulated by the several States.

The broad outlines of such a system are proposed below. It should be emphasized that the policy limits and deductibles used in the following description are *basically illustrative,* although the Department of Transportation's study would indicate that they are roughly in the right order of magnitude.

1. Compulsory First-Party Benefits

Under the ultimate configuration of the system, every owner of a motor vehicle should be required to carry insurance protecting himself, his family and every uninsured passenger or pedestrian suffering injury as a result of an accident involving the insured vehicle for all economic losses they thereby incur for the amounts specified. In addition, the insurance should protect the insured and all members of his family who are part of the same household against losses suffered when they are pedestrians or passengers in some other vehicle.

2. Required Medical Benefits

The goal of the ultimate system should be to provide full coverage for all medical benefits with a relatively small permissible deductible per accident but with very high mandatory limit. Any deductible voluntarily assumed by the car owner on behalf of himself and his household or any maximum coverage limit would not apply, however, to the medical losses of uninsured passengers and pedestrians. Included in covered benefits would be all medical rehabilitation expenses within the limits provided. Payment of benefits by a carrier under this coverage should automatically remove the obligation of any other insurance carrier to pay benefits to the extent that the costs are covered by automobile insurance.

3. Income Loss Protection

With full implementation of this plan, coverage should be afforded for a relatively high percentage of earned income of the injured or deceased auto accident victim. There should be a short permitted waiting period at the option of the insured for the start of benefits and a permitted monthly benefit ceiling by the insurer of perhaps $1,000. Voluntarily assumed deductibles or any maximum coverage limit would not apply to pedestrians. Higher benefits for the insured or his family could be made available at the option of the insurer and insured.

This coverage should pay wage continuation benefits whenever an injured person is prevented from working whether as a result of his disability or during his participation in an approved rehabilitation program. The fact that his rehabilitation program was not necessary for vocational objectives but only to deal with other handicaps should not excuse the payment of wage continuation benefits. The benefit program should provide for modification as provided contractually between the insurer and insured because of changed circumstances, e.g., the remarriage of a surviving spouse, surviving children reaching their majority, etc.

The minimum duration of mandatory income loss protection should, and probably could, be finally established only after some further investigation and experimentation. Initially, minimum duration might be set at three years, except for victims in approved rehabilitation programs whose protection might continue as long as necessary. Longer durations should be optionally available from the beginning and should also be considered for inclusion in the mandatory coverage as experience dictates. A lump sum burial benefit of perhaps $1,000 per person should be required. Any higher benefits should be optional on the part of the insurer and the insured.

4. Lost Service Benefits

The goal of the system should be to provide coverage for the cost of necessary replacement services for non-employed persons (e.g., housewives) up to a benefit of $75 per week with a permitted waiting period for benefits at the option of the insured of up to 60 days. Minimum duration of mandatory protection would be the same as for income loss.

5. Property Damage

Ultimately, with the full shift of economic loss compensation to first-party insurance, coverage of damages to property, including the insured vehicle, might be required, but with a permissible deductible referable to the vehicle only at the option of the insured of up to a rather high level, perhaps $1,000 or a third of the value of the car, and with a permissible limitation of coverage by the insurer of $10,000 per accident. There would be no deductible with respect to the non-vehicular property of others damaged in an accident.

6. Elimination of Action for Damages

The goal of the system should be that no recovery for any loss of a type covered by the applicable required coverage would be permitted in any private action for damages. The insured victim's sole recourse for benefits for wage loss, medical loss, lost services, funeral expense and perhaps property damage should be limited to the insured's required coverage and any additional optional coverages that he has elected to purchase, whether under an auto insurance policy or other voluntary loss reparation program.

To the extent that insurance purchasers are willing to pay for duplicate coverages for the same loss and insurers are willing to write duplicate coverage, the practice of cumulating benefits should be allowed. However, unless each policy is clearly stated to be cumulative, only one recovery would be legally permissible with the order of priority among private sources being: (1) auto insurance benefits; and (2) other insurance benefits. In this way, it should be possible to ensure a much better coordination of benefits, with duplicate recovery occurring only where both the insurer and insured had known and agreed about it in advance.

The existing right to sue for damages resulting from negligence in car crashes might be continued for intangible losses, and if so could be subject to one limitation: no person should recover for intangible losses unless he establishes that he suffered permanent impairment or loss of function or permanent disfigurement, or that he incurred personal medical expenses (excluding hospital expenses) as a result of the accident in excess of a rather high dollar threshold. Any dollar threshold initially chosen should not be considered inviolable but should be reviewed as to its appropriateness at regular, specified intervals.

Drivers should, of course, be permitted to continue to insure against this residual third-party liability.

C. Cost of Insurance

Almost without exception, every recent probe of consumer attitudes about automobile insurance has shown its cost to lead all other concerns. This is understandable inasmuch as the cost of insurance affects all policyholders, and they are far more numerous than accident victims, while victims are more likely to be affected by their treatment as claimants. An improved system of auto accident compensation such as described above should, once fully implemented, affect the cost of insurance in several ways:

a. The elimination of "overpayments" of small claims and of compensation of the less serious forms of economic loss should produce cost reduction.

b. The removal of most compensation decisions from the adversary process should greatly simplify claims adjustment and eliminate much legal and court costs, thereby producing additional substantial cost reduction.

c. The voluntary acceptance of deductibles by policyholders should produce more savings; the deductibles, themselves, while reducing insurance costs would not be true savings to the insureds, but the concomitant elimination of the insurance mechanism's related administrative costs would be.

d. The first-party nature of the mandatory insurance coverages should eventually allow insurance companies to rate vehicles as to the value of their protective features and their own damageability. If this encourages the manufacturing of safer vehicles, there would be further insurance cost reduction.

e. If the first-party nature of the mandatory coverages were to facilitate their marketing on a group basis, and if this produced administrative economies, there might be further savings for those who participate.

Obviously, some features of such a compensation system would work to increase costs:

a. More victims would participate in benefits and this would increase total costs.

b. On the average, the more seriously injured victims or the survivors of accident fatalities will receive much greater benefits, and this would also increase total costs. (However, since all drivers would participate in the system, more would be paying premiums, i.e., one analysis of auto insurance coverage in all but six States indicated that about one out of every five drivers was uninsured for auto accident liability.)

It would appear that the true costs of compensating the socially significant losses from motor vehicle accidents should be reduced, since more of the insurance premium dollar would go for needed benefits and less for system expenses. Obviously, the cost to the insurance buyer would depend upon the trends in the frequency and severity of losses, the benefit levels chosen, and his own individual risk potential. To the extent that some potential savings are applied to needed benefits for victims, this too should be counted as a plus. Adequacy and equity of a better compensation system should not yield to cost in our list of priorities.

D. Implementation

Without question, any revision of the system along the lines outlined above would entail major changes in existing institutions and practices. The orderly accomplishment of such changes would require further study, cooperation, understanding, planning and the dedicated effort of all concerned, especially of the insuring public.

Mere speculation without observation of the actual operation of a new system is an inadequate basis for immediate and fundamental changes of a national scope in an important area. Experience with diverse plans in the states is essential, and one state has already, this January, taken a step down the road. The states are the best arena in which to solve the problem.

Any new mandatory first-party no-fault coverages could be adopted incrementally, giving both the insuring public and the affected institutions time to gain the necessary understanding and make the necessary adjustments. How much and what kind of compensation should be shifted in any one stage, how many stages there should be or even how long the process should take, or indeed whether it will ultimately prove desirable to go all the way, cannot be answered doctrinarily. Trial will be the best teacher. The important thing is to get started with at least a reasonably agreed-on goal in mind.

One, but by no means the only way to go would be to have the first stage involve the shift of the required medical/hospital loss coverages to a first-party, non-fault basis. Coincident with this step should be the elimination of the right to sue for intangible damages other than those related to death, permanent disfigurement or impairment, or when personal medical losses exceed a given threshold. Before this step is taken, the estimated "cost savings" from the elimination of payments for noneconomic losses should be judged at least sufficient to affect any added costs resulting from the higher level of medical benefits. The public should be able to take this step with some confidence that, overall, insurance costs will not rise because of it.

A suitable period—hopefully no more than one year or two years—might then be allowed to elapse during which insurers can gain enough experience with these coverage and recovery rule changes so that insurance rates can be set with confidence before going on to a second phase of the program. This second phase should probably encompass the rest of the personal benefit coverages—the wage continuation, lost service replacement and funeral benefits. A final phase that would shift all or most of property damage losses to a first-party recovery basis would take place once the system had "digested" the change-over of the personal benefit coverages.

As each phase is entered, damages for the type of loss shifted to mandatory first-party insurance should be removed from consideration in private personal injury litigation, until ultimately only the specified serious intangible losses might still be dealt with in this fashion. Even here if experimentation by insurers with optional, voluntary first-party benefits for these specified types of serious intangible losses were to prove successful, their inclusion under a first-party, no-fault system should also be carefully considered.

Ultimately, the systems of the several states must be compatible. Although there are means available to overcome great diversity, these are cumbersome and a reasonable degree of national uniformity seems best for a number of reasons. Motor vehicle travel is an interstate activity of major proportions and a consistent minimum standard for accident reparations involving all of the motoring public, wherever they travel, would constitute sound public policy. If basic reparations system reform were to be left wholly to individual State initiative without some encouragement, guidance and, at least in an advisory sense, direction from a national perspective, meaningful change might be exceedingly slow in coming. Should experience with systems of the type we describe prove as successful as we believe it will, the first-party, no-fault concept should become as dominant in the states as the third-party tort system is today. As to the length of the time schedule, a period of perhaps five years seems reasonable, but this judgment can at this juncture be only tentative and certainly should change as future experience dictates. Use of a phased schedule would permit an evolutionary change with ample opportunity for the public policymakers to review and evaluate the performance of the new systems and make any modifications that experience shows are desirable.

E. The Expected Results

Once implemented, the plan should produce several beneficial results:

A system geared basically to serve the needs of auto victims directly rather than one designed to protect tortfeasors. The latter system obviously was never insurance for the victim; he was no party to the contract. A liability system can easily be defended against the charge that it does not serve all victims. Such a defense only begs the question of the need for insurance for all victims.

A basically first-party insurance system fulfilling the mission of insurance by substituting certainty for uncertainty, both in eligibility for benefits and in amount of benefits payable. As a basically first-party insurance system, the plan lends itself to the prompt, timely payment of benefits for economic loss without the delays associated with the adversary system. Because in most cases benefits would be associated with measurable or ascertainable economic loss, there would be a closer correlation between the loss or damages and the amount of recovery. Thus, the plan avoids having individuals with substantially the same loss reimbursed with substantially different amounts, except to the extent they have voluntarily chosen to be treated differently by employing deductibles or added coverages.

A system much better able to allocate benefit dollars available according to the varying needs of victims. The creation of a proper balance between payments for the less seriously injured cases and the seriously injured would, itself, put benefit dollars to work for a better purpose. The wide spread now existing between settlement amounts and economic loss could be greatly narrowed. The large share of settlements now going to plaintiffs' lawyers would be eliminated. Claim administration costs would be very sharply curtailed. Because general damages, including lawyers' fees, will no longer be looked upon as a multiple of identifiable losses, a vicious incentive to maximize the latter will no longer exist.

A system lending itself to sounder rating criteria. As an insurance system, the dollar amount at risk will be better known than under any liability system. What loss a liability insurance policyholder will cause is completely unpredictable because the injured victim is unknown, e.g., a child, a student, a housewife, a retired person, a person earning $3,000 a year, a person earning $100,000. To the extent policyholders can be converted from potential wrongdoers to potential beneficiaries in the event of loss, the characteristics of those potentially suffering loss will be ascertainable much more exactly and the consequences of loss more readily determinable.

A system better adapted to the customer's ability to pay. Because the liability system is geared to the potentiality of creating loss to others, premium rates bear most heavily on the youthful and, at least until recently, the aged. Because the potentiality of economic loss to the victim bears a relationship to his economic status, the cost of meeting that potential loss should also be related to his economic status. Moreover, while there is hardly universal agreement, many experts believe that there would also be some narrowing of the wide spread in premium rates that exists today, specifically between adult and youthful drivers and between metropolitan and non-metropolitan areas. A much to be desired corollary is that the public should find the insurance product substantially more available on a voluntary basis than is the current liability product. More applicants should become desirable to insurance companies as insurance risks than is now the case, including some classes who present special problems today, e.g., the youthful, the elderly and enlisted servicemen.

Greater service orientation of the insurance business. Unlike the liability system, a basically first-party system would permit the relationship between insurer and insured to be one of mutual respect and trust—an ingredient essential in an insurance system designed to provide security for the consumer.

A system without incentives to maximize costs. Any system that determines losses as a multiple of reported actual expenditures provides a well-nigh irresistable incentive to exaggerate, inflate or needlessly build up the actual expenditures, even to the point of providing margins for kickbacks to the providers of service. Such incentives are anti-social as well as the cause for squandering insurance funds and, hence, a source of excessively high insurance premiums. A basically first-party system, properly administered, would not contain such incentives.

A system lending itself to more flexible or efficient merchandising methods. The intensive and extensive degree of underwriting discrimination on an individual basis, the hallmark of the liability system, should lose the justification now ascribed to it. This change in itself would contribute to the effort now underway to exploit various methods of enrolling policyholders in groups that hold some promise of lower acquisition and administrative costs.

Encouragement of competition. Liability insurance companies now insuring about 80 percent of passenger cars and providing medical payments coverage in a substantial majority of cases, will obviously be in the best position in the market to merchandise an expanded first-party coverage. Some of these carriers, now restricting their auto insurance writings because of bad underwriting experience, may be expected to reverse their competitive posture from one of contraction to one of expansion. Other insurers, intimidated by the bearish industry attitude regarding all forms of liability insurance but experienced with first-party coverages, may be encouraged to enter the field. The overall prospect would, therefore, be one of increased rather than decreased competition. In this connection, relatively small insurers writing first-party coverages have proved viable as they have in the liability field [sic].

Effect on State regulation. If the greater certainty associated with a first-party insurance system led to a freer, larger, more competitive market, regulation of auto insurance rates as now known might safely be relaxed as long as regulatory safeguards against insolvency and unsound rate cutting to destroy competition were maintained. Rather, the energies and talents of State regulatory authorities could be devoted to policing the real substance of insurance administration, i.e., the assurance that the coverages being provided meet established socially responsible standards and that the benefits are being paid in accordance with the policy provisions.

NOTES FOR CHAPTER I

The Maw of the Law

1. United States Department of Health, Education and Welfare, Report of the Secretary's Advisory Committee on Traffic Safety p. 4 (1968).

2. N. Y. Insurance Department, Automobile Insurance . . . For Whose Benefit? A Report to Governor Nelson A. Rockefeller p. 3, note 5 (1970).

3. United States Department of Transportation, Economic Consequences of Automobile Accident Injuries, Report of the Westat Research Corporation, vol. I pp. 40, 118 (Table 11 Fs) (1970).

4. "Needed: A Basic Reform of Auto Liability Insurance," Consumer Reports, August, 1962, pp. 404, 406.

5. N. Y. Times, April 29, 1970, p. 81.

6. United States Department of Transportation, *supra* note 3, at pp. 37-38; A. Conard, J. Morgan, R. Pratt, C. Voltz and R. Bombaugh, Automobile Accident Costs and Payments—Studies in the Economics of Injury Reparation pp. 172, 186 (1964).

7. United States Department of Transportation, *supra* note 3, pp. 146-47 (Table 15 Fs).

8. Conard, Testimony before the New York Joint Legislative Committee on Insurance Rates and Regulations, printed in University of Michigan Law Quadrangle Notes p. 14 (Fall 1970).

9. United States Department of Transportation, *supra* note 3, at Table 25 Fs, p. 235.

10. Compiled from *ibid.*

11. American Insurance Association, Report of Special Committee to Study and Evaluate the Keeton-O'Connell Basic Protection Plan and Automobile Accident Reparations, Exhibit X (1968). *See also* United

States Department of Transportation, Automobile Personal Injury Claims, vol. I p. 114 (1970).

12. United States Department of Transportation, *supra* note 3, at p. 41.

13. *Ibid.* at p. 52.

14. New York Insurance Department, *supra* note 2, at p. 19, note 26.

15. *Ibid.* at p. 21.

16. Klein and Clements, *Judicial Administration—1969* pp. 601, 631-32 1969-70 Annual Survey of American Law.

17. Institute of Judicial Administration, State Trial Courts of General Jurisdiction—Personal Injury Jury Cases pp. vi-vii (Calendar Status Study—1970).

18. R. Keeton, Compensation Systems: The Search for a Viable Alternative to Negligence Law p. 33 (1969).

19. Bartlett, "Auto Insurance A Prime Reform," nationally syndicated column during the week of September 13, 1970, appearing, for example, in the Chicago Sun-Times, September 16, 1970.

NOTES FOR CHAPTER II

"Who Dunnit?"

1. Nixon, *Changing Rules of Liability in Automobile Accident Litigation,* 3 Law And Contemporary Problems pp. 476-77 (1936).

2. *See A $100,000 Teaching Experiment,* Trial Magazine, August/September, 1966, pp. 20-21. This and other quotes from the film are not precisely verbatim from the sound track but a close approximation based on careful notes made during multiple runs of the film.

3. A. Conard, J. Morgan, R. Pratt, C. Voltz and R. Bombaugh, Automobile Accident Costs and Payments—Studies in the Economics of Injury Reparation pp. 214-15 (1964).

4. W. Prosser, The Law of Torts p. 924 (Third Edition 1964).

5. Prosser, *Comparative Negligence,* 51 University of Michigan Law Review pp. 465, 469 (1953).

6. W. Prosser, *supra* note 4, at p. 428.

NOTES FOR CHAPTER III

Injuring the Injured

1. R. Keeton and J. O'Connell, *Basic Protection for the Traffic Victim* pp. 28-29 (1965).
2. *Ibid.* at p. 31.
3. Conard, Book Review, 13 University of California at Los Angeles Law Review pp. 1432, 1433 (1966).
4. As quoted in M. Bloom, The Trouble With Lawyers p. 125 (1968).
5. Vol. 2, F. Harper and F. James, The Law of Torts p. 1303 (1956).
6. H. Somers and A. Somers, Workmen's Compensation pp. 160-63 (1954).
7. F. Harper and F. James, *supra* note 5, at p. 1304.
8. See *ibid.* at pp. 1303-04.
9. J. Henle, Rehabilitation of Auto Accident Victims p. 4 (United States Department of Transportation, 1970), quoting from a definition adopted by the National Council on Rehabilitation at its symposium, New York City, May 25, 1942.
10. Taken from a private letter, dated May 4, 1964.
11. N. Y. Insurance Department, Automobile Insurance . . . For Whose Benefit? A Report to Governor Nelson A. Rockefeller p. 33 (1970).
12. J. Henle, *supra* note 9, at p. 13.
13. *Ibid.* at p. 18.
14. *Ibid.* at pp. 23-24.
15. *Ibid.* at p. 36.
16. Corstvet, *The Uncompensated Accident and Its Consequences,* 3 Law and Contemporary Problems pp. 466, 468 (1936).
17. As printed in Preliminary Draft of April 4, 1963, of the Report of the Committee on Personal Injury Claims of the State Bar of California, Part II, p. 86.
18. Address by Arne Fougner, Rehabilitation and Insurance—A Partnership In Progress, American Academy of Physical Medicine and Rehabilitation and the American Congress of Physical Medicine and Rehabilitation, Dallas, Texas, August, 1963.
19. Address by Paul Wise, President, American Mutual Insurance Alliance, at the Mutual Insurance Technical Conference, Chicago, Illinois, November 13, 1967.
20. Wall Street Journal, January 13, 1967, pp. 1, 11.
21. *Ibid.*
22. *Ibid.*
23. *Ibid.*

24. *Ibid.*

25. United States Department of Transportation, Economic Consequences of Automobile Accident Injuries, Report of the Westat Research Corporation, vol. I, p. 51 (1970).

26. N. Y. Times, April 29, 1970, pp. 1, 81.

27. United States Department of Transportation, *supra* note 25, at pp. 362-63 (Table 56 FS).

28. A. Conard, J. Morgan, R. Pratt, C. Voltz and R. Bombaugh, Automobile Accident Costs and Payment—Studies in the Economics of Injury Reparation p. 176 (1964).

29. *Ibid.* at p. 221.

NOTES FOR CHAPTER IV

Paying for Pain

1. M. Mayer, The Lawyers p. 255 (1966).

2. Warne, *Let's Hear From The Insurance Consumer,* 36 Insurance Counsel Journal pp. 494, 496 (1969). *See also* A. Conard, J. Morgan, R. Pratt, C. Voltz and R. Bombaugh, Automobile Accident Costs and Payment—Studies in the Economics of Injury Reparation p. 59 (1964).

3. Note, *Unreason in the Law of Damages: The Collateral Source Rule,* 77 Harvard Law Review p. 741 (1964).

4. United States Department of Transportation, Economic Consequences of Automobile Accident Injuries, Report of the Westat Research Corporation, vol. I, p. 146 (Table 15 FS) (1970).

5. *See* Foran, *Valuation Problems Where All Of The Property Is Taken,* 1966 University of Illinois Law Forum pp. 69, 70.

6. Bishop, Book Review, 69 Yale Law Journal pp. 925, 926-27 (1960).

7. *See* H. L. Ross, Settled Out Of Court pp. 108-11 (1970).

8. *Ibid.* at pp. 118-19.

9. *Ibid.* at p. 118.

10. M. Mayer, *supra* note 1, at p. 263.

11. A. Conard, *et al., supra* note 2, at pp. 214-15.

12. H. L. Ross, *supra* note 7, at pp. 108-09.

13. *Ibid.* at pp. 139-40.

14. American Insurance Association, Report of Special Committee to Study and Evaluate the Keeton-O'Connell Basic Protection Plan and Automobile Accident Reparations, Exhibit X (1968).

15. United States Department of Transportation, *supra* note 4, at p. 235 (Table 25 FS).

16. N. Y. Insurance Department, Automobile Insurance . . . For Whose Benefit? A Report to Governor Nelson A. Rockefeller p. 26, note 40 (1970).

17. R. Keeton, Compensation Systems: The Search for a Viable Alternative to Negligence Law p. 33 (1969).

NOTES FOR CHAPTER V

A Pound of Flesh

1. F. MacKinnon, Contingent Fees for Legal Purposes: A Study of Professional Economics and Responsibilities p. 116 (1964). *See also* United States Department of Transportation, Automobile Accident Litigation: A Report of the Federal Judicial Center p. 7 (1970).

2. F. MacKinnon, *supra* note 1, at pp. 116-17.

3. *Ibid.* at pp. 66-67.

4. *Ibid.*

5. *E.g.,* N. Y. Lien Law § 189 (7) (McKinney 1968).

6. F. MacKinnon, *supra* note 1, at p. 78.

7. *The Workshop Sessions: Summary Report,* 1967 University of Illinois Law Forum pp. 618, 622; also printed in Crisis in Car Insurance pp. 258, 262 (R. Keeton, J. O'Connell and J. McCord eds. 1968).

8. As quoted in M. Mayer, The Lawyers p. 261 (1966).

9. F. MacKinnon, *supra* note 1, at p. 209.

10. *Ibid.* at pp. 9-10.

11. H. Bernstein, *Reparation for Traffic Injuries in West Germany,* in A. Conard, J. Morgan, R. Pratt, C. Voltz and R. Bombaugh, Automobile Accident Costs and Payment—Studies in the Economics of Injury Reparation pp. 468, 471 (1964).

12. N. Y. Times, August 7, 1966, p. E 5, cols. 4-6 (News of the Week).

13. *Ibid.*

14. Bowman, *An Inspection of a Personal Injury Law Firm,* 51 American Bar Association Journal pp. 929, 930 (1965).

15. Prosser, Book Review, 43 University of California Law Review pp. 556, 557 (1955).

16. Duguay v. Gelinas, 104 N. H. 182, 185, 182 A. 2d 451, 454 (1962).

17. N. Y. Times, August 1, 1965, p. 6 E, cols. 5-8 (News of the Week).

18. R. Keeton and J. O'Connell, Basic Protection for the Traffic Victim p. 22 (1965).

19. W. Prosser, The Law of Torts p. 580 (3rd Edition 1964).

20. A. Conard, J. Morgan, R. Pratt, C. Voltz and R. Bombaugh, Automobile Accident Costs and Payment—Studies in the Economics of Injury Reparation pp. 191-92 (1964); United States Department of Transportation, Economic Consequences of Automobile Accident Injuries, Report of the Westat Research Corporation, vol. I, p. 48 (1970).

21. A. Conard, *et al., supra* note 20. *See also* United States Department of Transportation, *supra* note 20, at p. 49.

22. F. MacKinnon, *supra* note 1, at p. 116, note 16.

23. As quoted in Bloom, "When the Lawyer Gets the Spoils," Readers Digest, March, 1960, p. 106.

24. In re McCallum, 391 Ill. 400, 64 N. E. 2d 310 (1945).

25. F. MacKinnon, *supra* note 1, at p. 198.

26. *Ibid.*

27. N. Y. Times, February 18, 1968, p. 4 E, cols. 1-4 (News of the Week).

28. F. MacKinnon, *supra* note 1, at p. 199.

29. A. Conard, *supra* note 20, at pp. 280-81.

30. F. MacKinnon, *supra* note 1, at pp. 198-200.

31. H. L. Ross, Settled Out Of Court p. 81 (1970), quoting from R. Hunting and G. Neuwirth, Who Sues in New York City? p. 109 (1962).

32. Gair v. Peck, 188 N. Y. S. 2d 491, 504, 6 N. Y. 2d 97, 115 (1959).

33. As quoted in Bloom, *supra* note 23, at p. 108.

34. F. MacKinnon, *supra* note 1, at p. 70.

35. Trial Magazine, October/November, 1970, p. 53.

36. Franklin, Chanin & Mark, *Accidents, Money And The Law: A Study of the Economics of Personal Injury Litigation,* 61 Columbia University Law Review pp. 1, 13 (1961). *See also* United States Department of Transportation, Automobile Accident Litigation: A Report of the Federal Judicial Center p. 7 (1970). United States Department of Transportation, *supra* note 20, at pp. 304, 305 (Table 38 FS).

37. As quoted in M. Bloom, The Trouble With Lawyers p. 141 (1968).

38. Franklin, *et al., supra* note 36, at pp. 14, 30. *See also* H. L. Ross, *supra* note 31, at pp. 193-98.

39. A. Ehrenzwieg, "Full Aid" Insurance for the Traffic Victim—A Voluntary Compensation Plan p. 6 (1954); for a slightly revised version of the book, see Ehrenzwieg, *"Full Aid" Insurance for the Traffic Victim —A Voluntary Compensation Plan,* 43 University of California Law Review pp. 1, 10 (1955).

40. Conard, *The Economic Treatment of Automobile Injuries,* 63 University of Michigan Law Review pp. 279, 290 (Summer 1964)'.

41. LaBrum, *Can Our Judicial System Be Improved By The Elimination Of Civil Jury Trials?: A Panel Discussion,* 15 Federation of Insurance Counsel Quarterly pp. 18, 34 (Summer 1965).

42. F. MacKinnon, *supra* note 1, at pp. 117-18.

43. United States Department of Transportation, Motor Vehicle Crash Losses And Their Compensation in the United States: A Report to the Congress and the President p. 49 (1971).

44. *See* Lawyer Reform News, April/May, 1971, pp. 1, 4. For the estimate of number of lawyers in the United States, *see* Desk Book American Jurisprudence 2d, 1970, Cumulative Supplement, Document Number 98 at p. 134.

45. M. Bloom, *supra* note 37, at p. 143.

46. As quoted in M. Mayer, The Lawyers p. 231 (1966).

47. LaBrum, *supra* note 41, at p. 30.

48. Note 43 *supra* and accompanying text.

49. Scariano, *Remarks,* 1967 University of Illinois Law Forum pp. 596, 599, also printed in Crisis in Car Insurance pp. 236, 239 (R. Keeton, J. O'Connell and J. McCord eds. 1968).

50. Phelan, *The Defense Attorney and the Changing World of Insurance,* 15 Federation of Insurance Counsel Quarterly pp. 58, 60 (Summer 1965).

51. Ryan, *Where Do We Go From Here With Tort Litigation,* 25 Insurance Counsel Journal p. 500 (1958).

NOTES FOR CHAPTER VI

. . .To the Hounds

1. As quoted in M. Bloom, The Trouble With Lawyers p. 130 (1968).

2. The Philadelphia Sunday Bulletin, February 21, 1971, p. 1 col. 6.

3. *Ibid.*

4. The Chicago Tribune, December 22, 1970, p. 17, col. 1.

5. Illinois Revised Statutes, Chapter 13, Section 15 (1969).

6. J. Carlin, Lawyers on Their Own pp. 22-23 (1962); Monaghan, *The Liability Claim Racket,* 3 Law And Contemporary Problems p. 491 (1936).

7. J. Carlin, *supra* note 6, at p. 84.

8. As quoted in M. Bloom, *supra* note 1, at p. 131.

9. The Philadelphia Sunday Bulletin, *supra* note 2, at p. 11, col. 1.

10. J. Carlin, *supra* note 6, at p. 83.

11. Yoder, "How An Ambulance Chaser Works," Saturday Evening Post, March 23, 1957, pp. 19, 96.

12. J. Carlin, *supra* note 6, at pp. 87-88.

13. *Comment: Settlement of Personal Injury Cases in the Chicago Area,* 47 Northwestern University Law Review pp. 895, 899 (1953); Yoder, *supra* note 11, at p. 96.

14. Yoder, *supra* note 11, at pp. 93, 96.

15. J. Carlin, *supra* note 6, at p. 83.

16. *Ibid.* at p. 90.

17. The Philadelphia Sunday Bulletin, *supra* note 2, at p. 11, col. 1.

18. J. Carlin, *supra* note 6, at pp. 84-85.

19. The Chicago Daily News, February 3, 1971, p. 3, col. 6.

20. 117 Congressional Record, p. S 1851 (daily ed. February 24, 1971).

21. J. Carlin, *supra* note 6, pp. 74-75.

22. *Ibid.* at p. 75.

23. *Ibid.* at pp. 77-78.

24. M. Bloom, *supra* note 1, at pp. 143-44.

25. *Ibid.* at p. 144.

26. *Ibid.* at p. 143.

27. J. Carlin, *supra* note 6, at p. 82.

28. F. MacKinnon, Contingent Fees for Legal Purposes: A Study of Professional Economics and Responsibilities p. 68 (1964).

29. *Ibid.* at p. 70.

30. J. Carlin, *supra* note 6, at pp. 74, 79-80.

31. *Ibid.* at p. 80.

32. Yoder, *supra* note 11, at p. 96.

33. As quoted in M. Bloom, *supra* note 1, at p. 132.

34. From a forthcoming study tentatively entitled "Payment for Pain" by Jeffrey O'Connell and Professor Rita Simon of the University of Illinois Sociology Department; *see also* H. L. Ross, Settled Out Of Court pp. 168-69 (1970).

35. H. L. Ross, *supra* note 34, at p. 70.

36. *Ibid.* at pp. 49-50.

37. F. MacKinnon, *supra* note 28, at p. 203.

38. Llewellyn, *The Bar's Troubles, and Poultices—and Cures?* 5 Law and Contemporary Problems pp. 104, 115-16 (1938).

39. J. Carlin, *supra* note 6, at pp. 156-57.

40. For documentation that people with higher education and income tend more to retain lawyers and to recover a larger proportion of

their economic losses, *see* United States Department of Transportation, Economic Counsequences of Automobile Accident Injuries, Report of the Westat Research Corporation, vol. I, pp. 52-53 (1970); *see also* H. L. Ross, *supra* note 34, at pp. 241-42.

41. But for an indication that, under no-fault workmen's compensation laws, the availability of lump-sum payments has led to some ambulance chasing, *see* H. Somers and A. Somers, Workmen's Compensation p. 161 (1954). For the limitations on lump-sum payments under the Keeton-O'Connell Basic Protection No-Fault Plan, *see* R. Keeton and J. O'Connell, Basic Protection for the Traffic Victim pp. 7, 277-78, 319, 432-33 (1965).

NOTES FOR CHAPTER VII

Let the Buyer (not only) Beware (but be gone)

1. R. Keeton and J. O'Connell, After Cars Crash: The Need for Legal and Insurance Reform pp. 31-32 (1967).

2. N. Y. Times, July 6, 1970 p. 47 cols. 4-6.

3. N. Y. Insurance Department, Automobile Insurance . . . For Whose Benefit? A Report to Governor Nelson A. Rockefeller p. 41 (1970).

4. *Ibid.,* note 75.

5. *Ibid.* at pp. 42-43.

6. *Ibid.* at p. 42, note 78.

7. J. O'Connell and W. Wilson, Car Insurance and Consumer Desires p. 15 (1969).

8. Answers on file, Survey Research Laboratory, University of Illinois, Urbana Champaign.

9. N. Y. Insurance Department, *supra* note 3, at p. 43, note 79.

10. Consumer Reports, January, 1968, p. 9.

11. R. Keeton, Compensation Systems: The Search for a Viable Alternative to Negligence Law p. 2 (1969).

12. N. Y. Insurance Department, *supra* note 3, at p. 39.

13. United States Department of Transportation, Insurance Accessibility for the Hard-To-Place Driver, Report of the Division of Industry Analysis, Bureau of Economics, Federal Trade Commission p. 19 (1970).

14. *Ibid.* at p. 18.

15. United States Department of Transportation, Structural Trends and Conditions in the Automobile Insurance Industry, Report of the Division of Industry Analysis, Bureau of Economics, Federal Trade Commission pp. 8-9 (1970).

16. N. Y. Insurance Department, *supra* note 3, at p. 39.

17. Ridgeway, "Underground War on Auto Insurance," The New Republic, December 3, 1966, p. 19.

18. As quoted in an address by Cecil Mackey, American Bar Association Meeting, Philadelphia, Pa. August 7, 1968.

19. N. Y. Times, August 9, 1970 § 3 (Business and Finance) p. 1, cols. 6-8.

20. National Observer, March 11, 1968, p. 1, col. 3.

21. *Ibid.*

22. N. Y. Times, June 21, 1970, p. 7, col. 1.

23. *Ibid.*

24. Hearings on Senate Joint Resolution 129 before the Consumer Subcommittee of the Senate Committee on Commerce, 90th Congress 2d Session p. 54 (1968).

25. Ridgeway, *supra* note 17, at pp. 19, 22.

26. Hearings, *supra* note 24, at pp. 63-64.

27. As quoted in Consumer Reports, June, 1970, p. 342.

28. Wall Street Journal, October 10, 1967, p. 32, cols. 1-4.

29. *Ibid.*

30. *Ibid.*

31. *Ibid.*

NOTES FOR CHAPTER VIII

The Untouchables

1. Wall Street Journal, October 10, 1967, p. 32, cols. 1-4.

2. N. Y. Times, December 1, 1967, p. 29, col. 1.

3. Sharp, *Remarks,* 1967 University of Illinois Law Forum pp. 614, 615; also printed in Crisis in Car Insurance pp. 254, 255 (R. Keeton, J. O'Connell and J. McCord eds. 1968).

4. United States Department of Transportation, Public Attitudes Toward Auto Insurance, A Report of the Survey Research Center, Institute for Social Research, The University of Michigan, Staff Analysis of Consumer Complaint Letters Concerning Auto Insurance pp. 33-37 (1970).

5. Consumer Reports, June, 1970, p. 332.

6. United States Department of Transportation, Insurance Accessibility for the Hard-To-Place Driver, Report of the Division of Industry Analysis, Bureau of Economics, Federal Trade Commission p. 1 (1970).

7. *Ibid.* at p. 6.

8. *Ibid.* at p. 2.

9. *Ibid.*

10. N. Y. Times, June 21, 1970, p. 7, col. 2.

11. *Ibid.*

12. United States Department of Transportation, *supra* note 6, at pp. 50-51.

13. *Ibid.* at p. 59.

14. *Ibid.* at p. 60.

15. *Ibid.*

16. *Ibid.* at p. 2.

17. *Ibid.* at p. 66.

18. *Ibid.* at p. 70.

19. *Ibid.*

20. *Ibid.* at p. 29.

21. N. Y. Times, April 28, 1968, p. 36, cols. 1-3.

22. Testimony of A. Conard, Hearings on House Joint Resolution 958 before the Subcommittee on Commerce and Finance of the House Committee on Interstate and Foreign Commerce, 90th Congress, 2nd Session p. 83 (1968).

23. Statement of A. Biemiller, Hearings on Senate Joint Resolution 129 before the Consumer Subcommittee of the Senate Committee on Commerce, 90th Congress, 2nd Session p. 21 (1968).

24. The National Underwriter (Property & Casualty ed.), June 5, 1970, p. 2, col. 4.

25. Wall Street Journal, June 30, 1970, p. 7, col. 1.

26. Consumer Reports, June 1970, pp. 332, 339.

27. Consumer Reports, August 1970, p. 459.

28. Wall Street Journal, June 5, 1970, p. 8, col. 2.

29. Wall Street Journal, September 30, 1970, p. 32, cols. 2-3.

30. N. Y. Times, February 8, 1971, p. 1, col. 4.

31. *Ibid.* at p. 36, col. 5.

32. R. Mehr, Life Insurance: Theory and Practice pp. 341-42 (1970).

33. B. Webb, Collective Merchandising of Automobile Insurance: A Report to the Subcommittee on Antitrust and Monopoly of the Committee on the Judiciary of the United States Senate p. 62 (1969).

34. *Ibid.* at pp. 174, 175.
35. S. Heubner and K. Black, Life Insurance p. 526 (7th ed. 1969).
36. R. Keeton and J. O'Connell, Basic Protection for the Traffic Victim pp. 76-123 (1965).
37. S. Kimball and H. Denenberg, Mass Marketing of Property & Liability Insurance, Prepared for the Department of Transportation pp. 93-112, 161-86 (Appendix F) (1970); B. Webb, *supra* note 33, at pp. 136-73.
38. S. Kimball and H. Denenberg, *supra* note 37, at p. 62.
39. National Underwriter, (Property & Casualty Edition), April 10, 1970, p. 50.
40. Kimball, *Introduction: Unfinished Business in Insurance Regulation,* 1969 University of Wisconsin Law Review p. 1019.
41. S. Kimball and H. Denenberg, *supra* note 37, at p. 12.
42. Senate Bill 4340, 91st Congress, 2d Session. The bill appears in 116 Congressional Record pp. S 15265-66 (daily edition, September 14, 1970). As to agents' efforts at re-enforcing and extending stricter laws forbidding group auto insurance, *see* N. Y. Times, August 24, 1970, p. 50, cols. 2-5; S. Kimball and H. Denenberg, *supra* note 37, at pp. 74-77.
43. S. Kimball and H. Denenberg, *supra* note 37, at p. 112.
44. N. Y. Insurance Department, Automobile Insurance . . . For Whose Benefit? A Report to Governor Nelson A. Rockefeller p. 113, note 191 (1970).

NOTES FOR CHAPTER IX

No-Fault Insurance—What and Why

1. N. Y. Insurance Department, Automobile Insurance . . . For Whose Benefit? A Report to Governor Nelson A. Rockefeller p. 19, note 26 (1970).
2. Moynihan, "Next: A New Auto Insurance Policy," N. Y. Times, August 27, 1967, § 6 (Magazine), pp. 26, 82.
3. Conard, "Insurance Rates and Regulations," 15 University of Michigan Law Quadrangle Notes pp. 14, 16 (Fall 1970).
4. Consumer Reports, June, 1970, pp. 332, 336, 337.

5. Allstate Insurance Company, Adjuster's Work Book, Witness Portrait, pp. 171-78; N. Y. Times, October 19, 1968, p. 38, col. 2.

6. N. Y. Times, October 19, 1968, p. 38, col. 2.

7. A. Conard, J. Morgan, R. Pratt, C. Voltz and R. Bombaugh, Automobile Accident Costs and Payment—Studies in the Economics of Injury Reparation pp. 280, 287, 288, 289 (1964); Moynihan, *supra* note 2, at pp. 76-78.

8. Sargent, *Disaster Walks in the Guise of Social Reform*, Trial Magazine, October/November 1967, pp. 24, 25.

9. *E.g.,* Worcester (Mass.) Evening Gazette, September 5, 1967, p. 29, cols. 2-8.

10. J. O'Connell and W. Wilson, Car Insurance and Consumer Desires, pp. 22-23 (1969).

11. Conard, *supra* note 3, at p. 14.

12. From a forthcoming study tentatively entitled "Payment for Pain" by Jeffrey O'Connell and Professor Rita Simon of the University of Illinois Sociology Department.

NOTES FOR CHAPTER X

Lower Price—Higher Value

1. Nationwide Mutual Insurance Company, A Plan for Reform of the Automobile Insurance System, Part III, p. 2 (February, 1971).

2. T. L. Jones, Statement at Hearings on Automobile Insurance before the U. S. Senate Antitrust and Monopoly Subcommittee of the Senate Judiciary Committee, December 15, 1969, p. 18 (mimeographed).

3. N. Y. Times, March 11, 1971, p. 70, cols. 1-2.

4. Wall Street Journal, July 16, 1970, p. 20, col. 6.

5. Wall Street Journal, October 26, 1970, p. 1, col. 6, continued at p. 21, col. 2.

6. Wall Street Journal, July 16, 1970, p. 20, col. 6.

7. Wall Street Journal, October 26, 1970, p. 21, col. 2.

8. C. Spangenberg, Testimony at Hearings on Senate Joint Resolution 129 before the Consumer Subcommittee of the Senate Committee on Commerce, 90th Congress, 2d Session p. 102, (1968).

9. Fuchsberg, *Lawyers View Proposed Changes*, 1967 University of Illinois Law Forum pp. 565, 573; also reprinted in Crisis in Car Insurance pp. 205, 213 (R. Keeton, J. O'Connell and J. McCord eds. 1968).

10. American Bar Association, A Report of Special Committee on Automobile Accident Reparations pp. 97-100, 151-55, (1969).

11. National Underwriter (Property & Casualty Edition), December 18, 1970, pp. 1, 36-38; N. Y. Times, December 14, 1970, p. 33, col. 1. For a detailed elaboration of the proposal of the National Association of Independent Insurers, *see* Specimen Statute: Dual Protection Plan, dated January 26, 1971.

12. Davidson, *Remarks*, 1967 University of Illinois Law Forum pp. 454, 457-58; also printed in Crisis in Car Insurance pp. 94, 97-98 (R. Keeton, J. O'Connell and J. McCord eds. 1968).

13. Fuchsberg, *supra* note 9, at pp. 571 and 211 respectively.

14. Address by Bradford Smith, Jr., at the Mid-Winter Meeting of the Federation of Insurance Counsel, Miami, Florida, February 1, 1968.

15. R. Keeton and J. O'Connell, Basic Protection for the Traffic Victim (1965).

16. American Insurance Association, Report of Special Committee to Study and Evaluate the Keeton-O'Connell Basic Protection Plan and Automobile Accident Reparations p. 6 (1968).

17. N. Y. Insurance Department, Automobile Insurance . . . For Whose Benefit? A Report to Governor Nelson A. Rockefeller (1970).

18. For discussion of the Massachusetts Law, *see* Keeton and O'Connell, *Alternative Paths Toward Nonfault Automobile Insurance,* 71 Columbia University Law Review pp. 241, 251-54 (1971).

19. S. 4339, 91st Congress, 2d Session (1970), 116 Congressional Record pp. S 15262-65 (daily edition, September 14, 1970). Senator Hart's Bill has been drafted to make it clear that, as was intended (*see* 116 Congressional Record pp. S 15260-62 [daily edition, September 14, 1970] Remarks of Senator Hart), it would eliminate by federal standards all suits under the fault criterion in motoring cases for other than serious injury or death.

20. Specimen Statute: Dual Protection Plan, *supra* note 11, Article II, Section 1 (a) (b), pp. 13-14.

21. United States Department of Transportation, Motor Vehicle Crash Losses and Their Compensation in the United States: A Report to The Congress and The President p. 136 (1971).

22. A. Conard, J. Morgan, R. Pratt, C. Voltz and R. Bombaugh, Automobile Accident Costs and Payment—Studies in the Economics of Injury Reparation p. 144-45 (1964); the latest comprehensive discussion of cost is contained in Williams, *Cost Studies of No-Fault Insurance: Explanation and Comparison,* in Fault or No-Fault? Proceedings of a National Conference on Automobile Insurance Reform p. 35 (E. S. Maynes and C. A. Williams, Jr. eds. 1970); *see also* in the same volume Mayerson, Bailey, Hughey, Simoneau and Lange, *Cost Studies on Trial: A Panel Discussion* p. 55.

23. Harwayne, *Insurance Costs of Basic Protection Plan in Michigan,* 1967 University of Illinois Law Forum pp. 479, 486-87; also printed in Crisis in Car Insurance pp. 119, 126-27 (R. Keeton, J. O'Connell and J. McCord eds. 1968).

24. Harwayne, *Insurance Costs of Automobile Basic Protection Plan in Relation to Automobile Bodily Injury Liability Costs*, 53 Proceedings of the Casualty Actuarial Society p. 122 (1966); concerning this same study, *see* Keeton and O'Connell, *Basic Protection and the Cost of Traffic Accidents*, 38 New York State Bar Journal p. 255 (1966).

25. Wolfrum, *Remarks*, 1967 University of Illinois Law Forum, pp. 538, 548; also printed in Crisis in Car Insurance pp. 178, 188 (R. Keeton, J. O'Connell and J. McCord eds. 1968).

26. National Observer, February 22, 1971, p. 7; *see also* N. Y. Times, April 24, 1971, p. 45, col. 5.

27. There has been considerable confusion in the press and the public mind about court rulings with relation to this 15 per cent cut in rates. Originally the legislation applied the cut not only to personal injury liability coverage, which was affected by the no-fault provisions, but also to property damage liability and so-called collision, comprehensive, fire, and thefts coverages, which were not affected by the new no-fault law. Only with regard to the coverages *not* affected by the no-fault law was the 15 per cent cut protested in the courts by the insurance companies and struck down. *See* Aetna Casualty and Surety Company v. Commissioner of Insurance, 263 N.E.2d 698 (Mass. 1970), and Boston Herald Traveler, November 19, 1970, pp. 1, 10; Keeton and O'Connell, *Alternative Paths Toward Nonfault Automobile Insurance*, 71 Columbia University Law Review pp. 241, 251 (1971).

28. Boston Herald Traveler, August 24, 1967, p. 1, cols. 1-5.

29. A. Goldsmith, 21 Washington Insurance Newsletter, August 24, 1970.

30. N. Y. Times, March 19, 1971, p. 65, cols. 2-5; *see also* N. Y. Times, April 21, 1971, p. 77, cols. 6-8.

NOTES FOR CHAPTER XI

Defending the Indefensible

1. "A Matter of Opinion," Newark Star-Ledger, December 6, 1967; *see also* "No-Fault Insurance Proposal in New York Alarms Many Lawyers," Wall Street Journal, March 15, 1971, p. 8, col. 3; *see especially* Mintz, "[Capital] Hill Told of Lawyers' Efforts to Beat No-Fault," Washington Post, May 7, 1971, p. A2, cols. 1-3.

2. N. Y. Times, December 15, 1969, p. 41.

3. O'Connell and Wilson, *Public Opinion on No-Fault Auto Insurance: A Survey of the Surveys,* 1970 University of Illinois Law Forum pp. 307, 314-15.

4. J. O'Connell and W. Wilson, Car Insurance and Consumer Desires p. 9 (1969).

5. N. Y. Times, December 11, 1969, p. 107, cols. 5-6.

6. N. Y. Times, November 15, 1970, p. 70, cols. 4-5; *see also* N. Y. Times May 9, 1971, p. 60, cols. 1-3.

7. N. Y. Times, March 19, 1971, p. 65, col. 2.

8. N. Y. Times, February 19, 1968, p. 34, col. 1.

9. From a private communication.

10. Spangenberg, *At What Price* . . . Trial Magazine, October/November, 1967, p. 10.

11. 60 Mass. 292, 6 Cush. 292 (1850).

12. W. Prosser, The Law of Torts pp. 672-85 (3rd Edition 1964).

13. *Ibid.* at p. 538.

14. *Ibid.* at pp. 683-684.

15. C. Reich, "Reflections: The Greening of America," The New Yorker, September 26, 1970, pp. 42, 74, 80; C. Reich, The Greening of America pp. 18, 39 (1970).

16. *See* N. Y. Times, December 14, 1970, p. 1, cols. 1-2.

17. D. Klein and J. Waller, Causation, Culpability and Deterrence in Highway Crashes, Prepared for the Department of Transportation p. 213 (1970).

18. American Bar Association, Report of Special Committee on Automobile Accident Reparations p. 71 (1969).

19. United States Department of Transportation, Driver Behavior and Accident Involvement: Implications for Tort Liability p. 160 (1970).

20. *Ibid.* at pp. 160-61. Quoting Herman, *Mathematical Theory of Traffic Flow,* 1960 Proceedings, Institute of Traffic Engineers p. 76.

21. United States Department of Transportation, *supra* note 19, at pp. 189-190.

22. H. L. Ross, Settled Out of Court p. 199, note 34 (1970).

23. D. Klein and J. Waller, *supra* note 17, at p. 210.

24. James, *An Evaluation of the Fault Concept,* 32 University of Tennessee Law Review pp. 394, 398-99 (1964-65).

25. N. Y. Insurance Department, Automobile Insurance . . . For Whose Benefit? A Report to Governor Nelson A. Rockefeller p. 38 (1970).

26. Moynihan, "Next: A New Auto Insurance Policy," N. Y. Times, August 27, 1967 § 6 (Magazine), pp. 26, 78.

27. D. Klein and J. Waller, *supra* note 17, at pp. 74-77.

28. United States Department of Health, Education and Welfare, Report of the Secretary's Advisory Committee on Traffic Safety p. 76 (1968).

29. Joint Information Service, American Psychiatric Association and National Association for Mental Health, The Treatment of Alcoholism: A Study of Programs and Problems pp. 22-26 (1967). For an interesting exchange concerning the intractability of treating the problem drinker, *see* N. Y. Times, March 30, 1971, p. 1, cols. 1-2; Ubell, "Alcoholism: Challenge to the Theory That It's a Disease," N. Y. Times, April 11, 1971, § 4 (Week in Review) p. 7, cols. 6-8; a rebuttal in a letter to the editor, N. Y. Times, April 19, 1971, p. 34, col. 5; a surrebuttal, N. Y. Times, April 30, 1971, p. 36, col. 3.

30. If, however, those who object to paying insurance to the drinking driver carry the day in any legislative consideration, the solution is very simple under insurance such as the Keeton-O'Connell Basic Protection Plan, where you claim against your own insurance company rather than some other person: Just allow an optional exclusion from benefits for a person whose conduct such as drunken driving contributed to his injury. Thus, nobody is forced to buy premiums to cover injuries to someone else who is guilty of drunken driving, but if a person prefers to include coverage for himself if he happens to be involved in an accident while drinking, he must pay whatever premium is needed to have this coverage in his policy. A provision for such an option was included in the Basic Protection bill filed in Massachusetts for the 1968 Session. The terms of the revised section are printed in Keeton and O'Connell, *Basic Protection Automobile Insurance,* 1967 University of Illinois Law Forum pp. 400, 412-13, note 40; also printed in Crisis in Car Insurance pp. 40, 52-53, note 40 (R. Keeton, J. O'Connell and J. McCord eds. 1968).

31. *See* D. Klein and J. Waller, *supra* note 17, at pp. 136, 213; *see also* United States Department of Health, Education and Welfare, *supra* note 28, at pp. 73-80.

32. *But see* N. Y. Times, March 14, 1971, p. 72, cols. 1-4.

33. N. Y. Times, March 8, 1971, p. 1, cols. 3-6.

34. Rosenberg, *Court Congestion: Status, Causes, and the Proposed Remedies,* in The Courts, The Public, and The Law Explosion p. 29 (H. Jones ed. 1965).

35. As quoted in Main, "Only Radical Reform Can Save The Courts," Fortune, August, 1970, p. 111.

36. *Ibid.* at p. 114.

37. *See* Hearing before the Committee on Commerce, U. S. Senate, 91st Congress, 2d Session, on Automobile Insurance and Compensation Study, October 7, 1970, p. 17.

38. In unpublished remarks, Chief Justice Joseph Weintraub of New Jersey, in addressing a joint dinner in Newark of State Supreme Court Justices and Members of the New Jersey Press Association, opined that 51 per cent of civil cases arise from automobile accident suits, but that those cases occupy about 80 per cent of the total civil trial time and about 20 per cent of all trial time. In a letter to the author, Chief Justice Weintraub has further opined that "the actual impact of this litigation on a total court time is more than the stated per-

centages." Letter from Chief Justice Joseph Weintraub to the author, December 23, 1970; *see also*, recent Annual Reports by the Executive Secretary to the Justices of the Supreme Judicial Court [of Massachusetts], indicating that consistently about two thirds of the jury cases pending in the trial court of general jurisdiction in Massachusetts as "undisposed of" on June 30 are motor vehicle tort cases. Eleventh Annual Report, tip-in sheet between pp. 60-61 (1967); Twelfth Annual Report, tip-in sheet between pp. 72-73 (1968); Thirteenth Annual Report, tip-in sheet between pp. 68-69 (1969).

39. Burger, *The State of the Judiciary—1970*, 56 American Bar Association Journal pp. 929, 932, 933 (1970); Remarks of Chief Justice W. E. Burger, Testimonial Dinner Honoring Chief Justice John C. Bell, Jr., of the Supreme Court of Pennsylvania, Philadelphia, Pennsylvania, November 14, 1970.

40. *See* note 38 *supra* and accompanying text; *see also* Chicago Sun-Times, April 22, 1971, p. 18, cols. 4-6, reporting on congressional testimony of Benjamin S. Mackoff, the administrative director of the Cook County Circuit Court, indicating that Chicago's court systems have become "deluged by civil litigation arising out of automobile accidents."

41. Burger, *supra* note 39. Address by Earl Warren, Harvard Law School, Sesquicentennial Convocation, September 22, 1967, in The Path of the Law from 1967 pp. 215, 218 (A. Sutherland ed. 1968).

42. N. Y. Times, March 12, 1971, p. 18, col. 1.

43. N. Y. Times, March 13, 1967, p. 42, col. 1.

NOTES FOR CHAPTER XII

Where from Here?

1. Lawyer Reform News, vol. 1, no. 1, pp. 1, 4 (April/May 1971).

2. Main, "Why Nobody Likes the Insurers," Fortune, December, 1970, pp. 83, 121.

3. N. Y. Times, June 2, 1968 § 3 (Business & Finance) pp. 1, 5.

4. Hellman, " 'Your Policy Is Hereby Cancelled,' " N. Y. Times, November 8, 1970 (Magazine Section) pp. 32, 126.

5. Kemper, *The Basic Protection Plan: Reform or Regression?* 1967 University of Illinois Law Forum pp. 459, 469, also published in Crisis in Car Insurance pp. 99, 109 (R. Keeton, J. O'Connell, and J. McCord eds. 1968).

6. United States Department of Transportation, Motor Vehicle Crash Losses and Their Compensation in the United States: A Report to the Congress and the President, March 1971, p. 90.

7. National Commission on Product Safety, Final Report of the National Commission on Product Safety p. 70 (1970).

8. United States Department of Transportation, note 6 *supra*, at p. 6.

9. See *e.g.* N. Y. Times, April 7, 1971, p. 1.

10. R. Keeton and J. O'Connell, Basic Protection for the Traffic Victim pp. 189-218 (1965), for a discussion of foreign systems indicating a pattern of compensation for wage loss at modest levels under social insurance with a retention of fault claims for remaining losses.

11. Compensation for Personal Injury in New Zealand, Report of the Royal Commission of Inquiry (1967). *See also* Personal Injury: A Commentary on the Report of the Royal Commission of Inquiry into Compensation for Personal Injury in New Zealand (1969).

12. N. Y. Times, April 21, 1971, p. 77, col. 6; *see also* The National Underwriter (Property & Casualty edition), May 7, 1971, p. 1, col. 4.

13. Moynihan, *Changes for Automobile Claims?*, University of Illinois Law Forum pp. 361-62 (1967); also printed in Crisis and Car Insurance pp. 1-2 (R. Keeton, J. O'Connell, and J. McCord eds. 1968).

14. C. P. Snow and P. Snow, "Hope for America," LOOK, December 1, 1970, pp. 30, 33.

15. As quoted in TIME, November 23, 1970, p. 12.

16. Moynihan, *supra* note 13, at pp. 366-67 and 6-7 respectively.

17. *Ibid.* at pp. 368-69 and 8-9 respectively.

18. J. Frank, American Law: The Case for Radical Reform (1969).

19. Symposium, 47 Texas Law Review pp. 965-1038 (1969).

NOTES FOR APPENDIX I

Provisions for Property Damage

1. This material is adapted, with permission, from Keeton and O'Connell, *Alternative Paths Toward Nonfault Automobile Insurance*, 71 Columbia University Law Review pp. 241, 260-62 (1971).

2. Keeton and O'Connell, *Basic Protection Automobile Insurance*, 1967 University of Illinois Law Forum pp. 400, 412; also printed in Crisis in Car Insurance pp. 40, 52 (R. Keeton, J. O'Connell and J. McCord eds. 1968).

3. *Ibid.* at pp. 429-33 and 69-73 respectively.

4. American Insurance Association, Report of Special Committee to Study and Evaluate the Keeton-O'Connell Basic Protection Plan and Automobile Accident Reparations p. 6 (1968).

5. N. Y. Insurance Department, Automobile Insurance . . . For Whose Benefit? A Report to Governor Nelson A. Rockefeller pp. 88-89 (1970).

6. This device of having a traffic victim claim against his own insurance company on the basis that some other driver was negligent has been in use for many years. It is the key idea of Uninsured Motorist coverage, the very common supplementary coverage in most automobile insurance policies sold today under which the insured's own company pays him for his personal injury losses caused by an uninsured motorist *if* the latter was negligent and the insured was free from negligence.

Keeton and O'Connell, *supra* note 2, at pp. 431 and 71 respectively.

7. For the provisions of the statute, *see* Keeton and O'Connell, *supra* note 1, at pp. 265-66.

NOTES FOR APPENDIX II

An Optional No-Fault System

1. This material is adapted, with permission, from Keeton and O'Connell, *Alternative Paths Toward Nonfault Automobile Insurance*, 71 Columbia University Law Review pp. 241, 254-60 (1971). For a similar proposal, presented independently but simultaneously, *see* Calabresi, *The New York Plan: A Free Choice Modification*, 71 Columbia University Law Review p. 267 (1971).

2. Statement of John A. Volpe, Secretary of Transportation, before the Senate Commerce Committee Regarding the Automobile Insurance Compensation Study, 91st Congress, 2d Session, October 7, 1970, p. 8.

3. A draft bill for a compulsory Basic Protection Plan appears in R. Keeton and J. O'Connell, Basic Protection for the Traffic Victim pp. 299-339 (1965). A more recent draft, with comprehensive provisions fitting the act into a framework of existing state law, was filed in Massachusetts by Representative Dukakis and more than forty co-sponsors as House (Mass.) No. 610 of 1970. *See e.g.*, Boston Herald Traveler, November 11, 1969, p. 20.

4. House (Mass.) No. 4820 of 1968. Representative Michael Dukakis, who led the fight for compulsory Basic Protection in Massachusetts in

1967, also obtained a favorable house vote on House (Mass.) No. 4820 in 1968. With further refinements, an optional bill was filed by Representative Dukakis and more than forty co-sponsors as House (Mass.) No. 610 of 1970. *See e.g.*, Boston Herald Traveler, November 11, 1969, p. 20. For a description of an optional plan, *see* text accompanying and following note 7 *infra*.

5. *E.g.,* J. O'Connell and W. Wilson, Car Insurance and Consumer Desires (1969); United States Department of Transportation, Public Attitudes Toward Auto Insurance: A Report of the Survey Research Center, Institute For Social Research, University of Michigan, and Staff Analysis of Consumer Complaint Letters Concerning Auto Insurance (1970); United States Department of Transportation, Public Attitudes Supplement to the Economic Consequences of Automobile Accident Injuries (1970). *See also* O'Connell and Wilson, *Public Opinion Polls on the Fault System: State Farm Versus Other Surveys*, 1970 Insurance Law Journal p. 261; O'Connell and Wilson, *Public Opinion on No-Fault Auto Insurance: A Survey of the Surveys*, 1970 University of Illinois Law Forum p. 307. For a summary of a Gallup poll on public attitudes toward no-fault insurance, *see* N. Y. Times, April 22, 1971, p. 74, cols. 1-2.

6. Marryott, *The Tort System and Automobile Claims: Evaluating the Keeton-O'Connell Proposal*, 52 American Bar Association Journal pp. 639, 640 (1966).

7. The alternative is set forth in House (Mass.) No. 610 of 1970. *See* note 4 *supra*. Some key aspects of this alternative are set forth and discussed in Kozusko, *Reallocation Under Nonfault Automobile Insurance: Comments and Proposed Regulations*, 7 Harvard Journal on Legislation p. 423 (1970).

8. As to the working of the pool, *see* below.

9. *See*, Appendix I, *supra*.

10. For additional comments on the pool, *see* Kozusko, *supra* note 7.

NOTES FOR APPENDIX III

Complete or Partial Abolition of Fault Claims?

1. This material is adapted, with permission, from Keeton and O'Connell, *Alternative Paths Toward Nonfault Automobile Insurance*, 71 Columbia University Law Review pp. 241, 245-50, (1971).

2. R. Keeton and J. O'Connell, Basic Protection for the Traffic Victim pp. 299-339 (1965).

3. *See e.g.*, Keeton and O'Connell, *Basic Protection Automobile Insurance*, 1967 University of Illinois Law Forum pp. 403-04; also printed in Crisis in Car Insurance pp. 43-44 (R. Keeton, J. O'Connell and J. McCord eds. 1968).

4. R. Keeton and J. O'Connell, *supra* note 1, at pp. 274-76.

5. American Insurance Association, Report of Special Committee to Study and Evaluate the Keeton-O'Connell Basic Protection Plan and Automobile Accident Reparations (1968).

6. N. Y. Insurance Department, Automobile Insurance . . . For Whose Benefit? A Report to Governor Nelson A. Rockefeller (1970).

7. Davies, *The Minnesota Proposal for No-Fault Auto Insurance*, 54 University of Minnesota Law Review p. 921 (1970).

8. American Insurance Association, *supra* note 5, at p. 5; Davies, *supra* note 7, at p. 935.

9. For constitutional reasons, the New York Plan preserves fault claims in death cases. N. Y. Insurance Department, *supra* note 6, at p. 86 note 139. *See also ibid.* at pp. 88-89 concerning the preservation of fault claims "for damage to property other than another automobile—property such as the clothing and belongings of the passengers and pedestrians and such as roadside buildings."

10. R. Keeton, Venturing to Do Justice p. 136 (1969).

11. The Keeton-O'Connell proposed Basic Protection Act also has the $750 wage loss limit. R. Keeton and J. O'Connell, *supra* note 2, at p. 283. But the limitation is much less vulnerable to attack along this line because when the wage loss is well over $750 per month and the injury is severe, the recovery for the excess over the $750 per month limit would often be achieved under the preserved fault claims.

12. *See e.g.*, American Mutual Insurance Alliance Actuarial Committee Report on the Adequacy of the Costing of the American Insurance Association's "Complete Personal Protection Automobile Insurance Plan" (1969).

13. Inflation is much more likely to affect costs under the AIA and New York Plans than under Basic Protection because the former plans have no limit on payment, thus increasing the likelihood that payments will extend far into the future.

14. A. Conard, J. Morgan, R. Pratt, C. Voltz and R. Bombaugh, Automobile Accident Costs and Payment—Studies in the Economics of Injury Reparation p. 144 (1964). Conard's finding of a huge percentage of loss being suffered by those losing $10,000 or more in out-of-pocket loss gains support, it would seem, from Harwayne, *Insurance Costs of Basic Protection Plan in Michigan*, 1967 University of Illinois Law Forum pp. 479, 506-09 (1967) and accompanying tables; also printed in Crisis in Car Insurance, *supra* note 3, at pp. 119, 146-49. The importance of the $10,000 Basic Protection cutoff—and the concomitant expense in doing away with it—is also suggested by an observation of Professor Conard:

> Though the wage losses in such [very serious] cases naturally run up into the hundreds of thousands of dollars, the prevail-

ing [$10,000] limit on automobile liability insurance means
that very few victims ever collect more than $10,000 for an
automobile accident.

Conard, *Remarks*, 1967 University of Illinois Law Forum at p. 440;
also printed in Crisis in Car Insurance, *supra* note 3, at p. 80.

15. United States Department of Transportation, Summary Description
and Major Findings of the Study of Auto Accident Victims p. 3
(April 27, 1970). For the figure of $5.1 billion in compensable out-of-
pocket loss, *see* United States Department of Transportation, Economic
Consequences of Automobile Accident Injuries, Report of the Westat
Research Corporation, vol. I, pp. 40, 118 (Table 11 FS, with the figure
$5,126,595,000 rounded to $5.1 billion); for the figure of $2.5 billion
being repaid from all sources, *see ibid.* at pp. 146-47 (Table 15 FS,
with the figure $2,493,815,000 rounded to $2.5 billion); for the figure
of $1.1 billion being paid from automobile insurance, *see ibid.* at pp.
145-46 (Table 15 FS. From that table, if one adds the total amount
received from "Auto med" [so-called medical payments coverage]
[$108,414,000], "Collision insurance" [$140,567,000], and "Net tort"
[$813,105,000], the total is $1,062,086,000 which is rounded to $1.1
billion.)

16. For a description of the stresses on even a fairly well insured and
affluent family from catastrophic medical expenses, *see* "The Cost of
Illness," Wall Street Journal, May 7, 1970, p. 1, col. 1.

17. R. Keeton, *supra* note 10, at p. 138.

18. The manner in which the savings from the surrenders of fault claims
can be fairly distributed only among those who make the surrenders,
rather than providing windfalls to others, is discussed in Appendix II,
supra. A draft of a statutory provision for optional full protection
coverage as recommended here appears in Keeton and O'Connell, *supra*
note 1, at p. 265. Such a plan could also be drafted to preserve, for the
relatively few who might want it, the right to large no-fault benefits,
coupled with the right to sue under a fault claim for benefits not collected under no-fault insurance, such as those for pain and suffering.
See R. Keeton and J. O'Connell, *supra* note 2, at pp. 284-85, 278-80.
See also text accompanying note 19 *infra*.

19. R. Keeton and J. O'Connell, *supra* note 2 at pp. 285-86.

20. The text of this modification, as indicated in note 18, *supra*, is presented in Keeton and O'Connell, *supra* note 1, at p. 265. Also, because
of the low cost of removing the per-accident limit as indicated by cost
studies published since the original Keeton-O'Connell proposal was
offered, it would seem appropriate to eliminate the per-accident limit
on the basic compulsory coverage. (The low cost of removing per-
accident limits as found in their studies lead both the AIA and the
New York Insurance Department to eliminate per-accident limits in
their plans.) This change would remove the need for special provisions concerning allocation of per-accident limits in cases of multiple
claims—an additional welcome simplification. These special provisions
appear in § 2.7 of the proposed statute presented in R. Keeton and
J. O'Connell, *supra* note 2, at pp. 314-17.

21. R. Keeton and J. O'Connell, *supra* note 2, at p. 288.

22. *Ibid.*

23. *See* Harwayne, *supra* note 14; American Insurance Association, *supra* note 5. Note that the AIA Report calculates costs of the Rhode Island Basic Protection bill, which included $15,000/$30,000 of bodily injury liability insurance in the compulsory package. Note also that the scaled-down Massachusetts no-fault plan includes $5,000 per person/ $10,000 per accident liability insurance in the compulsory package.

24. Some have criticized the Basic Protection Plan because in providing no-fault protection along with the corollary exemption from fault claims, it does not cover, as does liability insurance, the costs of defending against liability claims, including a lawyer's fees. A plan in which the package of required insurance includes both no-fault benefits and liability coverage obviates this objection.

Index

Accident and health insurance
. duplication of fault insurance benefits...210
. fault insurance compared...8, 67-8, 102, 130, 133, 140, 142, 145
. source of payment for automobile accidents...29, 188

Accidents
. frequency...2
. inevitability...128-9

Advance payment...22-7, 181, 197, 200

Alcoholism...132-3

Ambulance chasing...44, 54-60, 67-8
. "brokering"...60-3
. claim padding...60
. fee-splitting...60-3
. referrals by doctors...58-9

American Academy of Physical Medicine and Rehabilitation...23

American Bar Association...44, 65, 196-7
. code of ethics...56, 59, 61, 63, 65-7
. Section on Insurance, Negligence and Compensation Law...125
. Special Committee on Automobile Accident Reparations...111, 128

American College of Surgeons, Committee on Trauma...18-9

American Insurance Association...79, 108, 115, 118, 158-9, 170, 204-6

American Mutual Insurance Alliance...22, 111, 116

American Trial Lawyers Association...10, 40, 42-3, 49, 53, 98, 111, 125

Arbitration of liability claims...187, 197, 200

Attorneys' fees...see Contingent fees

Automobile insurance
. costs...7, 28-9, 36, 37, 69-75, 84, 110, 130, 216-7
. federal assumption...141-3, 146-8, 193, 206-8
. legal necessity...69-71, 76, 91-2, 102, 188

Automobile safety...108-9, 193-4

Bankruptcy of insurance companies...86

Barber, Richard J....4, 26, 124

Bartlett, Charles...8

Basic protection plan, Keeton-O'Connell...115-6, 118, 119-21, 141-2, 157-60, 162, 163-75, 240 n. 30, 245 nn. 11 and 14, 246 nn. 18 and 20, 247 n. 24

Biemiller, Andrew...88

Blue Cross Association...5, 29, 98, 103, 110, 117

Botein, Bernard...48, 49, 64

Boyle, Judge John S....55

Bradshaw, M. B....88

"Brokering"...60-3

Brown v. Kendall...125

Burge, W. Lee...80

Burger, Chief Justice Warren...137, 138

Cancellation of insurance policies... 3, 76-9, 83

Carlin, Jerome...57-8, 60, 61

Class action suits...137

Code of Ethics, American Bar Association...56, 59, 61, 63, 65-7

Collateral source rule...56, 189, 196

Collision insurance
. comparable benefits under the Keeton-O'Connell basic protection plan...165, 166
. rating system...183
. supplementary no-fault insurance ...109, 130, 133, 188

Committee on Trauma of the American College of Surgeons...18-9

Compensation...*see* Payment

Conard, Professor Alfred...17, 87-8, 95, 97, 104-5, 118, 171

Consumer Reports...3-4, 72-3, 83, 96

Consumers Price Index...70, 72

Consumers Union...3, 29, 88-9, 95-6

Contingent fees...37-9, 43-53, 198

Corstvet, Emma...20

Costs of automobile insurance... 69-75, 84, 110, 130, 216-7
. allocation...7, 28-9, 36, 37

Courts
. delays in hearing automobile insurance cases...2, 6-7, 10, 12, 135-8
. time spent on automobile insurance cases...137, 240-1 n. 38

Cox, Charles K....141

Daniels, Edward...109

Davidson, Louis...111-2

Defense Research Institute...196-7

Delaware plan of no-fault auto insurance...121 n.

Delays in settling fault claims...6, 20-3, 26, 95, 96, 97, 181-2
. contingent fee as cause...45-6
. court tie-ups as cause...2, 6-7, 10, 12, 135-8

Dennenberg, Herbert...93

Department of Transportation studies, United States...4-5, 161-2
. allocation of payment from auto accident claims...50
. amounts paid for compensable out-of-pocket loss...171-2
. cancellation or refusal to renew automobile insurance policies ...83
. *Causation, Culpability and Deterrence in Highway Crashes*...127
. competition in the auto insurance industry...74
. court time occupied with auto accident cases...137
. *Driver Behavior and Accident Involvement: Implications for Tort Liability*...129
. insurance accessibility...83-4
. *Motor Vehicle Crash Losses and Their Compensation in the United States*...176-225
. no-fault insurance...121, 124
. payment of insurance claims...26
. *Rehabilitation of Auto Accident Victims*...19
. traffic safety...129

Direct writers...75, 140

Disabilities resulting from automobile accidents...19-20, 119
. hardening...20
. permanent partial...19
. permanent total...19, 20, 143
. temporary partial...19

Divorce laws, comparison with automobile insurance laws...12, 18

Drunk driving...34, 131-4, 240 n. 30

Ehrenzweig, Professor Alfred...49

Ellenborough, Lord...13

English law...13, 39

Erdman II, Dr. William J....23

Farnham, C. Eugene...120

Fault . . . *see also* Liability, Negligence
criterion for payment in auto accidents...128-31

. determination...3, 10-5, 34-5, 112-3, 128-31
. history of concept...125-6
. rehabilitation, lack of emphasis ...22

Federal auto insurance...141-3, 146-8, 193, 206-8

Federal Judicial Center...137

Fee-splitting...60-3

Fire insurance, comparison with automobile fault insurance...8, 98-9, 107, 130, 133, 142

Florida plan of no-fault auto insurance...121 n

Foungner, Arne...21-2

Frank, John...154

Frequency of accidents...2

Fuchsberg, Jacob...111

Gambrell, Charles W....78

Gans, Alfred W....51

General damages in auto accidents ...30, see also Pain and suffering

Gillette, Dr. Harriet E....23

Government automobile insurance... 141-3, 146-8, 191-3, 206-8

Group automobile insurance...90-3

Guest passenger statute...197

Hart, Sen. Philip, plan for no-fault auto insurance...116, 118, 237 n. 19

Harwayne, Frank...119-20

Health insurance . . . see Accident and health insurance

Henle, John...19, 25

Herrmann, Karl...77-8

Illinois plan of no-fault auto insurance...117 n, 121 n

James, Fleming...17, 18, 130

Jones, T. Lawrence...79, 108

Keeton-O'Connell basic protection plan...115-6, 118, 119-21, 141-2, 157-60, 162, 163-75, 240 n. 30, 245 nn. 11 and 14, 246 nn. 18 and 20, 247 n. 24

Keeton, Professor Robert...43, 73, 114-5, 157, 161, 169

Kemper Jr., James...141-2

Kennedy, Senator Edward...143

Kimball, Spencer...92, 93

Lawyers' fees...see Contingent fees

Lemmon, Vestal...82-3

Liability . . . see also Fault, Negligence
. absolute...187, 193
. clear...25
. probable...25

Life insurance
. comparison with automobile fault insurance...8, 98, 130, 133, 188
. duplication of auto insurance coverage...29

Lindsay, John...138

Llewellyn, Karl...65-6

Loss, out-of-pocket...3, 30, 35, 95, 118-9, 123, 170-2

Magnuson, Sen. Warren...79, 82-3

Maidenberg, H. J....141

Main, Jeremy...137

Marryott, Franklin...163

Massachusetts plan of no-fault auto insurance...99-100, 116, 120, 162

Mayer, Martin...28, 32

McKinnon, F. B....44-5

Medicaid...29, 172, 188

Medical expenses incurred in auto accidents...16-23, 30, 116, 130, 133, 145
    percentage of loss from traffic accidents...143

Medical treatment of injured...18-25

Medicare...29, 142, 172

Mehr, Robert...90

Mertz, Arthur...109

Mini-no-fault bill...see Massachusetts plan of no-fault auto insurance

Moynihan, Daniel P....95, 131, 148-9, 150-1

Myrdal, Gunnar...149

National Association of Claimants Compensation Attorneys...40, see also American Trial Lawyers Association

National Association of Independent Insurers...82-3, 109, 111,116-7, 184

National Council on Rehabilitation ...18

National health insurance...143-4

Negligence...125-126, *see also* Fault, Liability
. comparative...13-4, 187, 197, 199
. contributory...13, 56, 187

New York Insurance Department ...6, 70-1, 73, 75, 89,115, 131, 158-9

Nixon, Richard M....9, 12, 13, 130, 143

No-fault auto insurance plans... 199-208, 209, 213
. added protection...166
. American Insurance Association ...170, 171, 173, 174, 175, 204-6, 246 n. 20
. bodily injury liability...165-6
. Davies...170
. Delaware...121 n.
. extension to other areas...144-6
. Florida...121 n.
. Hart...237 n. 19
. Illinois...117 n., 121 n.
. Keeton-O'Connell basic protection...115-6, 118, 119-21, 141-2, 157-60, 162, 163-75, 240 n. 30, 245 nn. 11 and 14, 246 nn. 18 and 20, 247 n. 24
. Massachusetts...99-100, 116, 120, 162
. New York...142, 170-1, 173, 174, 245 n. 9, 246 n. 20
. optional...161-8, 173-4
. Oregon...121 n.
. property damage...144n, 157-60, 165-6, 205
. vehicle protection...157-60, 165

No-fault divorce laws...12

Nuisance value...34-5, 117

Oregon plan of no-fault auto insurance...121 n.

Out-of-pocket loss...*see* Loss, out-of-pocket

Pain and suffering...3, 30-3, 35, 39-42, 64, 95, 104-5, 117, 190-1, 200
. exclusion of payment...205

Payment of claims...2-5, 26, 113-4
. advance...22-7, 181, 197, 200
. amounts...16
. criteria...96-7, 128
. delays...6, 20-3, 26, 95, 96, 97, 181-2
. doctors' role in establishing...16-7
. duplication...97-8, 100, 102-4, 114, 117, 189, 210
. inequity...180-1
. legal expenses...37-8, 45-53, 198
. lump sum...16-8, 63
. medical expenses...16-23, 30-2, 50, 116-7, 130, 133, 213
. method...16-8, 22-7
. out-of-pocket loss...3, 30, 65, 67, 95, 123, 171-2
. overpayment...5-6, 29-31, 34-5, 98, 180-1, 212, 216
. pain and suffering...3, 30-3, 39-42, 64, 95, 104-5, 117, 123, 172, 190-1, 200, 205
. wage loss...16, 30, 117, 214

Peck, Judge David...43-4

Phelan, John D....52

Porter, Sylvia...60

Property damage...121n, 143, 144n, 157-60, 165-6, 182-3, 201-2, 203-5, 207, 209, 215

Prosser, William...13, 43

Rating of insurance risks...*see* Risk, assigned

Reforms, proposals for...*see* No-fault auto insurance plans

Rehabilitation of accident victims... 18-9, 23-5, 182, 211

Reich, Charles, *The Greening of America*...126-7

Reinsurance...167

Renewals of insurance policies...3, 76-9, 83

Report by the Committee to Study Compensation For Automobile Accidents...148

Risk, assigned...75-90, 106-8, 183-4, 185, 192, 208
. age discrimination...78, 79, 87
. employment discrimination...78-9
. marital status discrimination...78
. nationality discrimination...80
. racial discrimination...76, 78, 79-80, 87-9
. voluntary high risk...85-6

Rockefeller, Nelson...115, 205
Rosenberg, Maurice...51, 137
  The Courts, the Public and the Law Explosion...137
Ross, Professor H. Laurence...47
Rustin, Bayard...87
Ryan, Lewis C....52

Sargent, David...98
Savings under no-fault...94-5, 97-9, 102-4, 110-1, 118-20, 159-60, 162, 164-6, 170-1, 204, 216-7, 221-2
Scariano, Anthony...51-2
Senate, U. S....77, 78-9, 82-3, 120
Sick leave...29, 142
  . duplication of auto insurance benefits...98, 99, 117
Small claims...45
  . expense...189
  . nuisance value...34-5, 117
  . overpayment...5-6, 35, 212, 216
  . waste...117
Smith, Bradford...113
Smith, Reginald Heber...38
Snow, C. P....149
Social insurance...130, 144, 188, 191-3
Social Security...29, 144-6, 188
Spangenberg, Craig...111, 125
Special damages...30, 33, *see also* Loss, out-of-pocket
Stewart, Richard...115
Survey Research Laboratory, University of Illinois...71-2, 102-3, 123

Teamsters Union...99-100
The Courts, the Public and the Law Explosion, Maurice Rosenberg...137
The Greening of America, Charles Reich...126-7
Uninsured motorists...87
  coverage...165, 166, 188, 198, 207, 243 n. 6
United States Department of Transportation studies...*see* Department of Transportation studies, United States
University of Michigan study...4, 26, 97, 118
Van Voorhis, Judge John...48
Vehicle protection insurance...158-60, 165
Velde, James...55
Vertrees, Orman L....78-9
Volpe, John A....120-1, 124, 161-2, 176
Wage loss...16, 23, 30, 107, 115, 117, 143-4, 164, 171, 202, 204, 209, 214, 215, 217, *see also* Loss, out-of-pocket
Warne, Colston...29
Webb, Professor Bernard...91
Wise, Paul...22
Workmen's Compensation...18, 130
Young drivers...3, 33, 34, 76, 79, 82-3, 84, 85, 87, 107, 221